HENRY ROLLINS

SEE A GROWN MAN CRY

NOW WATCH HIM DIE

2.13.61

P.O. BOX 1910 · LOS ANGELES ·
CALIFORNIA · 90078 · USA

2.13.61
P.O. BOX 1910 · LOS ANGELES ·
CALIFORNIA · 90078 · USA

2.13.61 Publications, Inc.
P.O. Box 1910
Los Angeles, CA 90078

JOE COLE 4.10.61 – 12.19.91

See
A
Grown
Man
Cry

Tired dog's legs running
Treadmill
Endless life
Shovelful after shovelful into the hole
Grey day
Weak struggle ahead
Dirty air
Breathing in orders
Half dead fish, hole in its lung from the hook
Slaps its tail against the floor of the boat
Cold eyes staring through and past
Needles in the skin, nails in the feet
Nightmares in the head, hate in the eyes
Long way down
Falling short
Falling in love
Falling asleep
Falling in line
Falling into the hole for good reason
For no reason
For real
Forever
Bullshit
Bull's eye

✠ ✠ ✠

Sometimes I like to watch those movies
The ones where they believe all that shit
For awhile I believe it too
Then the movie's over and everyone leaves
Sometimes I think about that bullshit like it was real
It's what I call a junkfood thought
Not all that good for you, but it gets you through somehow
You can taste the fake truth
The illusion is poison
All of a sudden you're on your own
It's easy to get cut off
Lost in the cold moon night

You reach for the poison
You don't care if it's killing you
As long as it gets you out of this

✠ ✠ ✠

Tonight I'm an old satellite
Emitting weak signals from far away
Low output
Where are the planets tonight?
Think about the spaceman blues
Lonely on the moon
Imagine walking out of your room
And finding you're on the moon looking at Earth far away
After awhile it might not be so bad
At least they couldn't hurt you from there
Memories stick like napalm and keep burning
Years later I still burn

✠ ✠ ✠

I'm hot
I'm heat
It's hot out tonight because I'm alive
Breathe in the smell of your body
Other bodies
The heat makes me want to destroy myself
Makes me want you
Catch fire like a disease

✠ ✠ ✠

I remember the cold nights up there
Never had enough clothes
All those punks on speed
Trying to look worse than Billy Idol
Pulling it off
All those dead girls walking around
You said they were junkies
I remember the time I spent with you
You told me that my cum tasted like chocolate milk

You write me every once in awhile
You all do at some point
I like it better when you don't
I like to forget a lot these days, it's like throwing stuff out
Getting rid of you is a good thing, that's why I don't write you back
I'm vomiting every memory from my system
You make me remember
When I felt more alive than I do now
Everything we say now is a lie
We could only talk about a time that didn't happen
No one could have had it that good

✠ ✠ ✠

I am punishing myself tonight
Three in the morning, can't sleep
I need to get out of here
Today I went through all kinds of domestic bullshit
Tiny rules for tiny lives
Tonight I'm living all their little hells
I'm going to do the best I can out there this time
I want to be that which overcomes itself
Listening to them makes me weak and small
I watch them go out and fuck each other
They tell me that I'm crazy
The years scar me
I don't want a smooth ride
I want the crushing wheel
Their glass grinds my guts
They watch you bleed to death and call it show business

✠ ✠ ✠

There were gunshots outside tonight
They were close
The streets here are filthy, everything is covered in spray paint
This town is a joke, a worn out paradise
It's been gang raped into shock

✠ ✠ ✠

I got thrown into a fierce fire
I found myself in a place that you had lost a hold of
I got a grip where you lost yours
I have a calming hand in the middle of a storm
I inhale the sun
I exhale the total absence of light
I am the number One
Burning

✝ ✝ ✝

She is untouchable
I wrap my arms around her and I find myself alone
She is alien
I try to understand her and I start to lose my mind
She is the most beautiful thing I have ever seen
I destroy myself when I am with her
I leave all my blood at her feet
Dreams of her rip through my head like bullets
Looking at her makes me want to rip my eyes out
She is a hollow space that cannot be filled
I have emptied myself out and caved in

✝ ✝ ✝

I want the hard nights to destroy me
I want the long haul to define me
I want to disappear beneath the crushing wheel
So little time left
Fierce awareness burning always hungry
Looking to get destroyed
Inside myself I am strong
Tonight I am napalm

✝ ✝ ✝

I'm standing on the edge and looking down
Everything's on fire and glittering
I am alone and looking down and through
I come from the war in my dreams
There's a wall of fire between me and everything else

Tonight I'm walking down streets that are hot and long
I feel good because I'm alone and burning
I don't like talking anymore
I'm going to cut it out and send it to a stranger
I don't like looking into eyes
They make me feel cheap
I live inside the war reality
Glad to be all one

✚ ✚ ✚

I get lost in the nights
I get lost in all the stories
They envelope me until I can't see or think
All the hot nights
The glittering eyes that don't sleep
The stories the memories the dreams...
I'm standing around in this empty night
I'm waiting to get taken away
All the madness all the rooftops
All the heat there ever was in a summer night
Roaring through my veins right now
The hot nights will unfold themselves soon
I'll be wrapped in moist shrouds of solid unending night
In the dark corner of some night I lay ravaged
Glory's teeth have scarred my flesh
I've become addicted to the unending thing
Sirens of the night that scream inside my brain
The nights keep coming
The thunder screams inside me
I feel like I could catch fire
The black fever night
The animals of vision come forward
A woman once said to me:
I want to kidnap you and take you someplace special

✚ ✚ ✚

The answer to my hunger is starvation
The answer to my self doubt is action

I smash hope with confrontation
Confidence is a guess
I'm here and we'll see if I fall or not
At the end of all of this we'll know the truth
The gun isn't loaded until all the bullets have been fired

✝ ✝ ✝

In my cold box room
Playing the game again
Waiting night after night
It's breaking my heart
Every minute in here kills me slow and cheap
The phone calls me
Talks bullshit to me and stops
I pull it off the hook
I go outside, hear the bullshit, smell the stench
Come back to my room and sit
I'm not lonely mad or anything else
I'm waiting
Coming off the road to this place
Is like coming home to a wrecked car
It's all fucked up and going straight to nowhere
It's Friday night
What a burn out

✝ ✝ ✝

Today I crossed the Mississippi River
It was covered with ice and kept Illinois from moving
Grey cast iron sky driving snow falling dirty
Empty houses dip backed horses pigs graveyards baseball diamonds
A large building, the paint so worn away I could barely read
Smith and Wilson - Embalmers
The windows were broken out
The sun started going down
Darkness crept in slowly
It could have been death taking a breather

✝ ✝ ✝

Do you know them?
The little insult hurling embodiments of weakness
The ones whose voices resemble small dogs
The ones who run in circles
The ones who peck like the birds that pick shit off rhino's backs
Their words and gestures mean nothing
Without the strong they couldn't exist
Every once in awhile one of them gets crushed
Or better yet, back handed at a restaurant
A few drops of urine go down the leg
They get called a few names and get a different job
Spineless

✝ ✝ ✝

I can feel things breaking inside me
Show after show, night after night
It feels like glass in my guts
My head feels like I've been wringing out a washcloth
At the end I'm left in a desert
I don't know who I am
I lose big parts of myself out there
I do my best to get them back
I don't know if I pull it off
Or if I'm lying to myself
Or trying to make it real for lack of nothing better to do
At night I throw bricks at my soul
I cut myself on the splinters
And sit in quiet rooms trying to find myself again
It never ends

✝ ✝ ✝

I don't love you
I did for a few minutes but even then
It was just me loving myself with your body
I do that sometimes
So do you

✝ ✝ ✝

My thoughts turn into blades
I cut myself on myself
I work hard to protect myself from my self destructive nature
Sometimes I think that I only maintain myself
So I'll have something to kick very hard
My thoughts turn on my thoughts
I eat myself alive
I vomit myself into myself
I make myself sick
Sometimes I think that I could rupture all my blood cells
By thinking the wrong thing
It's a good thing I have a short attention span
It allows me to forget myself from time to time

☩ ☩ ☩

When I saw you the other night I wanted it to be different. I wanted
to go back to years ago. When I see you, part of me longs for that
time. When I see you now, I only feel a slight ache. I get mad at
myself for not feeling that overload that used to run through me.
Perhaps part of me has died or given up. Now you're just someone I
know. When I see you, I look closely. I hope to see a spark of what it
was that inspired such heated unrest. There's part of it I can't let go.
It's the third arm that beats me. You're beautiful and you make me
feel old and confused. I don't know who I was. I only know who I
am.

☩ ☩ ☩

Hating you makes me hate all the others
Hating you makes me hate the whole idea
It frees me so I can see you
Your attempts to infect me obviously didn't work
So you turned on yourself and called it something else
Like oppression
Or getting screwed by the powers that be
You make me laugh as I watch you sink
Finally meeting yourself and not recognizing the face

☩ ☩ ☩

I sign my name to all my flights
All my break downs
All my calamities
I cannot disown them as others do
That would be like looking at your arm
And saying it wasn't yours
Because you didn't like the way it looked
I have no separation, no distance
I can register the destruction of thought
I know the alien and the enemy
I cannot turn it loose into the streets
And not recognize it as my own
I cannot abort myself
I cannot disown myself
I'm locked in here
If there was a key I never found it
If I did I would have thrown it away

✝ ✝ ✝

The man telling the story about little kids blowing up in Vietnam
His anger fear fueled insanity doesn't escape me
The lines of eyeless wordless ones punished by existence
They don't escape my eyes
The vet who started to strangle me
As he went back to the jungle to bayonet babies
While we sat in the park
I can't take my eyes away
Sometimes I think I'm going to explode from what I see
It makes me want to tear my arms off and help
It makes me want to walk away
And never see another thing that breathes
Get a gun and wait for death

✝ ✝ ✝

You don't make me feel like you used to
That's why I'm leaving
That's why people leave each other
They come to their senses and get selfish again

✝ ✝ ✝

I saw you last night
It's hard to believe I felt so strongly about you
I feel very old right now
Have you ever experienced something so great
That years later you regretted the whole thing
Seeing the hole it left in you?
I remembered how I used to lose sleep over you
When you made me hate everything
It was glorious
Now it's nothing
When we see each other we cover each other in dust
Some wars are over
Peace sickens me
I am an archaeologist searching through my own ruins
I can see the sun setting in your eyes
How dimly they shine through the dust

✝ ✝ ✝

Nothing you do blows me away
I read your papers
Fifteen year-old boy found with three bullet holes in his head
You assholes torture each other every day
All your wars make perfect sense to me
Your acts of love are just acts
Kids dealing crack to kids
World War III so what
I don't hate you idiots for it, it's just the way you are
All your pain and suffering leaves me cold
This is not the time or place to be in need
Fuck all of you

✝ ✝ ✝

Let's do a song about the girl in college who fucked the frat boy and
got knocked up. The one who died screaming and convulsing in her
room from septic infection from the abortion.

About the kid from Nebraska who went to Vietnam and watched
his guts cool on his legs before he died a virgin in the jungle.

About the girl who has been in a mental institution for nine years and has been stuck with needles so many times she thinks she's a messenger from god to take the word's pain on her shoulders.

About the man on Death Row who has not touched a woman for fifteen years.

About the boy who was made to fuck his mother while his father watched.

About the man who came home from work to find that his wife had cut their infant son in half and shot herself in the head.

About the mother who was too high on junk to see that her baby had fallen down the side of the bed and smothered to death.

About the boy who is beaten regularly by his father and is afraid to tell anyone because he fears the fucker will kill him.

About the rich kid who fucked the girl, killed her and got away with it.

About the woman who threw her baby into a dumpster and when she heard the sound of the child's skull hitting the iron floor she ran away screaming and vomiting.

Let's sing

✝ ✝ ✝

Touch me
Kick me
Make me crawl
Do something
Make me see that I'm alive
I need it bad
I feel dead
Stick something sharp into my flesh
Rip the lids off my eyes
Make me see
Torch me
My burning body will light up the night sky
It will make the sun jealous

✝ ✝ ✝

Black summer night
Incinerator breathing hard
Calling me down
I want it
Take me all the way
I have nothing else to want for
Except the chance to burn
I want a life time of summer nights
Seduce the sweat from my pores
Like a killer
Turn me on
Turn me up
Turn me loose

☩ ☩ ☩

She calls
It's ok if you don't want to have sex with me
But let's not throw the friendship away
I hung up on her
Friends?

☩ ☩ ☩

It's getting dark out side but I can see clearly
The world around me is falling apart but I keep it together
The walls are closing in but I can still catch my breath
I can see my death
I can see myself at the end, wearing out like a common fool
Right now I am the shadow man
I know that this will end
But right now I am the endless scar
I know that I will get old and easy to kill

☩ ☩ ☩

Her eyes were always cold
By lying to myself
I could make believe they had some warmth
She was cold and wooden
I don't know why I stuck around

Maybe I was trying to prove how wrong a person could be
It's easy to cut yourself on your own edges

✝ ✝ ✝

Beware the night
It has sharp teeth
It knows the ways of stealth
It carries a sharp blade
It cuts deep
The night has me in its spell
A shadow that follows me
Silent assassin
My reason for living
Come closer and let me see you
Before you kill me
I want to see myself in your eyes

✝ ✝ ✝

Nothing will happen to you
You will emerge from all this totally unscathed
They will not destroy you
All the things that you heard they do to others...
It's all a lie
Those things don't happen to real people
They only happen to those in the other world
They get hired by killers to get killed
You're safe from all storms
In case they get you mixed up about those people
Like the ones that die in plane crashes
—They pay extra to have that happen
They didn't want to die alone
Imagine the woman that lives in the rooming house
One who slashed her wrists and left no note
You'll never have to do that
Your life will be long endless bliss
Good night, angel

✝ ✝ ✝

She's got cardboard tears
They fall from her face
She's got plastic emotions
She turns them on and off
She is energy efficient
She has glass eyes
She sees blindly, selectively
She has television instinct
I love to hear the sound she makes
When she short circuits herself
For a brief blinding instant she is real

✝ ✝ ✝

That city is a wasteland
With all the cars whizzing by my eyes
With all the people moving up in the world
It's a wasteland
A gutted animal raped and devoured
A land of empty and filthy rooms
Your jaded dream is not a vision
The wasteland is not wonderful
It's a space pushed over by vicious children
Land of a thousand addictions
The endless suicide
You chainsmoke abortions
You drink dead water
You speak a dead language
You bought the whole thing
You don't even exist

✝ ✝ ✝

It's raining in the desert tonight
I'm on the Southwest Chief going east
I'm looking at the black window
My face stares back
Good to be out of the room

Every once in awhile you get a break
I'm happy to be free and alone

✝ ✝ ✝

4.20.88
Driving through Georgia
Shirt getting wet
Been moving south since noon
Saw the first palmetto an hour ago
The sides of the road are flooded
The green is exploding
We nosedive south
Palm trees, pine trees
Last week I was in Boston
We pull for Tallahassee
Every road greets me
Like a black vein that runs through my marrow
After this is over I will be dead
But right now...

✝ ✝ ✝

Georgia: Burnt down house. Fat white man, fat black man sitting on
the front porch playing checkers. Sheriff at the gas station. Old
woman in a rocking chair. Child playing in the dirt next to a trailer
home. Old church. Man driving a tractor down the side of the road.
Green trees, brown fields. Abandoned shack, swamp. Man burning
garbage. Small lake with rowboat on shore. Three men and a boy
looking into the motor of a Model A. Sign for Cairo, GA. Central
High Yellow Jackets football field. Stubborn unmoving sun.
Thomasville train station. Endless two lane road cutting a path
through impenetrable foliage. Days later: New Mexico. Flat rock
plateaus. Red clay. Brush. Dry, hot, cloudless. Huge sky with black
birds.

✝ ✝ ✝

Her laughter grates against the air
She sounds like the end of one thousand nights of chain smoking
She's the dregs of a bad dream

Ex-junkie
She sucks me in and spits me out
She tells me about all the guys she's burned in the past
How she used them and the things they believed
She laughs and says, "I'm a pro!"
Lies fall from her mouth to the floor
They fall into the ashtray
Her perfume smells like death and longing
Her eyes hunt and consume
They steal, they are the hungriest eyes I have ever seen
It's as if she's dying and she's sustained by what she sees
She hates men but she says that I'm different
She works her mouth across my waist
She looks up and tells me she knows what I like
Insane

⊹ ⊹ ⊹

He learned about pain by studying the faces of others
He would go off by himself and try it
He didn't feel anything that made him want to stop
He couldn't feel pain
Everything felt good
He hired a guy to depress him
The guy got mad and left
He couldn't get our boy to stop laughing
One day he laughed so hard he choked and died smiling

⊹ ⊹ ⊹

The ballad of no man
I am void
I am all things compacted into nothing
Countless ghetto sunrises see my incendiary eyes
Watch my burning footsteps
Don't get too close or I'll take you nowhere
I am all the empty rooms
Cheap light
Exhaled air

My heart is a lead bell ringing
My thoughts are pieces of broken glass
I'm getting out
I am that which can no longer be destroyed
I suck tears from the corpses of dreams
I am the emptiness
I sing the wordless tuneless dead song
This is my song
Listen to it rot

✢ ✢ ✢

California highway at night, the last ditch for strangers
The two of them strapped in while the car burned
1978 Pinto wagon turned incinerator coffin
They just sat there taking it
The flames screamed against the sky
I watched the paint burn off the license plate
I've never seen anyone go like that
Up on the embankment the palms hissed laughter
Say good bye to the night
What a human way to go
All consuming fiery arms wrap yourselves around me tonight
Hold me
Burn the whole night through

✢ ✢ ✢

Alone looking for the quickest way to get to pain
I am my soul smasher love call death trip
I slashed the wrists of Destiny and took total control
I watch the night strangle the sun
Hail night
Darkness, my brother

✢ ✢ ✢

Fucking without kissing without talking
I bite your shoulder
You claw my back
Later you come out of the bathroom with a cigarette in your mouth

You say goodbye and I hear the engine of your car fade
I stare at the ceiling
Some might find that a bit shallow
Not you and I
We like it that way
We think that we have it beat by mutual denial
I like it when you're cold to me, it makes me respect you
If you ever showed me anything other than your animal need
I would never see you again
I don't want to know about your problems and your life
We are the real thing

✠ ✠ ✠

He tells me he's doing better now
It's been a long upward crawl up from the sewer
The bottom floor was hell for real
He used to be addicted to junk
Now he's addicted to talking about
How he's not addicted to junk
Counting the days he's been clean
He talks about junk more now than when he was using it
Makes me think that no one gets away from it all the way
The more he talks, the more I see the monkey
Breathing down his neck
Singing sweetly in his ear
Telling him to come home
No one ever gets away
No one ever crawls all the way out
They become living documents
Tributes to the overwhelming claws of the ten ton monkey

✠ ✠ ✠

He stood on the roof
Threw a penny off and listened
A few seconds went by
Then he heard the faint bright sound of it hitting the cement
He looked up into the night sky

Clear, no planes, no clouds, nothing but darkness and stars
He threw another penny off and listened
He spat and listened to the barely audible splat
He threw himself off
All he heard was the wind

✠ ✠ ✠

Come to my funeral
Sing me your dearest song
Climb into this funeral bed with me
Love this corpse
Play me your real music
It's alright
I won't tell anyone, I'm dead
I'll never betray you, I'm dead
Everything I say is final, get it?
Touch me, hold the corpse
It's cold I know
Fuck the memory, taste what was
I'm dead, hold me, make me miss life
Breathe into my mouth
Sleep with the dead
Look into my dead eyes, tell me the truth
Your one truth
I won't tell anyone
I'm dead
Where I'm going, no one cares to know
Touch this dead thing
Lie down with this rotting figure
Feel your thoughts melt
Your memories turn on you
Turn you into a self inflictor
Ride with the dead tonight

✠ ✠ ✠

I am Dead Man
I am un-numbered, un-filed

I am untouchable
I laugh at you everyday
Everything you do falls short of me
You can't kill me, I'm Dead Man
I threw myself away before you could get to me with your disease
You fucking cripples
I am the great failure
The endless botched suicide attempt
The super charged embarrassment
I am all the things that fell short
I am all disappointment
I manufacture all the things that you hate in yourself
I am all your secrets
You'll never get to me
I'll be the hot monkey on your back for the rest of your life
I am king of the modern day car crash
I am the ten-ton alienator machine
I inject hope into you like a disease
I drain it from you to cause you pain
I make you cause yourself pain
That's the way it should be
You're always eager to blame others for your discontent
I like to run you up against yourself
Watch you drown in self pity
I breathe on you so hard your back wants to break
When I kiss you, you're gone forever
You hate me?
No
You don't deserve to hate me
Learn to hate yourself better
I'm here to help you until death motherfucker

✠ ✠ ✠

You see what they do when they get the chance
They rape and kill and steal
Can you feel their disease?
Do you ever feel like a prisoner?

Like you're being sucked dry?
Do you ever feel hated?
Do you ever feel you're destroyed by them everyday?
They are not your friends

✠ ✠ ✠

It's hard to keep shit together
Depression is always there, waiting to hammer down
Makes it hard to be around others for any sustained period of time
When I extend myself to others I always regret it
At the end of it I always feel I said too much
I get mad when I feel the need to communicate with them
They ask questions like tourists walking around my face
It's a constant battle to hold back the anger and the rage
Sometimes when I see them I want to kill them all
Some of the things they have done to me over the years
Burned me with cigarettes and were allowed to walk away
Seems to me that you should get killed for doing shit like that
I know this and that's what keeps me separated from them all the time
I know I'm a freak
They don't like it when they see themselves in me
It makes them violent and makes me stronger

✠ ✠ ✠

Streets full of eyes checking me out
I listen to the report
The black guys on the basketball court think I'm hot
They laugh and cheer as I pass
Like I really need this shit
I feel like I got the wrong planet
When I try to be close to someone
I temporarily forget that they are one of them
Rooms full of eyes
Always looking
I don't like them like I used to
They don't get to me like they used to either
They used to get me all wound up

Then one day I realized that it's all nothing
Now I see them differently
I see right through them
I don't hear them the same way either
They sound like little dogs yapping
It doesn't count
It doesn't matter
It doesn't exist

☩ ☩ ☩

I see them yes I see them
Like pale hairless cattle
Packed into subway cars rushing off to the circus
They all want to get in the center ring
Sick and scared I see them running
They sweat when they're cold, cold blooded
You would think they would have a little more imagination
I have no desire to die like my father and mother died
They way they died thousands of times
Corralled, fed shit, made to stand in line
Sent on errands and degraded by clowns
I don't want to go up on any of the crosses
I'm tired of hearing about the crosses
The tired, empty, tiny pain
Don't try to make it matter to me
Have you ever seen a man running to catch a bus
An overweight man running like he's going to die
Could you imagine how that would hurt
Your heart pounding
Sweating for the boss
Eyes bugging out
They got tricked a long time ago
Tell me it's not that way for you too
Don't tell me that they made you hard and steely eyed
Jaded and short of breath
You have to be careful
They're everywhere

☩ ☩ ☩

Those who know are the lucky ones
The ones that don't look lucky really are
It's the ones that know they're sick that stand a chance
They know there's a war on
The world is a bad place that kills people
The strong are killed along with the weak
The weak take longer, they hide in the cracks
It's easy to see the sick ones
The ones choking on life
Trying to choke the life out of life
Battling the elements
You see the cowards and their doctrine of cowardice
They peer timidly from their tombs
They feel convenient pain
Something for a thrill
The strong live
The weak take years to die
My heart goes to the ones that struggle
The ones that search and destroy
More savagery, more beauty, more life

✝ ✝ ✝

I keep telling myself that I'm not bitter
That their poison has not gotten to me
That I have risen above their petty timid reality
That they have not mutilated my mind
That I have not been broken and made to crawl
I am filled with burning rage
I feel it rise inside me and it makes me choke
I think back to the past
I see that I was taken for a ride by them
Friends, parents
My father calling me "mister"
I spend a lot of time spitting out pieces of myself
Pieces that have been ripped and torn
Ridding their blood from my blood
Wondering who I am underneath the scar tissue
After all this, what will be left

Will I be able to recognize myself
Will I know what to do?

✢ ✢ ✢

I see your face in my mind and I pull away from myself
It's like I'm spitting on my soul
I cause myself pain by thinking of you
I think of you and it's the worst
Usually people don't mean that much to me
You're different
I think of you and I fall into a hole
I see your eyes in other women
It makes me small and foolish
This has no punch line
It's just a locked groove
I miss you

✢ ✢ ✢

The room is my helper tonight
The walls stare me down
I turn on myself, can't stop turning
The room is a womb that kills
Makes me an expert in the making of high grade depression
I'm tired of talk
The sound of their voices makes me want to scream
Maybe I can sit in this room until I die
That would be so good, so gutless, so fitting
I would know myself so well by then
I wouldn't have to think

✢ ✢ ✢

This place fills me with hate
They try to tell me about love
I can't see it on this road
Screaming about love as they run forward with knives
I had to get rid of love to survive
Love was trying to kill me so I learned hate
They can't stop the fire that burns inside me

They can't stop the hate machine
You tell me that love is the answer
Has it ever occurred to you
How fucked up you are?
They took your identity
The rest came only too easily
You crumble
All your books will not help you now
I can't wait for a lot of years to pass
I want to be the one to see you and your sad face
As you drag it to the death you fear so much
And do so much to hurry forward

✠ ✠ ✠

Tonight depression beats down on me with lead hands
The night holds me prisoner
Inside my brain I smolder with violence
I'm on a slow burn that's turning me to ash
I don't sing love songs
There's too many holes shot through them
I don't feel lonely
For who, for what?
They'll sell you out in a minute
Hate is the only thing that lasts
Hate is always at the bottom of the cup
You see hope running out of the house
With blood streaming from its asshole
You see hate standing on the front porch
Laughing, zipping up its pants
Love lies and never pays the rent
Neither does hate but it never makes you think it will
So I'm here tonight, unmoved

✠ ✠ ✠

I know what I'm doing
I'm killing myself slowly
It's an addiction to destruction
These places I go, these death houses

Endless highways to death
All roads going to death
All the time rattling my bones
Dying over and over
Looking for the big rise
It's one big scream
The big night
The huge overwhelming dark
Sucking the air out of my lungs
Scorching my dreams
Driving down a dark throat
It's nothing but a death trip

✠ ✠ ✠

Sometimes the only thing that sees me through is hate
It make me see clearly
Love makes me blind
I always regret love
I have never regretted hate
In the middle of nowhere with all against me
I use hate to endure
I like hate better than sex
It makes me burn brightly
Hate makes me think I'm a genius
It's like an aspirin for my soul
No money, strangers in my face
Good thing I have hate
Hate keeps my stitches from ripping apart
Sometimes it feels good to be alive
The rest of the time it's a joke

✠ ✠ ✠

Budapest
Night time
You and I standing against a wall
We are burning
Your breath on my neck
Your nails in my shoulders

Our bodies locked and grinding
Your boyfriend in the apartment
Drinking vodka, listening to rock and roll
He knows that we're gone
There's not a lot he can do about it
I've been on both sides of this one

⊹ ⊹ ⊹

PASSING THROUGH

—The factories torture the evening skies of Coventry.

—The filthy, grinning wino clutches a large bottle of wine and staggers into an alley in Leeds

—A woman passes me, her perfume is the same as the shit my step-mother wore. It makes my stomach turn.

—I look into the window of the house where I wrote all the songs for Hot Animal Machine. It has a for rent sign up. The table is in the same place, the same postcards are tacked to the wall.

—A bum blocks the sidewalk. He wants money for a cup of tea. His breath reeks of liquor.

—The flight attendants make jokes about the large breasted passenger.

—The factories are full of square eyed windows. I see smoke, flames and steam. I smell the stench. I think to myself that someone will be working in there for fifteen years without quitting.

—A car load of gay boys pull up next to me as I walk and ask me if I want to go for a ride.

—A man and a woman search a dumpster for food. They pull out rotting vegetables. A van pulls up, a man with a suit gets out. His suit makes him seem impervious to the fate of the garbage eaters.

—I sit in a public park and look at the teenagers smoking like there's no tomorrow. They look over at me and I start laughing in their faces.

—A beautiful woman gets out of the driver's side of a Jaguar. A fat little man gets out the other side. I wish she would drop him and take me with her. I'm waiting for the bus with a 12 oz from 7-11. I am dirty and crazy looking. She eyes me with disgust and walks away with the worm man. He looks back at me and smiles.

⊹ ⊹ ⊹

I got hit with a stone that was thrown
Through the wire of a long distance telephone
Static on the line couldn't get through
She told me she didn't want to see me anymore
Then she hung up
I sat down on the bed of 100 hotel rooms
Everything got hollow and back to normal
I guess I'm free to go out and make other mistakes

✝ ✝ ✝

Child of the fist
Here lies the lie of experience
Hard heat and heavy step
Aware, ready to wince recoil and attack
Constantly in the corner
On the ropes
If you were thinking about it I wouldn't do it
His hostility is handed down
He was stepped on and nearly destroyed
The eyes give him away every time
You can see the animal rising
Child of the fist
Lord of the solitary refinement
The ear mark of destructive genius
Genius through brutality and fear
A man in touch with the ultimate perception
Instinct

✝ ✝ ✝

The filth
The pool of dried vomit at the bus stop
The jeering youths in the passing car
The man getting busted by the pigs
Scar maker
Big cement fist to kiss
Alienator
Disease spreader

Bruises into my flesh
Welts rising in this bad exhaust dream
In this pummeling madness
It gets easier to die and fail
Your feet find themselves in line
My cancer heart!
It was always like this
Pull back the scar curtain
Roll back the iron lining
You'll find someone who remembers other times
But one who also crouches and waits
For the cheap bite of the weak
Who live and sneak peeks
At the strong who aren't long for the suicide song
Amen, good night, come here, I won't hurt you
Yes I know it's bad
But you get good at lying to yourself

✠ ✠ ✠

Something
Someone
Some power, force, unrestrained act of will
Take me out of here
I want to feel myself in your grip
If you're going to crush me go ahead
I can't find anything to live for
I'm not interested in their trophies
They're turning all the songs
Into tarnished coppers at the bottom of a tin cup
So smash me
Reality
Big soul incinerator
So run me
Road
Big time stomper
I want blood
I want a 10 star storm

Blow me into the next time zone
I'll see you next time
In the next crime
I'll burn and freeze alone
But don't leave me here
To eat dust and drink lie filled water
I don't want the shallow mind grave
I need something deep
Take me and destroy me
But don't leave me in this

☩ ☩ ☩

The mission
The burning idea
Blinds me to obstacles, numbs me to pain
Turns me mute, makes them into strangers
I know the flesh is weak
It falls away
So easily swept and cleared
There's one thing that can carry us through
The idea
The idea makes us strong
Embrace the power
The world is full of creeps
Watch them crawl
Don't get too close
They'll pull you down
Keep the idea intact
Get to that power
I'm not talking about money
I'm talking about power, the idea
You'll never have to crawl
You'll never have to be one of them
If you keep the idea, embrace the power
I know that skin is only skin deep
Look past it
Don't fool yourself

Don't go insane
Get to the power

·I· ·I· ·I·

2 a.m. bus ride
Heading east on Hollywood
The dead men are riding tonight
Going to Crenshaw, Lawndale, Long Beach, Echo Park
It's all the same, a shit pit
The lucky ones are getting off work
They get on like hollow numbers
The occasional wave of recognition
Drinking beers from paper bags
A hard ride to the bottom

·I· ·I· ·I·

Year after year your cities continue to destroy themselves
I watch them stab themselves, use dirty needles
Cities chew you up with iron teeth
Nowhere men, nowhere women
You whore yourselves daily
You can never kill yourselves enough
Always looking to get the latest disease
I spit on your heads
You're turning people like me into heroes

·I· ·I· ·I·

For so long I resisted, I told myself that I was wrong about you. A
long time ago my hatred spoke to me in clear simple words. I saw
things for what they were and it filled me with hate. To see things as
they are is to hate. For a while I tried to fit into their world of love
and blindness and found it to be violent and filthy. I was filled with
dirt after listening to their words of lies and desperation. I became
part of their losing world. I can't see how they take it year after year.
Perhaps they're so numb that they don't even feel it. This morning
my hatred came and filled me with light and clarity. I want to drop a

bomb on this shit. I think at this point it's the best thing I can do. My hate burns clean.

+ + +

Dream for the future night
I walk your streets
My breath is filled with the stench of garbage
You might as well shit on yourselves
You wait for the other pigs to hose you off
When I walk your streets I think of bombs
I want to see the whole shit house go up in flames
It would be good to see you burn
Burn all the way to ash
It would be good to see you do something all the way
I should line you up and shoot you in the street
Right in front of your fucked up apartment building
You could fall right in with the other pieces of garbage
I am right about this
I live to destroy your world
I'm the best thing that ever happened to you

+ + +

The Rhythm of Decline
Your world is crumbling
Falling apart in front of your eyes
All things beating in the Rhythm of Decline
Soon it will all be over
You'll wonder why as you get shoved into the train
Smell the garbage
Shake your own hand
Now bite it
Congratulations
You're a success
I am the Sanitation Engineer
You can call me Almighty

+ + +

When we're together we play tapes
You put in yours and I put in mine
We press play
We have a relationship
We can fuck
But can't look each other in the eyes
Pathetic

✠ ✠ ✠

From hell to hell on a rope I swing
So many sets of eyes before I pass
Night after night rips across my flesh
Confession after confession
I feel rung out at the end of each one
I manage to find new parts of myself to destroy
Memories come like assassins
I want to smash all mirrors
Enough reflection
When I think too much
I stab myself in the back
I must move forward
I look for the rope to swing to the next hot place
It's getting harder to see the explosions
They are moving in, castrating the thunder
Turning it all into wall paper
They kill my nights
Memories get me when I'm weak
I Must break out of this room

✠ ✠ ✠

There's a small part of my heart that's always sad
Part of me that walks with a slow aching step
Forever longing
The beauty of that
To be forever longing
Too much joy makes the time pass too quickly
A bit of sadness slows things down so you can see it
Makes the sun set slower

The poison of joy
They cannot imagine a beauty in sadness
They stay away
They never get past the surface
When I fall down inside I find new parts
It's like digging for soul's gold
I never want to become a stranger to the downside
That which moves me when I cannot be moved
The great longing, the great sadness
That's my inspiration
Filling the void
Filling the grave
Filling out the time card

✛ ✛ ✛

I told her so much tonight
I told her of the great longing
The endlessness that I feel
I told her the things that mattered to me
And how hard it is to find things that matter
I thought I was making a lot of sense
When I saw the cold door of her eyes
I stopped talking and went back to my jungle
I feel homeless in their eyes
Surrounded by a wasteland in their embrace
Their everywhere is my nowhere
I'm tired of feeling lost and empty in their oasis
Life is not too short

✛ ✛ ✛

Once they get in they never seem to get out again
They get trapped like roaches in a roach hotel
The big house of love
A big run down house that never sleeps
Life waits outside
I see the few crawling survivors
On their hands and knees going out the back door
Cut and bleeding they curl up and die

Some of the fools try to get back in
They try to break in the side window
They get their ass kicked and swear it's the best
It looks like a torture chamber
I don't play that shit
They can call me anything they want
I always see through
I always look at them as they crawl
They're lost in love
I'm lost in something else

✝ ✝ ✝

I don't know when it happened
Parts of me died
I don't know if they all died at once
Or if it was in installments
Maybe I killed them off
Too many nights trying to destroy my weakness
In front of strangers
Maybe I did it in hotel rooms dotted all over
When I look into your eyes
I don't feel the way I used to
It's not you, you're beautiful as always
It's me, I'm dying piece by piece
Things don't seem as good as they used to
Maybe I'm growing old
Remember when someone's touch
Could send you to another world?
When it was the only thing you needed?
I feel like a soldier finishing the mission
I don't know if I'm as stupid as I used to be
Half of life is fucking up
The other half is dealing with it
If I had tears
They would be hollow

✝ ✝ ✝

Some nights I try not to think too much
Loneliness creeps into my thoughts
I see how alone I am
On the good nights I'm distracted
On the other nights it's all there is
That's why I keep busy all the time
I make things to do to take up the time
The more I do the more I see the emptiness
On a lonely axis I turn
Sometimes I want to paint all the windows black
Somehow thinking that it will all go away
It's hard to be here

☩ ☩ ☩

Keep walking these battered streets
Scared and sullen streets
They gotcha
You try to stay clean of the full on disease
But they gotcha
They run the game
They're in charge of all that good looking shit
This city turns people into losers
There's no escape, no outlet
People hacking off parts of their souls
They give readily to the great castrator
As time passes
The machine gets more refined
Easier to get to
More deadly
A world of whoredom

☩ ☩ ☩

Take me into your heart
Swallow me whole
All the way down
Let me run wild in your dreams
Let me go and tear through you

Let me see what you're made of from the inside
Let me take hold
Let me wrap my hand around your soul
Only for a little while
A life time isn't all that long
You can't keep me out
You thought you had a choice
You thought you had a thought of your own
I think I'll destroy you and waste your time
I'll make you think I'm all there is to life
I use you up as you go down the line
I am lust

✠ ✠ ✠

The streets by my house are covered with garbage
Every few blocks there's a pile of safety glass
A human broke into another human's man-made car
The city chokes on black blood and old needles
Cheap gasoline and red wine
We get the drugs flown in
We kill ourselves exotically
Outside the bars, there's sometimes blood on the sidewalk
Someone got stabbed down the street recently
Made the Times
The sidewalks make hollow sounds when I walk
I know it's ready to cave in
I don't want to forget
One scream, one gunshot
I want to remember it all
The place I'm going doesn't have time for decadence
My television has no channels
You can't touch me
You can't sell me anything

✠ ✠ ✠

She kept telling me about how she had been going to the clinic and
staying clean. It's all she talked about. She said that she had to stay

away from all of her friends that were still doing it. They should hand out manuals with dime bags telling you how to creatively lie to your straight friends and make them think that you're clean so they'll hang out with you and let you into their houses even after you've ripped them off a couple of times. I hear the same shit from junkies. They're always so in control. She came stumbling out of my bathroom high as shit. She passed out on my couch and didn't get up until the next morning. She told me she was straight even when I gave her back the cap to the syringe she had left in the sink. As I was kicking her out of my house she asked me what she was going to do. I gave her bus fare and told her that I had no idea. Junkies always seem to come up with something don't they?

✠ ✠ ✠

The maggots boiling in the can of meat
They tell me about what happens
To things that are set out to rot
Why do I smell smoke in my dreams
They'll kill you with your own secrets
Anger boiling in the American ghettos
Nothing will come soon enough
Nothing will make enough sense
Nothing will be strong enough
Nothing will be there to wipe the slate clean
Open up my head and find this

✠ ✠ ✠

Where I live is filthy
Even the cement is rotting
I pass the hotel
There's a woman sitting out front
Her knees are scabby and she looks like shit
She sees me and gets up to hit me for change
I sidestep and keep moving
I will not help the disease
I pass the spray painted walls
Barb wire, razor wire, vacant lots

Los Angeles is rotting
I see a palm tree with a poster tacked to it
"Stand Proud!"
Sure, but don't get any dogshit on you
Don't be late
Don't get shot
Don't be here after dark

+ + +

You thought that they were your friends
You're on the ground and sinking
You see that you were wrong
No one will pick you up
That's what they do best
They let you fall
They tell you that you're beautiful
Can't you see what they've done to you
They wrecked your beautiful face
They sold your smile
They turned you into garbage
You fell hard
I came running
It was too late
They stole the jewels from your eyes
The last time I saw you
You were a museum piece
A history lesson
A walking book on how to be ugly
Who to stay away from
It's too late for you
Hollywood kills another
Nice young thing from the midwest

+ + +

A man sits on a public bus on his way home from work. He is exhausted. The bus is hot and the smell of human sweat is almost overpowering. He thinks of the stranger he married, their child who will have cold strangers as parents. He thinks that the last person who he would want for a father would be himself. The apartment is too small and the walls are too thin. Time is running out and things didn't turn out the way he thought and hoped they would. Not as if he had a clue as to what it was he was supposed to do with his life. No direction. Swept up in the winds of carbon monoxide and pain. He stares at the floor and inhales. His head explodes.

☦ ☦ ☦

We were walking on a trail
You looked into my eyes and all you could see was jungle
There are some people that you can't get close to
You find that you can't find them
They hide themselves too well
Ones who paint the walls of their rooms with their eyes
Ones that fill endless hours of silence
With the sound of their breathing
Alone in any place, in any embrace
Beyond heartbreak
Beyond love and hate
Invisible people
Terminal strangers
We walk on time's outer crust
Enveloped in shadows
Encircled in pure jungle

☦ ☦ ☦

Be careful with your face
Be careful with your eyes
Be careful with what you say
You can't retract a single thing you do
Every action is true
Some people don't care about apologies
When you lose your temper
You throw in all your cards
You give them everything they need to pull you apart
Be careful with what you let show

Be careful with what you hold back and how you do it
Some people can read faces like headlines

✠ ✠ ✠

I sleep on floors of people's houses
Always moving, always displaced
I was walking down this road today before soundcheck
I was thinking about this endless shuffle
Always moving
A lifelong haul
I'm a constant stranger
But I always know where I am
Always moving

✠ ✠ ✠

I hate to think of you
I hate the memories
They always lead up to the part where you dumped me
Last week you sent me a letter
Telling me that you have been thinking about me
And how you want to be my friend
Your beauty is a disease
A sharp blade that keeps cutting night after night
Scar tissue is stronger than normal flesh
You are turning me into a living scar
I don't know whether to thank you or myself

✠ ✠ ✠

The great emptiness
After the show is over
I come out on the stage to load out the gear
An hour ago the place was full of people and noise
I look up at the roof
I can see the ghost of the music
All of a sudden it all seems so futile
I feel empty like the dance hall
I feel wooden like the floor

When the equipment is loaded out
And the exit door has been slammed shut behind us
I feel extinct

✝ ✝ ✝

In these places I see them
Dead drunks
Choking on the booze
Tiny pig eyes that squint to check me out
Ugly and fat, waiting for death
They bang their glasses and yell
When they are told to shut up, they do
They are broken
Spirits stomped to death by dirty shoes
The urinal stinks all the way to the entrance
All the way back to their hovels
The way they look
I don't think they know it's happy hour

✝ ✝ ✝

Tonight you smell gunpowder in the air
The street sounds are ripping through your head
You think about killing yourself as you stare at the ceiling
Ignore it
It's just a tiny disease that the city gave you
The streets give you poison dreams
Little seeds that sprout in your mind
Everything starts to talk to you
Sirens sing to you, brakes call out your name
The water pipes chant
It's hard not to hear it when they speak so clearly to you
You can't tell anybody
They don't know what you're going through
But you and I know
Don't let the cities fool you
You see how they glitter and lie
The glass eyed women who chew you up and spit you out

They leave you cut and broken in spirit
The filthy air fills your lungs with fire
The eternal hell of your room
They speak to you in rational tones
Be careful of yourself

✠ ✠ ✠

Are you still alive?
Open your eyes upon this summer blackout
You know the summers are scarring us
Year after year they drag us down the molten streets
The sunsets burn down our backs
I was out tonight, looking at the blinking moaning city
I know you're out there somewhere
I wonder if you're thinking what I'm thinking
Do you ever think about you and me
And the summer nights we passed through?
They were some of the best times of my life
I inhale this night
It always smells the same and it fills me with longing
Do you ever sit outside and look into the black heat
And think about this?
Do summer nights ever break your heart?

✠ ✠ ✠

I'm on the floor of some guy's house
I don't know his name, I call him "Hey Man"
I smashed my nose playing tonight
Bled all over myself
Now I'm here all crashed out with two people snoring next to me
I look at my dirty pillow
I see new and old blood stains
All mine
I had a sheet awhile ago
It had a lot of blood on it
A girl bled on it one night in I forget where
Nice girl anyway

My nose hurts and I'm all alone
Sleeping on a mildewed sheet
My back and knee are in pain's embrace
I got no complaints
Except I wish we got out on the road earlier this year
Good night

✠ ✠ ✠

I'm the straight man
Walking with a slight limp down crooked streets
I am the set up man
Your jokes fly by my head
They aren't funny
They don't penetrate the skin, skull or anything else
What do you look like turned inside out?
Put your hand in a vice and crank it tight
Speak the truth like a dog speaks the truth
I'm a bit worn down from the process of definition
At the bottom of your eyes I find a shaking uncertainty
I know you by your cracks and infirmities
They shine like badges
I eye you calmly
There's nothing you can do that doesn't warn me

✠ ✠ ✠

I used to sing myself to sleep
I was raised on my own voice
I would talk to myself on my paper route
When someone talks to me
I often answer myself back
I'm the one I have come to depend on
I figure the more self involved I become the better
On the outside, people will just wear you out
I write letters to myself
I wish there was a way to call myself on the phone
When I need to see a face that understands me
I look into the mirror

When I was growing up I would be alone in the apartment
I would talk to myself
Strangers are too strange

✠ ✠ ✠

Tonight my thoughts go out to the woman
She has no name
Because she has all their names
I stare at a blank wall
I can see her face
My thoughts fly from my skull
They crash and burn in the night
I sit in the darkness as my soul starves
Every sense sharpens
I can articulate my starvation for touch
She becomes more beautiful
Her eyes burn brighter as the nights pass
Her features become clear
More nights pass
She starts to decompose
She wears away to black night still moving air
I starved her to death
I destroyed that longing

✠ ✠ ✠

They're all over me
I smell their beer breath mixed with my sweat
I can't answer all the questions, I can barely think straight
Now I'm alone in the room
To be hard you must be alone
To withstand this shit you must be hard
The logic works itself out right in front you
Be alone as much as you can
If you want to hit like a ton of fire
You have to get to the essential number
One

✠ ✠ ✠

Road
Looking out of the window of the van
It's night and we are speeding through Germany to Austria
I look out and see lights and fields
It could be Wisconsin
I think to myself as the lights strobe the median
This is my home
The road passing underneath me
The truckstops, the weary faces, the road, the movement
The miles slam through my eyes
Crease my face and harden my jaw
I can't think straight unless I'm moving
I sleep in hotels and on floors and I sleep soundly
The road is cold, lonely and true
It gives me life
One long road stretching out in front of me

⊹ ⊹ ⊹

I have no problem with hostility
I was raised with it
I was taught to be hostile or be destroyed
The other night when you threw the lit cigarette
The hostile brother came out
Last night when you tried to fuck with me
I sent you to the hospital
You sent me to the police station
As I was sitting with the pigs
I was thinking that I'm not fit for society
You tease the animal and it smacks you
You can't handle so you call the police
You make me lose control

⊹ ⊹ ⊹

In these brutal times honesty leaves scars
I can see why so many of them stand in line and lie
I can see what the truth has done to me
I'm not as old as I used to be

I feel farther away from them now
Than when I hated them all

✠ ✠ ✠

What does it take?
Do I want to know?
Do I care anymore?
Can I say that the scars on my hands don't exist?
From all the times I reached out
Can I say that I like it anymore?

✠ ✠ ✠

When I go outside I feel stupid
I look at them and I can't see the reason I'm here
It's like being in a bad movie
So I stay in the room and wait to go back on the road again
I went out to see a show tonight
As I pass people I hear them say my name
I run back to them and ask them what they want
They look at me like I live in a museum
I go back to the room and wait to leave again
I don't get it
This place rejects me

✠ ✠ ✠

Waiting at the bus stop on Santa Monica Blvd.
Cars pulling over to check out my dick
I stand away from the curb so I don't get confused with the rental
meat
Besides, it's easier to dodge the bullets
I was in a club waiting to see a band
But they were going on so late I couldn't take it anymore
Having to look at people trying to look cool
As they died from boredom
On the way out I heard this guy give the bouncer a raft of shit about
the wait in line. The bouncer told him that there was nothing he
could do. The guy kept it up and the bouncer got mad and said that
he was having a bad night and he'd love to take it out on his narrow

white ass. I thought that was a great line.
I look at the others waiting for the bus
Dull and covered with LA's spit
No place on earth bakes and destroys them like here
This is the alienator land
You have to learn the prison shuffle
It's the only way to get along
It all looks like a jail to me
I look at the skinhead with the incredibly ugly girlfriend
They start to kiss violently
Where the hell do you think they started out from?
Where are they going?
What are their dreams?
Human machines getting the life squeezed out of them
I don't want to go out like this
I don't want to go out near this desert hell

✝ ✝ ✝

Where are you tonight my loneliness?
I sit in my room
I keep the music loud to distract my mind
There was a woman here last night
It was hard to not walk out in the middle of the whole thing
Where is the echo in my heart?
Will I ever meet someone
That will take the bitter taste from my mouth?
I am loneliness
I wish I had someone to miss

✝ ✝ ✝

Alien boy
He is ugly
It gets worse
He has bad skin, is too smart and sensitive for his own good
He lives in the mid west, Russia, Paris, you name it
He feels it
The silence of his room
The occasional rage

The desire to touch
Sometimes it gets to be too much
He claws at his flesh
He's everywhere
I saw him last night at a show
He told me about the writers that he likes
I could tell from the way he was describing them
That these books were saving his life
I get letters from him all the time
They don't understand him in Berlin
He can't identify in Portland
He can't get the courage to talk to a woman in New York
He tells me about the music he likes
His favorites never come to Mississippi, N. Dakota or Alabama
He says he lives in his room
He writes a lot
Maybe he'll send me some if I want to see it
Alien boys, rock steady

✠ ✠ ✠

I want to thank you
You taught me not to need or want you
I took the lesson and went on
You forced me into myself
You made me see myself
I learned not to depend on anyone for anything
I remember you told me all this stuff
About how you needed me
I took it all in
I wanted to be with somebody
And then you took it all back
It's all a lie
A commercial for something
So now I'm out here in the free zone
It's no ghetto

✠ ✠ ✠

They are not deserving of my hate
I don't hate them
I hate the disease that's eating them alive
I hate the thing that makes them what they are
I hate the machine that causes them so much pain
My hate is a grand scale machine
A full and wonderful event
Not to be squandered on some punk
Some weak powerless fear victim
No
I'm taking mine to a higher place

✠ ✠ ✠

12.2.88 12:58 a.m. LA CA:
I walk down the street to dump the last of the day's mail
The air smells like something huge has died near by
Maybe everyone in the city died and no one told me
I see a couple looking into their car
It got broken into
There's safety glass on the sidewalk
I was in the studio all day
Seven hours of listening to myself
My body hurts
I have band practice early in the morning
I called a girl tonight, to make some contact
I'm still wondering why I did something so stupid
She put me in my place
I know better now
Like I really have something to say to a girl
I cross the street
I see several girls leaving a club
I think of a man sitting in his room
He puts a gun in his mouth and pulls down
He hangs himself
He lies in bed with a beautiful woman
Whenever I see this pitiful stretch of Sunset Blvd.
Bathed in crime lights

I know that I'm in the deadest place on earth
It's where dreams come to die
My house is right up the street

✝ ✝ ✝

Last night playing that show in LA
The pain got me good
My entire body was consumed
Every movement I made was accompanied by a cramp
By the last song I could barely stand up
I fought myself to stand up straight
I could feel my body rebel
My own body turning against me in front of strangers
I went backstage and sat in a corner
My legs felt so fucked that I didn't trust them to stand
That's my religion, power through pain
Today I woke up sore and strong
The other day this woman told me
I was wrong, negative and violent
I couldn't make her see where I was coming from
I would rather die than take all the shit she does at her job
I would rather lose the whole thing tomorrow than sellout

✝ ✝ ✝

Alien song
Where do I fit in?
It must be a place I've never been to
I don't understand what they are saying
They don't make me feel anything
I can't get close
I don't know where to go
I stay inside my head
Words choke me
I've learned to destroy parts of myself
I kill the parts that feel
I'm afraid of them
I feel like I must be a different species
I feel lonely but I'm working to get rid of that

I'm working hard not to want anything from their world
It's hard going, but I'm getting better all the time
Sometimes I feel like I'm falling
Sometimes I feel like I'm on ground so solid
Back to the wall with all the answers
Having seen heard and felt enough of their world
I am alien

╬ ╬ ╬

Do you remember the last time?
The great crash, the big depression?
The one that felt like a storm had ripped through you
And left four days of mud in your guts?
Maybe you were in your room
Nothing made sense
You couldn't hide from yourself
Something came in
And stole all the parts of your brain that didn't hate you
Self doubt was coursing through your veins
Do you remember that one?
Nothing worked
You tried playing your good records
The ones that got you through the last one
Iggy, Lou, The Godfather of Soul
The real thing
Even they couldn't get you out of the hole
You couldn't think of one thing to change the situation
All of a sudden you didn't know yourself anymore
You started hating the stranger you were alone in the room with
Do you remember that one?
Me too

╬ ╬ ╬

The memories come and wash pain, sadness and regret over you
They have sharp eyes that stare into yours without flinching
They cut ugly shapes into your flesh
The night moves slow like your oncoming death
Like a car crash that won't quit

Can you forget, can you get rid of it?
You're left with no choice but to deal with yourself
The memories track you down like assassins
You're amazed at the cruelty you inflict upon yourself
You're some kind of criminal
You hold your head in your hands
Feeling for the on-off switch

✠ ✠ ✠

Picture this
You're walking down a long hallway
On the walls are many pictures
Pictures of people you know
Pictures of yourself
All the good times
They taunt you with their silent stares
They start to talk to you all at once
You walk faster, trying to get away
It doesn't matter how fast you walk, the pictures won't stop
You recognize the faces the places, the times, all the things you were
All the things you were thinking
You hear yourself say:
I love you, I'm never going to die, I want to kill myself
You can't escape your life
You scream, you want to be someone else, something else
Someone without a face, without a name
Someone that never knew anyone, who never felt the pain
Someone that didn't have to exist all the time
Your history becomes your enemy
You run, you fall exhausted
But in your ears and eyes
The times that will never leave and never come back
They all come crashing in on you
Your body feels like a prison
You start to drown in yourself
Where to now?

✠ ✠ ✠

Strung out looking for a friend
Feeling sick, no one understands
You're a hero in disguise
Monkey chewing on your ear
Your body and its vile needs
Call a ghost on the phone
All of your friends have become strangers
You mutated, dipping low, lower
A race for the bottom
You're the only one on the trail
Grey sky, cold walls
Everything sounds like WW3 in a cement mixer
They never did understand

✟ ✟ ✟

There will be no Valhalla for you
There will be the television set and the beer
Waiting for you like a trap
There will be no glory
There will be re-runs and ulcers
There will be sleepless nights
Looking at all the women and thinking
Regrets hopes and dreams
The thoughts of a fighter on his way down
But you threw the fight
There will be no real life
There will be the alcohol circus
The sadness, the jealousy
There will be nothing at the end of your line
Except maybe a commercial
Father

✟ ✟ ✟

The noise they make sends me running
Sends me running and makes me feel alone
Their words hit me like hammers
Don't look, don't see me
Don't hurt me with your recognition eyes

You don't know how much it hurts
Don't talk to me
It reminds me of the distance
The cold room, the window I look through
The echo in my heart
The shallowness of my world
My cowardice
I like you
Don't tell me your name
Don't touch
I break too easily

✠ ✠ ✠

City
I will kill you
I will kill all of your friends
I will run them down like I'll run you down
Doesn't matter what you do
I don't sleep
I live to kill you
I am an institution, a way of death
Think of how napalm sticks and burns
I will hunt you, stalk you
I will infect your dreams
I will make you want me, need me
I will make you love me and then I will kill you
I am the definition of relentless
I win, you lose, always
I keep you plugged into my life support system
And then I cut you off
You die like some creep
Withered, polluted and destroyed
Give me your children, they taste good
So strong, so stupid
Me, so hungry, so beautiful
The perfect killing machine
I invented suicide
I am the ultimate disease

I suck the blood right out of you
You thank me for it
The sun never sets on my empire
Thanks to you, I work

✝ ✝ ✝

I am not in a state of confusion
I don't get hung up on emotion
My coldness will freeze the tears off your face
I see what love does to you
I see you drinking yourself into the floor
I see you destroy yourself
You try to deny your hate
You put it below you
You become a stranger and an enemy to yourself
See you in the real world

✝ ✝ ✝

I walk these streets
I see you
You don't see me, I'm a stranger
I see the desperate war you have going on
I walk the streets and observe
You hide your fear and call it something else
You're addicted to all the things that make you weak
I work hard to get your filth away from me
For awhile, your fake pain was all I had
Your words are antiques
Your movements are but gestures
You have made this place small and dirty
That's the way of the weak
The blind leading the crippled to the cliff
And then charging money to let them jump
You make suicide illegal so you can make a buck on misery
Your circus stinks
Fuck it
The storm is coming

✝ ✝ ✝

The days go on, I see them fall away
They tell me why I should follow them on the burnout path
It seems like internal drive is a disease
I thought they were like me
I see that I'm wrong
All I can do is get on with it
If you want to get things done
Stay away from people
They'll slow you down and break your heart

☩ ☩ ☩

Things are different now
They guard and distance themselves
They used to confront, now they hide
They have cultivated arrogance
I see through it
It's hard to see them retire before they're dead
At the end of the trail all hearts will be broken
All promises will be crushed
All bones will be turned to dust

☩ ☩ ☩

I watch the music play
I watch the fat liar with the untouchable money
These bands take all the people that like them
To a place that bleeds painlessly
And then there are people like me
People that you throw peanuts at
I see you, yes I do
I must endure your shallowness daily
How can you lie to yourself like that?
How can you go for this shit?
This guy told me I should take some time out to smell the roses
I am the things that you deny
I am all the things that you hate the world for
I wish I wasn't alive as much as you are dead

☩ ☩ ☩

1.2.89
Ugly machine
Take me up
Pull me into your giant cylinder
Tear me up
Reduce me to the component parts
Show me what I'm made of
I want to know

✝ ✝ ✝

The woman in the jar
Her friends gathered in a circle
To wish her well into the next world
Dead a week
Cancer
It was a clear day
I could see the Hollywood sign

✝ ✝ ✝

These hotel rooms
Lost rooms
Every night a new place to sleep
Reinforce the emptiness
Clarify the alienation
The nights rip by
Layers of distance coat my brain
These sterile un-lived in rooms
Stacked, looking over the neon sprawl
Terminal jet lag

✝ ✝ ✝

The fields of pain have opened my eyes
Riding Death's highway to the end of the line
A brutal dream has been inflicted upon me
A darkness runs through me
This evil life
I have found ways to mutilate you
To make you show your true colors

I see you dancing without a brain
Mindless energy multiplying like car wrecks
I poke my fingers into you
Ball you up and throw myself away
An alien is born free and burning
The poison desert sings tonight
Slamming wind and metal together
The sparks fly and it's real
I learn from what was
I hear music in the ruins
I find harmony in the ashes
The safety is off
The One is straight ahead

✝ ✝ ✝

Anything for a rockstar
I was wrong, I thought you were different
I let down my guard
I thought it was your kindness that was drawing me out
I was just walking the plank
Talking like a fool trying to get it all out of me
Peeling my skin off and cutting myself to pieces
And then you asked me if I wanted a ride to the hotel
I said ok
You said: Anything for a rockstar
It became clear that you were just another one of them
You put a quarter in the talk box
I was a good evening of human entertainment
Now you can tell your friends
You're all the same to me

✝ ✝ ✝

Decay
Weakness falling inwards
Pushed up against the wall
Alcohol disease
Too stupid for reality
The booze gives you the soft edges

The throat waiting to get cut
Tonight I watched you crash slowly
So this is the place you picked for your slow death
Ah, fuck it
Just shut up and drink
Your life's not much

✣ ✣ ✣

In Brisbane Australia
Backstage
A large cockroach runs through my clothes
The room is lit with florescent bulbs
The opening band is almost finished
Out there, about two hundred people
Drunks walking in circles
There's a mirror over the sink
I can see my face spotted with rust
Sometimes, like right now
I feel empty as the hull of an old boat
Just a ribcage waiting to play
Sometimes I feel like such a goddamn fool

✣ ✣ ✣

Every night on this road
A perfect ugly brutal blade
Stabbing hacking, deciding that what is, is
A good night rips its claws down your back
You feel this beast
And you know you'll miss it when it's gone
You'll go looking for it somewhere else
In someone else
In your broken knuckles or bleeding mouth
Getting off, getting out
Getting onto the next one
Pull yourself from one to the next
Line to line, vine to vine
You're swinging now, singing now, bleeding now
Time never ends, it just finishes you

Recline on this beautiful mattress of endless feeling
You haven't fallen until you can't get up
You aren't beaten if you can still take a beating
The night is my friend because it's always here
Or on its way
Gotcha

✝ ✝ ✝

My eyes grow clearer as I walk the trail
I cut through the thick jungle searching for the beauty
That will fill my shoes with my blood
No, I'll do it myself
It will be my tiny statement
My extension, my grasp
My elbow will snap broken
Don't you feel it, the need to cut deep
The urge to stalk
Discipline, strength, straight lines
Silence, stealth, calculation
Discrimination and the lunge
There's nothing to explain
You have no questions for me
But you have questions filling your pockets
Destroy them one by one
Eat them, fuck them, enjoy them
But answer them yourself

✝ ✝ ✝

Nijamegan Holland
Forgotten thrown away
Cold raining outside
Hendrix blasting this bar
An asshole in the corner hands pounding the bar off time
I was here five years ago
Watched these guys beat each other up
It was more interesting than the set
Soon the hash bar will open

Grubby nicotined fingers will deal to grubby nicotined fingers
The night will close in damply
Like a slow moving coward
Another show, another stop on the train
Romance quit, got a real job
Pouring beer and coffee
In a building covered with spray paint
Look at all these people who traded in life for this
Lives lightly crumpled
Placed gently in the garbage
Not decadent
Just lazy and indifferent
Crumbling, teeth falling out
Trying to look cool
As the whole thing passes them by

✠ ✠ ✠

Cockroach 20th Century Fox
After we have destroyed their world
We'll come out of our holes and meet again
You'll wrap yourself around me
After the storm has cleared
We'll find each other
In the new jungle, in the new garden
After the storm, we'll crawl out of our holes and start again
We'll take back what was ours to begin with
We are the true masters of the earth
We rise so strong
We are perfection
They destroyed themselves

✠ ✠ ✠

Wheels and Wings
I walked down the ramp into the plane
London to Frankfurt, raining outside
Traveling alone eyes aching
Five subways shut down barely made the flight

Put on my headphones and put on a soul music compilation
Almost cried into my coffee
Looked at my face in the bathroom mirror, exhausted
I'm so tired, so lonely
I think of what I would say if I was with a woman
I'm so burned out, the only person I can stand is myself
I'm the only one I would put through this
Wheels and wings
The ride is everything
I'm all I've got
I'm all I can take
Another day has destroyed part of me
So far so good

✠ ✠ ✠

Montreal
I'm a ghost shuffling through these hallways
Train stations, endless tracks
In and through nights
Tunnels of shrouded walkways
Silent roaring separates me from all lives
Up flights of stairs, in lines
They don't know me
I'm a ghost
Through these dying cities I float
The Blvds. of whores
Needle parks
Looking for where the freak show's at
Finding myself there, meeting their eyes
Re-affirming the distance
Widening it, strengthening it
The more I see, the more I know, the deader I get
I don't exist sometimes
Times like right now
In this hotel room
Not wanting for anyone
Killing futility by starving it

I fed it to itself
I wait for daybreak to move to the next space

✠ ✠ ✠

One way conversation
Yea, hi I thought I'd check in
This house I'm at is full of bugs
There's lots of things that I don't tell you
Lots of things that don't have words to wear
The light in this place is really bad
I'm thinking about your eyes
Hell, we're tied up in this shit you know
Stuck behind walls, frozen in doorways
I hope these bugs don't get into my food
If I could remember where I was
I could tell you where I'm at right now
I'm in someone's apartment that's all I know
I spent the night talking to a lot of people from a stage
I don't know who I am
A voice, an answering machine
One lining it through life
Yea sure I'm hung up, aren't you?

✠ ✠ ✠

Chicago Bus station
Waiting on the 6 p.m. to Fort Wayne Indiana
Lines of people
A lot of them with pillows
The PA system booming
Jacksonville, Lexington, Richmond, Atlanta, Dallas, Hell
Destinations days away
This place fills me with filth
On the top floor
I thought if I heard one more plea for money
My eyes would explode
But down here where the busses take off
Overheated, the smell of popcorn
She's telling them all about how she's been there all day

All the way from Appleton WI
Her kids all over the place screaming
Eleven years ago a man chased me and Ian through here
Never understood why, but it scared us good
The depression in these places
Can squeeze the marrow from your bones
The road, the distance, the people
It drills a hole into your brain
I've been here for hours
I left the house I was staying at
They were trying to get me to talk to them
I had nothing to tell them so I split
These rides coat me with distance
Make me mute
People ask me where I've been
I tell them here and there
I feel bored out
Fills me with pure blues
Another night shuffling through the hallways
Onwards to nowhere
Can't think of anyone I want to be with
Though still I'm lonely
The bus will be thirty minutes late
I will be late for this show in the middle of nowhere
It's going to be a long night

✠ ✠ ✠

Yes it's getting to me
I want to pawn my eyes
The cities starve my sight into a corner
Sullen indifference is the result
I think of how you might smile at me
How you might kiss me
Some nights I want you so bad
My imagination is like a curse
Loneliness is like a curse and a gift

✠ ✠ ✠

In my room for the first time in seventy-one days
Trying to unwind
Trying to get back to normal
Forgot what that's like
Falling into this room
Last night was good
I was in the Road's choke hold
Now everything is moving slow
A new choke hold as the night drags its feet

✢ ✢ ✢

Strange stranger reaching out
Grabbing hold in this mindless blindness
I search and destroy for kindness
That sits in my imagination's mind
Across a burning field
Across a drenching jungle
Strange stranger strangely as you go
I've always never seen you
But you're the only one I know

✢ ✢ ✢

Don't touch me
I'll feel too good
I'll fall apart
The only thing holding me together is my pain

✢ ✢ ✢

Willie Loman
You got sold out
Bad news for a salesman
You thought you were dancing
But you were just getting pushed down the line

✢ ✢ ✢

3:30 a.m.
Another burnt wasted day closes out
I'm alone in my room

It's good company
When I don't sleep alone
I feel that I have somehow sold out
For me it's better this way
You have to get used to your own company
After you do things make more sense
I've got nothing to say, nothing to feel
I like being alone
Alien is as Alien does

+ + +

I sit at every bus stop in the city
Trying to understand on all levels
The noise and dirt settles on me
Roaring motorists detached going nowhere
At night I listen to the sirens, helicopters
The strange television violence knifing through the air
The lazy, indifferent gunshots
That salt and butter our block to taste

+ + +

Torn
On an edge
Between falling apart and winding up tighter than ever before
One hand on the phone
In need of a human voice
I'm cold, talk to me
The other hand in a fist
Feeling like it could crush the world like an insect
I need someone, no one
For a moment, a breath
And then it's over
I pound myself into submission
I wait for the next day to start

+ + +

Show me your scars tonight
Break down in tears

Fall apart in my arms
I need something to hold me together
Come undone
Show me
I will heal your wounds
The deeper they are
The better you'll feel when I'm done
Life is such a bitter pill
They hurt you and they tell you lies
They try to destroy you, but not tonight
Not here with me
All the walls you have built around you
All the defenses you have to protect you from them
Let them fall like concrete clothing
I will hold you
I will listen

✠ ✠ ✠

When the world wraps its iron hands around your throat
When the poison ink night nearly pulls you down
When no one thinks and feels like you do
When you think you're alone with your pain
When you know that you have nothing in common with any of them
Think of me
The Alien
I know how it feels to need to speak and have no words
The need to scream and have no voice
We have a silent voice together
You and I sing the perfect painful harmony
Together alone
In our rooms, cells, lover's fierce embrace
We come from the same place

✠ ✠ ✠

Remainder man: This night will go away. It will give way to the day.
It won't have the dignity to go out with a bang. It will fade into the
dawn like a coward shrinking away from the fight. But now, tonight,
I'm here breathing it all in. Lungfull, cupful, gut full. Walking

through it, endlessly walking. This night will fade into their world, their zone. The time will become theirs. After that, another night will slam itself into my guts. In out like a slot machine. Like a fuck, like bad luck, like a ride to the same place. The nights come like slow wave music. I feel the night from far off. When the sun starts to take its seemingly endless leave, when it stops polluting my life with its brightness and warmth. Liquid night, to swim in the night, bathing in ink. I hyperventilate, trying to get as much night air into myself as possible, as humanly possible. What a shallow concept. Human anything, don't remind me, it hurts enough already. At night the phone becomes the magic tool, the voices of the night might call in. Tales of the day sound good, like the wreck that we survived and crawled away from, the beast that didn't eat us alive. The fools who didn't destroy us. At night we become secret and electric, open to suggestion and truth. It all looks good at night. Violent sexual and ultimate. You look good at night, you look like the only thing in the world that matters. Show me your dances of abandon. Let your hands outline my body, hurt me, scar me, make me remember you forever, turn into a lyric, a living dream. Right here in this night, this deep place, this high-ceilinged crawl space.

✠ ✠ ✠

What, this hallway, this shuffle?
An endless series of doorways
All these strangers passing, passing
The idea of home
What a handout of an idea
What a vagrant lie
To think that we ever sit still
To think that we belong anywhere
You're telling me that this is the way it is?
You and I are the same
Tenants
Renters all
We are the ones given the task of passing time
Killing time
Getting away from ourselves

Getting away...
Another mongrel idea
An insult to life itself
No one gets away
Just lost, sidetracked, detoured
Success
Is the most distorted, insane, violent monster of an idea
Either you make it your life
Or you try not to laugh yourself to death
Some people think
Their deeds will be written in stone forever
I don't know about deeds
It all looks like an act to me
Saying something to get to something else
Like the man who says I love you
By putting a gun in his mouth and pulling down
In making the connection we lose the connection
Losing
Perhaps the most honest thing we could ever do
The first loser must have been a genius
A true human pioneer
So tonight don't tell me of your great plans
Don't tell me of your journeys and the lessons learned
Your glory is just an echo
Let's just lie here and look up at the stars
Do your best not to think at all
Can you feel yourself moving?
You're moving all the time
Passing through at the speed of time

+ + +

Freedom
Isolating, freezing, total
Falling in every direction at once
You don't belong anywhere
No place has possession over you
You hold yourself prisoner

As protection
Like the inmate who calls the pig to lock him in
Security
Free to lose all freedom
Too much thinking involved
Reality becomes an enemy
Freedom, the huge night colored vacuum
So cold

✠ ✠ ✠

My killer
I walk to the mail box late at night
Three gunshots sound behind
I step into the shadows trying to do the invisible man
I see a figure running up the street
When I can no longer see him I come out and keep walking
If I didn't mail these postcards
I would be accused of being a stuck up rock star faggot
And we couldn't have that
Better to risk death
Better to get a glimpse of my killer
My killer, my LA man
I never now when I'll run into him
It's going to suck
My killer will have no passion for his work
He'll waste me and think nothing of it
The detachment is so thick you would need...
Hell I don't know
A sixteen year old will cut me down to impress his brother
Hello killer, see you soon

✠ ✠ ✠

Breathe in this hard luck perfume
The bars are full tonight
I walk down Sunset Blvd.
Laid back loneliness
This place fills me with dirt and emptiness
I try to get a thought from the air

All I get is tarnished and devaluated
I never feel more alone than when I'm on the streets
On these busses, in their arms
I've never been to a place like this

☩ ☩ ☩

Can you walk through the streets and keep your head?
Can you escape the poison cancer minds that bark and shriek?
That welcome, love and fuck you?
Can you see them as enemy stranded?
Looking for a rat that's not drowning
Looking to introduce, infiltrate ingratiate and drain
Can you discriminate?
Can you see and feel their disease?
Do you understand the danger of a killer who works without passion?
The one who learned detachment in the womb?
Can you survey the decadence without apathy?
Can you deal with the confusion coming at you with a crooked eye?
Can you put litter in its place?
Can you resist the downward pull of the modern noise?
Do you fully understand your role as a modern contemporary?
Can you recognize the new model street warrior business man?
Can you see the meat for sale?
Can you distance yourself from it all?
Can you remember your name after a day full of this?
After a few lives full?
Will you be able to keep it up?
Do you understand the new meaning of stamina?
It's different than when your parents were young
More efficient automatic and deadly
Pity our flesh
It hasn't advanced as fast as the decadence around us

☩ ☩ ☩

Outside:
Four gunshots
A scream

Some one yells: Run, run
Then silence
No pigs
Nothing

✝ ✝ ✝

Across the school yard down the street from my house
A female night scream:
Oh god, oh my god
I wonder if she's partying down or getting raped
Watching someone get stabbed or skinned alive

✝ ✝ ✝

The man across the street empties his gun
Sends man made shooting stars into the sky
Everything gets quiet
The night creeps into my pores

✝ ✝ ✝

One hundred plus homeboys fill the parking lot
Of a Hollywood mortuary
Someone got wasted
To see these guys
Dressed down
Cool and steel eyed
You figure even their DNA is mean

✝ ✝ ✝

I tell you, you're wrong
I did reach out to you
But my arms were too short
I called out to you but my voice didn't carry
You told me that I was insensitive, unfeeling, uncaring
Your eyes filled me with wordlessness
The closer I tried to get
The more I became trapped in myself
I wish I knew how to ask for help
I wish I knew how to talk

Then I could make you understand
Tonight I'm alone in my wasted planet room
Walking through the wreckage of myself
I was thinking that if you could see me
You would know what to do
I don't think I'm desperate
But I think that the blood of all these nights is filling my shoes
Maybe you could say something that would make us both laugh
Maybe you could teach me something about myself
I don't know if I'm telling the truth or if I'm lying all the time
I wonder if the truth would kill me right now
I reach for the phone to call you
My arm is too short again
I wish I knew how to ask for help

☩ ☩ ☩

Phone call:
She writes to make sense of it all
She has a filthified point of view
Last night she drank and punched holes in the wall
She pan handled for food money and bought some rice
She fights with her mother
She says her room is alive with roaches
She doesn't kill them because she hates the landlord
Insanity is the best way to communicate your deepest felt truths
This is a nasty stretch of land
A bad place to get shot in
Easy to get lost
Something to drink about
LA, the coveted death machine
Amazing to see what we'll put up with and protect

☩ ☩ ☩

The stranger knows you, he sees you strange
He comes from a strange place
He locates you
He knows what you went through

Talk to the stranger
Touch the stranger
Marry the stranger
Kill the stranger
The one in your bed
The one on the bus
So what that it has a name
Anyone can name themselves
What do you understand?
What did you ever understand?
Blinded and brainwashed by orgasm
Now you're a stranger too
That's all you get
Talking in code and calling it something else
I call it a lie
That's why I stay on the outside
I'm tired of the codes
I'd rather take my chances in the outland
Outnumbered outmanned outlawed, fuck it
I know you very well, it breaks my heart
I see you clearly, it's truly ugly
The saddest song I've ever heard

✠ ✠ ✠

When the dogmouths start to speak
I become a one man rejection society
This guy telling me about the next life
What, I have to do all this shit again?
The next life, the next lie
This one is enough
I get starvation first class
Weeks of the shit
I like it, it tells me what I am
Long periods of time when no one touches me
I become starved for touch and things get clear
I stare at women and they don't like it
Especially on trains
Where the hell are they going to go?

I feel bad about it
I don't know if I would want
Someone to look at me like I'm their next meal
The ones with boyfriends bum out the worst
They can read the violence in my eyes
The hunger feels good
It's something to hold onto
Sometimes I like the pain that loneliness brings so much
I avoid contact with women
Like I've got this great roll going
And don't want the pain to end

☩ ☩ ☩

No one had touched me for weeks
I was starving
I met you in the middle of nowhere
I think of my hands on your body and I stop breathing
I remember melting into you
Everything was perfect
I am thinking of you through this bladed night
That doesn't have the guts to take me out
Will I ever see you again?
If I do will it matter?
There's only one road
One night at a time, one time at a time
Life has a way destroying you
Takes you out of the picture little by little
Ghosts you, fades you
Tracks you down and makes you speechless
Talking too much
I can't get you out of my mind

☩ ☩ ☩

Tonight she's drinking
Calling everyone she knows and telling them the same stories
Tonight she's crying, her soul is full of bitterness
Life has become a huge and confusing weight
She tells him that she hates him

She tells him that he is the reason she wants to die
Quietly he listens patiently
Patiently he listens quietly
He listens he stays on the line
He stays on the line and listens
He listens
Tonight she's bumping into things
A glass crashes behind her as she goes to the bathroom
She sits on the toilet and cries into a handful of kleenex
It's the loneliest sound in the world
It comes through the walls
A tiny sad light in the middle of nowhere
She's so alone
She's not handling it well
If only there was someone with her tonight
You should see the house
Everything is rusted, sprained, low on batteries and cold
Ten days from now she will shoot herself
(Shot herself in 1996. -Ed.)

☦ ☦ ☦

The last American song
Over and over
Broken glass litters the street
Two in the morning
Three guys in a car buy it
His teeth are on the dash board
He can't feel his legs
He passes out for the second time
The paramedic puts the iv. through the window
His two friends stand outside the car in shock
One tries to talk to the pig but can't find his mouth
Only then does someone notice his jaw is broken
He looks at the car and tells the pig:
My friend is drunk, I think he's fucked up
Mutilated puppets
Friday night entertainment
Los Angeles is a contest

A wrestling match
The night birds sing like sirens
Three in the morning
It's dead quiet in my hood
Then four shots followed by two return shots
The all's quiet again
It's 1989
I wonder how long until the magic runs out

✠ ✠ ✠

Alienated turned alienator
Alienator turned alienated
The child of dislocation
I grow distance in a rock garden
Alien turned cold animal in a distant hotel room
Turn off to turn off
Turned off by turn-ons
Turned away from everything that's warm
Warmth lies until it gets kicked out
Then it grows strong and cold
Or it dies
Facts are cold
The facts are in my distant hotel room life
Cold animal turned machine drill
Thought generator
Sometimes lies are necessary to deal with liars
Life leaves no clues
Life forgets me but will not let me forget
Holds me down and tells me that I'm free
I crawl from piece to piece
The ceiling has understanding eyes
Stares me down
While I make gestures in this still and silent life

✠ ✠ ✠

Last night I touched you
Tonight I don't know you
I can't stop the blood

Roaring in my ears, staining my sight
Shifting strangers walking point through jails and ghettos
They can't stop the blood
Moving down the hallways of brutality
Slaughterhouse circus antiseptic-minded
Numbed and partially destroyed
They can't stop the blood
Highway patrolmen holding handkerchiefs to their faces
As they look at the dead body they found
The pigs can't even stop the blood
Damaged from the start
Jaded before the first breath, burned out in minutes
Later dragged down, foaming at the mouth
Handcuffed and beaten beyond human limits
The blood seeps through the cracks, through TV screens
Through love and hate dreams
Last night I knew you
Tonight I destroy you and your memory
I can't stop the blood

☩ ☩ ☩

Walked east on Sunset down the line of crime lights
Everything was bathed in pollution death pink
Naked and burning
Through the haze downtown looked like it was burning
Three in the morning and I'm walking east
What the fuck am I doing
Looking to get shot?
I walk until I see a pig chopper chase a car
I take my shirt off and let the air pass over me
No sound except the birds
Then a Pig chopper breaks it up
I live in Los Angeles

☩ ☩ ☩

Performing
We are good performers

Good onstage
Good thing we're good
We can't seem to get ourselves off the damn thing
Like when you're involved in the relationship
How much of it is the real thing
How much is it tapes from the last time around?
Something you heard on television
Do you know when you're being real and when you're acting?
It's something to think about
Did you give them a good one?
A good show
What happens when you fall off?
You find yourself with yourself and you freak out
We love each other steeped in lies
When does it end?
Sometimes the mask slips and falls off
We see each other's real faces
Do you ever got the urge to get real and feel more lost than ever?
When you're alone and lonely
Do you want someone to be with
Or just someone in the audience to see the next show?

✠ ✠ ✠

I've been gone a long time
So long that I forgot I had a face
Forgot that I had a voice that you could hear
When you tell me how much I mean to you
And you want to know how I feel
I see my silence spit in your face
I didn't mean to throw a rock into your reflection
Maybe some things are better left broken and scattered
Veiled in darkness, secreted in bitterness and self doubt
I should have known better
Than to start something that I couldn't finish
That I couldn't care about
That I couldn't remember starting in the first place
I don't want to know you

You went years without me
You might as well keep going

✝ ✝ ✝

Don't act with re-action
Re-act with action

✝ ✝ ✝

Swimming in a lake of emptiness
Walking on the dark road
Staring out the window
Monitoring the train wreck in my head
Insomnia
Ten years of dead cities
Barking
Echoes clapping
Waiting to be blessed with sleep
Staring at the wall
Feeling the strings attached to the backs of my eyes
Aching stones
I try to put on paper the ship wrecked starvation
That I feel inside
Have you ever spent an entire day amongst them
And not been able to figure yourself into any of it?
Ride on a train
Wonder if you exist
Watch the grey rush by
Try to find a thought that ignites you
In the eyes of your reflection
Ride a lifelong train
Tread water while you sit
Isolation
Not knowing what to do with yourself
Your stupid tool hands
That heavy face trying to slide off your head
If someone were to come into your room right now
And wrap around you

You would still think you were alone
And you would be right

✝ ✝ ✝

Check in on the night shift
Calling all thoughts!
Fill up this vacancy
Nullify this paranoia
Clarify the monster thought
Give it all the weapons it will need
So it can try to rip me to shreds
Hard to find yourself as the end-up story
Looking at yourself
Seeing something that started and ended
Completion
Is terrifying

✝ ✝ ✝

Tonight the entire room stands on my head
I am not the battle
I am the battle field
Brain wiped clean
Shot through with disinfectants
My will stripped to a brittle wire
I look at the phone thinking about calling out there
There's no one to call
Just voices
Other worlds
Sometimes I feel so thrown down
So used up and vacant
That I have to let time pass me by

✝ ✝ ✝

An outsider can laugh at them all
The alien walking outside the wire can look at them
Their torture sessions
And laugh at their bitter tears

Like the guy in the room
Not knowing how to deal with it
He hates himself because he can't stop it
He feels stranded and used
He sees himself sitting in a chair
In the middle of a desert
His thoughts throw him into new ghettos
To avenues of ruin that he never knew existed
Yea, well it goes down all the time
The Alien walks the night trail
Looking through the man's thoughts
I laugh at you all the time
I am from your lost thought collection
When you go all the way out of yourself
You're with me
Look at the broken and the stranded
The road is littered with them
Pathetic wastes of energy
Mutilated pieces of human performance art
Years of denial for nothing

☩ ☩ ☩

I smashed out the windows of my room
No more natural light
Night time all the time
I am tired of the voices
The faces
The act
The windows of my room are broken
My world smiles now that you're gone

☩ ☩ ☩

I am looking at a picture of myself
In the picture I'm smiling
I know better than that
I wear a mask
On the outside that's what they see

I don't want to talk about the rest of it
I don't want them to ask about me
I don't want them to know me
I put a magnifying glass on myself
I dissect, I look closely, too closely
I fall silently into myself
Self perpetuated, self involved, self destroyed
I don't want for interaction with others
That kind of perspective is not true
It's true to life, not true to me
Time to go outside
Where's the mask

✠ ✠ ✠

Tonight turns the hands into fists
Shoves them deep into my pockets
Sends me out to the streets to walk
Sends my brain into rewind
Forces my head under one more time
I can't believe that I haven't drowned in my sea already
Always ready to take one more selfless plunge
Imagine diving into a pool of broken glass
A girl once said to me:
What's your problem, it sounds like you got burned once
I told her that I'm just burning
What the fuck does she know about me
Shove the world up your ass tonight
No one knows you
Don't let them tell you what your life is about
I tell myself this as I walk
Still I find myself listening to them
Trying to understand myself through them
Tonight attaches a leech to every blood cell that I possess
Punches me in the face with the past
Opens new wounds
Dissolves scar tissue
Sends me further into myself

Deeper than I thought I could go
Over and out

✠ ✠ ✠

Look inside the wound
What do you see?
The many headed night
The endless ever shifting possibility
Rip away the covering
See what you're made of
See the damage done, it's all you
Crawl inside the wound
Something wonderful is going to happen
Something terrible
Wrap the wound around you
Become the wound
Choose it before it chooses you
See motherfathermonster
Violentbloodhatebreeder
Inhale
It slams you
Sizes you up and magnifies all the bad stuff
The truth
Live the wound
Wounded in the womb
Pounded into the tomb
Walk the perimeter of the wound
It's that Abyss that looks through you all your life
Find shelter in the wound
Get away from them
They'll never understand you
They're too busy with their wounds
No matter what you think
They only get a glimpse
Some more than others

✠ ✠ ✠

Gone too far to be forgiven
Can't undo what I've done
Can't repair what or whom I broke
Gone too far to change
People don't change
They find better ways to cover themselves
Gone too far to take the lines from my face
Can't not see what I saw
This is it
There's a long trail behind me
A shorter piece up ahead
The brightest lights have shone
The loudest roar has been uttered
And now I'm getting down to it
Instances of time flash and pass
They get suspiciously similar
I see the same things
With different names in different places
Gone too far to ever love your world
Know too much to ever call it home
Gone too far to not see the fist in my hand
Know enough to know that I'll always come crawling back
To learn the same lessons in pain
I've gone too far

✝ ✝ ✝

Don't let the despair crush you
When it comes crashing in it wrecks you
Smash Ugly Tragic Destroyed
Can't handle the nights sometimes
I take it one breath at a time
Can't talk to anyone
The despair comes to you like a disease
Don't let it control you like it controls me
You can tell by looking at my eyes
The only thing stopping me...
I fear prison

I don't fit into this world
I don't like to look at women
For hours at a time all I can think about
Hurting myself and others
Anything that can feel
Anything that can register pain
I am lonely and I want to see it in someone else's eyes
The gunshots outside tell me
Others have reached their limit
Everyone has their own way of dealing with it
Don't let despair mutate your flesh
Look at my twisted stumps of thought
See the fingers, listen to the voice
I am slowly becoming the end of the line

☩ ☩ ☩

Paranoia climate
Nice out tonight, wind in the palm trees
I can smell the ocean from here
A car with tinted windows slowly passes
Everything tells me to
Run hide duck dive lock load attack
And there's you
You're beautiful tonight
Infinite and full of possibility
What do you want from me?
How many ways do you know how to hurt me?
Where's your knife
I don't believe your smile
Maybe you want to kill me
Maybe you want to use me
What do you see in me
What are you looking for
I don't know if I should let you do
Or if I should do to you first
I know me but I don't know you
This night is real
The Crips hanging out down the street

The crack headed woman picking her face
The neighbor's pitbull foaming away
Beautiful
But not as beautiful as you

✠ ✠ ✠

The night is alive with gunshots
Where are wounded tonight
You know the feeling
You've seen the invisible clawmarks rise
Your thoughts have been run over in traffic
I am thinking about thoughtlessness
I don't want to think of you anymore tonight
The impossibility of you and me is hard to take
Truth can break your arms while you sleep
I wonder if your beauty wounds you as it does me
Where are the wounded tonight
If I didn't find myself, everything would be alright
But I always do find myself
Ugly and cheap
A freaked out violent human mess
I am sure your touch heals wounds
Someone else's
A cannon blast outside
I think of blood, brains, your face, the moon
End this pain

✠ ✠ ✠

So leave me to the black hours
I will watch the air shift
You're right, let's not waste time
Don't talk, just leave
Alone makes sense
It's all I know
The rest of the time I'm faking it
Doing television outside of the glass eye

✠ ✠ ✠

So what happens to you when the dreams have been destroyed?
When you have chased cornered and ripped them limb from limb?
When you walk away to a desert inside yourself
I fell into the vacuum of my room
The darkness tortured me
Sucked the air through the cracks in the floor
Time scars my thoughts
I have thought about calling or writing one of you
Trying to reach out and touch one of you
I never get to it
I can't get out of myself
I couldn't find the right words to show you where I am
It used to be terrifying
Talking myself out of shooting myself in the head
Now it's just conversation
The night brings the silence and lies
With which I keep myself alive
I hold myself in fragile arms
I'm not strong
I'm a rat holding on one handed to the screen of the drain

✝ ✝ ✝

Electric coffee night
Black and unfolding
Full of promise
The lie that life provides
Keeps me cutting myself
Keeps me drawing darker blood
My brain is getting the fat trimmed
I'm breaking smiles on the street
Breaking bones, breaking light
Insanity fills this small hot space
I don't read character into it
Carbon monoxide has choked the pollution from my thoughts
I wait like a human for the last shove

✝ ✝ ✝

I'm sick of cities
Dirt rising off the streets
The air red with maniac words
I am sick of not cities
Quiet undisturbed crippling landscape
I need weakness to feel strong
Perspective of the impatient loser
I'm sick of in between cities
Motion sickness keeps me hanging on
Swinging by Death's eyes
I'm sick of stagnant time
My blind, raged, weak life has swallowed me whole
I am sick of myself

+ + +

New Zealand Hotel Jet Lag Blues
Don't want you to follow me
Don't want anyone to follow me
Into the wound
This room is dark
Spinning
You can watch
You can touch
But you can't come
The world doesn't care
It chews and spits
I walk alone into the wound
All the darkness
Madness and ruin

+ + +

I've see it happen so I know this for a fact
They will throw themselves at your feet
Lie and belittle themselves
To seem large enough to impress you
Waste time and lose sleep
Spend money like it's nothing

Transform themselves
Into vile human superhero shit heads
Hoping to make you smile
The rest is up to you
If one doesn't please, another one will come soon
To flagellate himself for your viewing pleasure
You can destroy them with a smile
Your touch can make them hot blooded idiots
When that gets boring
You can play them against each other
Make them hate blindly
So you can laugh
At their seeming stupidity
It was easy to figure men out
A few mistakes at first
But now it's together
I played that shit game for awhile
I didn't mind
I knew it was a game
Some of these poor bastards think it's real life
And let themselves get taken to the cleaners
You see what happens
Heartbroken damaged wrecks in human suits
And you see what happens to you
Broken jaws and black eyes
Decomposing bodies discovered by hunters
And all the other women who do not share
Your terrifying traits
And instead are real people
Have to take the rap for you
They will always be around
Risking death and humiliation
I am not one of them

✠ ✠ ✠

So fuck it
Keep destroying until it all falls apart
Take a look at a world that overloads and distorts

That filthifies and fictionalizes
Prolongs life in order to torture and infect
Pull back and rip your eyes out to see
I don't see any fucking soul
You want love?
Go talk to your mother
She's choking on it
I ride my overdriven headache until I'm ready to explode
Walk the streets trying to let the pieces fall to the bottom
I don't see any of the soul you're spitting on yourself for
Here it is:
Human until dead
So fuck it
Destroy
If you want to end it
End it
End me
Stop this trail of burning footsteps
End yourself
Find a method to rip the pain away
Find a way to see through the lie
Clear your camp
There's no fucking soul here

✠ ✠ ✠

I'm glad you don't respond to me
Days are passing
I'm forgetting you
I'm going on without you
It hurt for a lot longer than I thought it would
A lot longer than I was willing to admit
I get stronger as time passes
I move with time
We both forget you
The self inflicted wounds that spell your name
Are healed and gone

✠ ✠ ✠

Fuck it
Life is an embarrassment
Every breath threatens to pull your pants down
The lies are stacked in obscene piles
Makes me think of a dead man
Swinging in an apartment by an extension cord
The note in his pocket reads:
I stopped it, it did not stop me
I'm not going to grow old
I'm not in love with this heap
I will stop it
It will not stop me
Language falls out of my mouth
Ritual habit
Love hates
Truth lies
Blah blah blah
The convenient torture methods
Stacked layered and crammed in to every pore
Until you're forced to stand next to yourself
On bended knees
With all the smirking clown faces
Without motion and confrontation
Without my hand around life's throat squeezing
Forcing definition from this diseased confusion
Life is an insult
So fuck it
I'm taking it down the cinder trail
And I don't want to hear about
What you think you stand for
Because it's nothing
Furniture, boxes, bonfires, lists
A cast of renters
The embrace, the kiss, the long look
Falls to the floor on death row
Life is an embarrassment

✠ ✠ ✠

It's 1991
We fuck at her boyfriend's house

✟ ✟ ✟

Some things are too embarrassing
I could never tell you
I could never tell anyone
How much I think about you
How it scares me
Every morning as insomnia's grip loosens
I stare at your picture
I think of your painful shyness
Your ravaged self opinion
Your incredible beauty
How drawn I am to you

✟ ✟ ✟

You are the reason I don't want to die all the time
When I am with you life is worth living
Time away from you is strange and full of pain
When I look into your eyes
I can see how life has savaged you
It's ok if you fall
I will be there to catch you
Anyone that would want to hurt you
Would have to kill me to do it
I will never be able to pound words into lines
To match the velocity of your presence

✟ ✟ ✟

I will never let you know how much you hurt me
No, I will never tell you
The last few months have sent me into myself
It's not easy to forget you
Time is healing me
I keep my feelings to myself, it helps
I don't understand you or your kind

I end up getting myself messed up
I can't take anymore beatings like this

☩ ☩ ☩

In dead hours
Sitting in my room
Face in my right hand
Music playing
Thinking about him
His hands in your hair
The scent of your skin
Making his eyes close
Your breath on his neck

☩ ☩ ☩

It was all in my mind
You were never there at all
I wanted you to be though
When you would smile at me
It made up for years of wounds
They didn't matter
Now I see that it was just me
Losing my mind again

☩ ☩ ☩

As she becomes
Away
I watch myself try to hold onto her
I have never known a pain like this

☩ ☩ ☩

When you go insane there will be nothing
When you go insane there will be no one
Nothing to hold you
No one to love you
No one to talk to you
But it won't matter
It won't matter if the walls are grey

Or that time is hollow and lonely
And passes whistling and hissing like wind through high weeds
I'm laughing and shrugging all the way to death
I've never known a moment of real life
Watch me as I run mindlessly and directionlessly
Forward

⊹ ⊹ ⊹

If I thought it would help
I would stay with you for as long as it took
I would show you something different
That I was telling you the truth the whole time
As it is right now
I have taken all I can
Your shallowness has thrown me into a deep hole
It would be better for me to hate you I know
But I can't
I try but I keep thinking of you sitting alone
Seeing yourself as pieces of broken glass on the floor
Your inverted rage is hard to be around
Good luck

⊹ ⊹ ⊹

My loneliness is so large that it has outgrown me
It walks beside me, a wasteland that keeps in step
Sometimes our shoulders touch
It feels like teeth sinking into my flesh
A new and strange stretch of desert opens before me

⊹ ⊹ ⊹

If you want to hurt them and their children not yet born
Tell them the truth always
When you meet them
Stare deep into their eyes
Take those who wish to dominate you
Turn the game around and play it on them
Don't spare them a thing

Make sure you tell them about the blood and the pain
They can say what they want
You will trigger all their responses
It's all blood and death from here
You won't be kept waiting long

✠ ✠ ✠

To take a step into this vast emptying desert
This lit up hope filled expanse
This space that reduces us to the truth
To embrace this life extinguishing process
To constantly fuck with death
To live through this slaughter without killing yourself first
Here is dot dot dot

✠ ✠ ✠

For me it's the ever widening shadows
A silence that steadily increases in volume
Separation from myself
So that I walk alongside my body
I hear their voices like wind in high grass
Darkness is rushing forward

✠ ✠ ✠

If I could I would melt into your arms
I would fall like ten dead languages
I would not front
I would not lie to you
I don't think I could lie anymore
I have grown too old for such youthful pursuits
I want to love someone before I die
Hurry
It won't be long now

✠ ✠ ✠

All we do is eat sleep and worry about the rent
Somewhere there is real life
And those who live it

What about the rest
Paralyzed by television and police choke holds
Alas
Life widens and grows distant

✝ ✝ ✝

Burn the fat out of the tissue
I don't want to blunt the pain
I'm so tired of fucking around
I think that's why we live so long
The bullshit keeps us alive
If that's the case
Fuck this place

✝ ✝ ✝

The loneliness that the world generates
We keep it going all night long
Waiting for a dull moment, or a lot of dull moments
To sneak away from the pain
During these unmoving silent nights I feel its crushing wheel
Is there anyone in the world who I can know?
I am tired of knowing myself so well

✝ ✝ ✝

No drugs, no pain killers
Nothing to dull the pain
I want the Abyss
Straight no chaser
I want to see clearly
For once, for real
So what if it kills me?
So what if it tears me to pieces?

✝ ✝ ✝

I am the silent shell
Crashed out after a show
I watch the sweat run off me again
The silence is untranslatable
Farther away from them I go

On my way to Casualtyville
I am harder than loneliness
I scare it, it leaves me alone

✠ ✠ ✠

When we're not killing each other
We kill ourselves step by step
There will always be someone
To help you
To fill your shoes with blood
To fill your mind with idle time killing time
Sometimes it's you

✠ ✠ ✠

The singer in the other band was drunk
He slurred his words
The crowd loved this pathetic insult
"I drink because there's so many assholes."
I watched the pretty girls wave and scream
I was born too late
I should have been a samurai
Aspiring to the sword and death
These days people are withered
The spirit has been made to whine
They'll never get me

✠ ✠ ✠

The Iron is my friend my hero
Detects my weakness
Shows me where to go
Strengthens my number
Never fails
The Iron makes life worth living
Stabs self doubt
Mutilates depression
Opens gates of light
My body aspires to the Iron

✠ ✠ ✠

Need is a disease
Makes you crawl
You'll end up hating yourself
And you'll need something else
To take the pain away
And then you'll need to forget it all
And then you'll need to get back on track
And then you'll be another 24 hour a day need freak
I needed to tell you this

✠ ✠ ✠

Germany
My body is covered with road stench
Diesel, tobacco, sweat, grease and dirt
Men's room, rasthaus, no sleep
I don't want to wash it off
It's a second skin
Keeps my back straight
It insulates me from disease
Tonight I will sleep with it on

✠ ✠ ✠

I don't want to know you
I have nothing for you
I don't even have a self for myself anymore
People pick at your body like crows
You want a friend, go hang out with a big rock
It's not me you want
No matter what you think

✠ ✠ ✠

The road is a disease that bites your bones
Mostly it infects your mind
You think you're a mass of speeding electric velocity
You tell yourself that you're living
But you know you're just chasing shadows
Calling them spirits
I'm waiting for the dust to settle

For language to die
I want to breathe for the first time

✝ ✝ ✝

I am immune
Too exhausted to notice
Too paranoid to sleep or wonder for too long
Too self abused and withdrawn to help myself
Real life doesn't come close to this

✝ ✝ ✝

Welcome to this pure example of perfect human sadness
Your life in the finite ghetto
Yes your life is short
Yes your days are numbered
No you'll never escape
Touch the invisible wall of the ghetto
Man made
Run wild and get your wings singed
Find yourself in my arms
Your blood maniacally racing
Not even it can escape the ghetto

✝ ✝ ✝

Love heals scars love left
We're all hypocrites
Searching desperately
Before our ability to attract
Takes too much effort to use
Or disappears much to our horror
We die trying to impress each other
I'd rather be respected by a bolt of lightning

✝ ✝ ✝

I like my world
Right now it's all I can stand
Get too close and they'll take you to the bottom
They fuck me up

I go to the store and I have to listen
It's a non-stop tragedy
The night is here though
No gunshots
I wish the sun would take a vacation
Leave me in darkness for awhile
Let me heal
Let try to figure out why I'm fucked up

✝ ✝ ✝

Life sees through me
I walk on a tightrope of vertebrae
Ten years of spine
Take a photo
At this point it's an x-ray
Life passed through me
Left me here
I'm figuring out what to do
With the remaining time

✝ ✝ ✝

I'm obsessed with documentation
I must record every drop
I have good equipment
I don't miss much
It's a sickness
An obsession with contempt for life
We all need a sickness to live
A way to show our fear of death
I've got hours of conversation trapped
Pages of words in lockdown
Video on double life
Doing forever
Don't end up in this place

✝ ✝ ✝

It's all important and meaningless
Depression drives a car into my back

It gets worse with time
Sometimes I can barely speak
The phone is almost impossible
I tried talking to a woman tonight
In the first thirty seconds I wanted to get away
Tour starts in a few days
Start the tour or kill me
At this point I'd take either one

+ + +

No more television
No more radio
Selected input
Must be careful to avoid the polluting leech
They call real life
I can't take the beatings like I used to

+ + +

There's a lot of prisons around here

+ + +

I learned
Sometimes it's better to shut your mouth
And listen to the other fool

+ + +

Humiliation is a great source for inspiration
Gets you out of bed in the morning
I shake my head from side to side
Rage comes through every pore
Re-wind the tape and remember the first time
The first time you felt the lump in your throat
You understood where all those mass murderers got off

+ + +

Letter from the stripper
They want to touch your body
They never get to

It makes them want to kill you
But their words and eyes leave scars
I could show you something else
Maybe you're too far gone
Too fucked up to feel anything
Besides strange disconnected bitterness
A hollow wooden gut that confuses your instincts
Maybe I'm just another man
Who wants to check your flesh and leave
I will fall short of all your expectations

✝ ✝ ✝

Life neither remembers nor forgets
It is valueless to itself
It doesn't care about you
You see how easily it leaves the room

✝ ✝ ✝

At this point I reckon I'm clean
Stripped of youth's fat
Staring unflinching into the Abyss
I'm paralyzed there
Under the impression I'm flying
Tapping my bones for marrow
Thinking silently
And without the need to impress others
Life is the same always
It's the surroundings and their lure
That have become so serious
I bait my own trap
And wait for myself to walk in and trip the mine

✝ ✝ ✝

Bones
Moon shining blue off bone
Hold someone so tightly their bones crack
After the flesh is burned and hacked off
It's down to the bones

After we've said all the bullshit
Love lines/romance/drama/compliments
After we've carved our way through the sex
Tried to give it meaning and failed in silence
After choking on life's putrid breath
A breath of grey room suicide and sun light vacancy
Let's take it down to the bones
I wonder what your skull looks like
I could cook your ribs in my oven
Your juice running down my face
A head bone in a million pieces
.45 in the face
Take me to a better place
Skeletons dancing and grinning
Shuffling on the floor of my room
Take the bones of all the dead Viet vets
March'em down Pennsylvania Avenue
Send me the bones of my father
I'll beat my mother to death with them
Break her arms with his arms
Skin the kid next door
Build a scarecrow with his bones
I want to see my teeth in a cup
My skull in my hands
I laugh with death
I have no hope

✝ ✝ ✝

The cars passed me
I watched their red lights rip across the black top
I was walking along some high way
I don't really know where I am tonight
Some hotel in Virginia
Most of the nights are like this
Alive and not sure where
The silence in this room is good
It's all I can take of them right now
Out there they want to know what's the matter

They have questions and they don't care about you
It's their noise that sets me on edge
Pulled into their lives
In the middle of tonight's nowhere

╬ ╬ ╬

Lollapalooza
The air is moist in Orlando FL
8.21.91 2:54 AM
The show let out at 10:15 PM
Denny's is still full
They watch me eat
I cash out and listen to the rednecks
Talk shit about people's hair
My head hurts from running it into a guitar
Cars beep and wave as I walk down Colonial Ave
The hotel is full of kids
They're drunk noisy and hanging out
How can you not like them
I don't know them
I don't want to know them
But I like them still
Four more shows to go
Makes me sad to see it slowly end
Seems like a long time since Phoenix
My brain dulled from one hundred and forty-eight interviews in five weeks
I'm exhausted and I hate everything
I know one thing though
The day I'm flying home from Seattle
I'll wish we were in Phoenix
Doing it all over again
It's the nature of Motion Sickness

╬ ╬ ╬

I tried to let the wall down and let you see me
I tried but the other one started talking
All I could do was listen to my voice talk you away from me

You're not the first one
It always happens
I think that some people don't fit and never will
They have to find a different way to get through it
It makes them look stupid and mean
Lost and reckless
To them, you're the one who's lost
I ran out of ways to deal with you
I ran out of shit to say to you
That's why I just stare and silently curse you

✠ ✠ ✠

You would rather deal with someone who's not as real as pain
Someone who doesn't sweat as much
Someone quieter and more prone to all the normal bullshit
Someone that makes you feel superior
Life needs a little fakeness in it to make it easier to swallow
That's where the make-up smoke machines come in
I live in a different world
You will remember it as tragic
Painful and simple
I want to feel the muscle come off the bone
Exhaustion and insanity pound me
It's the reward and the punishment at once

✠ ✠ ✠

There's no night like tonight
They're all different
I went out there
I could taste the air
The power lines buzzing
I became part of the current
Like I knew exactly what was supposed to happen
So when the pig ran the stop sign
And nearly ran my ass over
My heart didn't skip once
I watch the man across the street watch me

He's plugged in too
We're both riding the current
It's not paranoia
It's just being on
Connected by the eyes
The eyes flash like knives
In the 7-11
I watch the man behind the counter
Try to lower the voltage of the drunk
Who's challenging his nationality
The drunk's eyes are glassed and out of control
He's ready to blow out
On the way back my entire body hums
I think that I'll never get far away enough from this
Do you ever feel the need to go somewhere
Forget everything so you can remember yourself?
You get a good way down the road and then the phone rings
Not tonight
A night for nights
Dried blood by the bus stop
A car patching out in the parking lot of the market
Where the hell could I go?
No, I'm plugged in
Hooked

⸸ ⸸ ⸸

Seeing devil's tails
I see'em twitch
In the corner of my eye
There's tunnels and hallways
Lines and chutes
The hallway to the back yard
That would have been the place to have shot him
With his own .38
To have seen his face
Pulling down three masks
Recognition, Fear and Relief

I walk down Death's tunnel
I can tell you what it's like
It goes at a slight downhill angle
It looks like it's always about to get bigger
And then it just gets smaller
Sometimes its tail is around my throat
Rooms become holding cells
People turn into garbage jokes
They offer me love
I give them back parts of their fingers
And thirty years of sharpened abuse
It sticks like jellied gasoline
And makes them just like me

✝ ✝ ✝

Bring in your gods
Before they rust
Young man
Born
With holes in his pockets
Left to scream
On the Avenue
Pick a city
Any city

✝ ✝ ✝

Silent terror disease
I don't speak human
I only scream
Machine number criminal
Soon they'll rape themselves
They'll stand in line
To fuck machines
Anything
To die clean

✝ ✝ ✝

You're alive but in this room you're a ghost
The last few nights you have come to haunt me
It's 4:19 a.m.
The room's getting smaller
I think about what they did to you
I tried to make you see that I was different
Maybe you saw something I didn't see
Perhaps you saw them in my eyes
I'll never see you again
It's never been the same
I feel so fallen
So old and final
This night breaks Time's nose

✝ ✝ ✝

Prince charming got dragged
Four city blocks by his dick
She shone like a beacon
Decaying behind blood and urine colored glasses
Ten princes left skidmarks the next day
She never moved an inch
What did you think she was going to do
She was only taught how to survive
Cruelty is all in your mind
So just don't think

✝ ✝ ✝

Sad rituals
I think I'm above it all
Somehow got past, through or around it
I couldn't be more wrong
I accidentally punish myself
It keeps me busy
I don't know what else to do with time
I always have to be abusing something

✝ ✝ ✝

I remember my mother's boyfriends
One in particular
Drives me into silence
Makes me want to sit in rooms
Clenched silence
Funny thing
Every night now I'm visited by Suicide
It's like an Armed Forces recruiter
I keep so much under the surface now
It's never been like this
A lot of things
I can't speak about out loud
Life haunts me now
Draws all the faces pale
When they talk
I know what they're talking about
And at the same time I have no idea
I feel like I'm going to slip and fall into a hole
Choke myself in a dream
Sometimes I wish I never happened

✠ ✠ ✠

I wonder where all this is going to end up
Can you make yourself so much of a fortress that you can't get out?
Because you've crushed the keys under the weight of your self hatred?

✠ ✠ ✠

Hey Superman
Hey Asshole
Hey Terminator, Mr. Action, Iron Man
You look hunted
Did you think you were something special?
Now all the assholes you spat on
Are running your life
They call your name and you come
All the shitheads know your name

You don't shine like you used to
You're not so slick
You look scared and old
Frozen with the shit still stuck to your smile
The dogs at your heels just ate your shoes
Ambition?
You never had any
You just wanted them to like you
So you could conveniently hate them
And now you'll do anything
To get them to give you a free breath

✠ ✠ ✠

I lie to myself here in this room
My descending box
I make it up inside so I don't go insane
I lie to myself constantly
It makes life easier
I make up reasons to live
Fake romances
Dead parents
I never liked much anyway

✠ ✠ ✠

Howard Johnson's right off the 80
Loneliness was outside my window tonight
I heard it's voice
It's the loneliest wail I ever heard
It was the sound of trucks roaring by
I lay in my bed and stared at the black hole ceiling
Loneliness clawed the glass again and again
I know better than to let it in
It always ends up staying too long

✠ ✠ ✠

Sharks: There was a drive by shooting in the neighborhood today. In
the store tonight a guy I know told me that there were some Bloods

in the parking lot. They had been seen driving around looking for Crips. They ran their cars up and down my alley. The growl of their engines were predators stalking the cement. Out looking. Smelling blood sweat and fear. I sat in the dark and waited for the gunshots and the sound of frenzied rubber grinding garbage into powder.

⚔ ⚔ ⚔

The fire pulls the flesh back
The fire turns the flesh black
Light the fire
Burn it all night long
Call me up if you want some pain
Call me if you're tired of talking
And just want to scream
Hang them from light poles by the collar bone
Let me know when you're on fire
I'll be right over
Walk with death all night long
Swing it
I see the fire in your eyes
If you want to see some of my blood
I'll show you
You gotta walk with death
All the time
All the streets know your name
Can't you tell?
Swing death like a watch on a chain
When you want to die
Call me

⚔ ⚔ ⚔

Please stay alive
I think about you coming down from that last tour
Wondering how you're making it
I never want to read about you overdosing in your room
I don't want to have to defend you to people who will talk shit
I would do it though

Always
So take good care of yourself
If you forget how
Call me
I'll remind you

✝ ✝ ✝

Lost son walk alone through the autumn leaves
Think about if you had a friend
Would it be a he or a she?
What would you talk about?
Good not to be in prison
The rest sounds like leaves scratching the sidewalk
Lost son like you ever had a chance
You know the pain and silence
The long walks alone
Trying to retain sanity
So young and already so rusty
Buried for years
What happens when you finally explode?
Lost son whatever you do don't hang yourself
Don't get hung up on the words that they throw
They don't know what they're saying
They don't know anything at all
Lost son do you ever wonder when
Real life starts
Or did they pick pocket your mind
So you no longer know what life is?
Lost son look for me tonight
I'm lost and I can't see
All the bright lights
Have taken my eyes away from me
Lost son be careful out there
Those smilers are crooked
They'll fuck the taste right out of your mouth

✝ ✝ ✝

I live in the cult of the night
Go out there in the day time
You must be crazy
I did it today
It's like a war waiting to happen
Fuck that
Give me the night
Panhandlers and pigs
Gangs roving the streets
Night time in this neighborhood
Is like the deep black sea
Sharks, killers
Not a problem unless one of them is hungry
And then it's nothing but a problem

✠ ✠ ✠

The nights pass over me
They hover above me
Silent specters
Bed cloth on top of me
I sweat underneath
Eyes of sadness upon me
I'm in the center of a flesh hurricane
The nights pull blades across my face
No one can see the scars
I can feel them though
This time around, life puts humps in my back
Makes me beg
Please
A feeding hand to bite
Until I feel bone stop my teeth
Tonight
Stop my mind from wounding me
Maybe you could somehow touch me
And not make me want to skin myself
I know about the Abyss
I could tell you stories about

Unending darkness
But then I'd see your stupid mute animal eyes
And all I'd want to do is break your fucking arms
And throw you off the balcony
Watch your meat hit the parking garage roof
And call it another night

✝ ✝ ✝

Don't come close
I'll hurt you
It's all I know how to do
I can't translate the pain into words
That don't cause pain
Don't tell me you love me
You'll make me think of my mother
And one thousand broken windows
Years of knotted screams into the bed
So much hate it would break your ribs
I put the miles through my eyes
I slam silence into my brain
Anything to get away
Walk away from me as fast as you can
Never speak of me or to me again
It's too late
For all that
Death is the only shadow on my road

✝ ✝ ✝

Men hugged him
Women asked him to come home with them
The money rolled in
He was so lonely it was pathetic
If they knew how he lived they would laugh
Sometimes he saw it all as punishment
Never escaping the humiliating inferno of his parents
The parents are gone now
Now he gets paid to humiliate himself

He constantly disgusts himself
In the name of telling the truth
Loneliness and alienation choke him
Hc tclls people to stay alive
He tells himself to die

✠ ✠ ✠

I live behind a wall of scar tissue
Scare tissue
Scarce issue
I don't like to think of myself
I like lifting those weights though
I like the feeling of pain
Nothing else
I am rescued from my mind
The nights are painful again
I can't do anything with that kind of pain
It's bad
Behind the wall of scar tissue
Hemmed in tight
I don't want them to know me
I tell them everything so there will be nothing left
That's the part I'll keep for myself
I figure the deeper I get into the pain
The better I'll be at dealing with it
That's how bad I hate this shit

✠ ✠ ✠

One hundred women left me tonight
I didn't take it too well
I kicked myself for letting it matter
I kicked myself for letting it go so far
I lost myself in the shuffle
Now the room is cold
All of a sudden it's Saturday night
There's no magic
Too dangerous to go outside

No shit
I pride myself in being the loneliest man on earth
Damn

✠ ✠ ✠

December 19 1991
Part of my life ended
My best friend was murdered
On my front porch
He never hurt anyone
The man who shot him in his face
Never knew his name
I am still alive
Sort of
From now on
My life is totally fucked and without purpose
Without inspiration
A mask that I will die wearing

✠ ✠ ✠

After dark I wait for something horrible to happen
I figure I'll have people shooting at me for the rest of my life
Like a drama in installments
Nightmares delivered to my door
Darkness comes and I wait for more horror
I figure we'll be friends for life
I'm swimming in an animal bag
Everything smells like meat
Everyone is a killer
I look at all of them now
I search out their eyes
I let them know that I'll kill them back
They take one look and they know I mean it
I lock the door behind me
Everything that moves begs me to attack it
I know how people are now
They take your money

Break your heart
Or try to kill you
Now I walk the streets like a secret animal
Some of them know
But not all of them
The one who fucks with me
Will lose his throat
He'll have no idea what he's fucking with
I live on the outskirts of humanity
I am scarred for the rest of my time here
That's all it is to me
Time left here
Time spent walking the city filth
Breathing in and out and keeping my teeth sharp
Waiting for something horrible to happen again

✝ ✝ ✝

Every slow dance took my breath away
Pinned my heart to the wall
I believed every slow song
I was intoxicated by the smell and the movement
Every one of them broke my heart a little
Now there's nothing but wise bitterness
Fatigue from seeing the whole thing
The pool of blood in the dirt
The end of real time has begun
It's all legendary from here

✝ ✝ ✝

The detectives went through my house for hours
I was at the pig station
I didn't know until later
They went through the food in the kitchen
I got back to the house and all kinds of shit was turned over
My best friend's blood was all over the front walk
They're looking for something to bust us for
The pieces of shit even went through the attic

They were curious as to why I had so many tapes
He talks to me and makes me think he's my friend
I look at him and know he thinks I'm scum
If I give these pieces of shit the time of day then they win
You know
There's so many pieces of shit in the world
It's amazing anyone gets by
The pigs asked if me and Joe were faggots
They were so relieved when they found out we weren't
Fuck you pig
Like I have to prove myself to you
I can't think of a more fucked up situation
I have to talk to these shitheads all the time now
They still ask other people about me
Like I might have been up to something
I'm some kind of suspect?
Nah, but you sure are some kind of pig

☦ ☦ ☦

Joe you should have seen the tabloids talk about you
They really love the fact
That your father was married to the bitch in Charlie's Angels
They talk about her sorrow
How you two were so close
Like you hung out all the time
How you were twenty-nine and in Black Flag
One of your father's piece of shit friends was lying
Talking a lot of shit
You looked great in the Enquirer
Good pictures of you and what ever the fuck her name is
I saw her at your wake
I wanted to spit on her
Your father had it at Gazarri's
All his AA friends were there
After all these fake ass people who didn't know you
Had spoken and congratulated themselves on their acting
And talked a lot of shit about God and AA

Your father stood at the end of a line
So people could come up and talk to him
Your mother didn't know anyone there
She just stood to the side
With her husband and your step-sister
They weren't used to the Hollywood sickness
It was gross
After that we went and looked at your body
Your father didn't go
He didn't go to your funeral either
Don't know why
Maybe because there would be too many people
Too busy with their own grief
To compliment him on his
I miss you man
I look at pictures of you and I can't take it
Yesterday I wanted to crawl inside the pictures and be with you
I have been thinking a lot of dying myself lately
Life is pretty boring without you around
I have to tell you Joe
I did it all for you
I was hoping that if I went out there and did something good
You would see that you could do something magnificent
Like I told you the night before you died
You have such a great talent
It's because you didn't lie
I admire that truth
You will inspire me for what's left of my life
I see now that it might not be all that long
That piece of shit took you out
In less time than it takes to turn off a light
When I was looking at you on that gurney
That bullet hole in the side of your head
All filled in with mortician's clay
All the powder burns on your face
What courage you have to be dead like that
This thing that we all fear the most

And there you are pulling it off like it's nothing
You even had a slight smirk on your face
But you were cold and you smelled like formaldehyde
It was so hard to leave that room with you in it
It took me three times I think
I kept coming back to say something else to you
It never seemed to be enough
It will never be enough
Please come visit me in a dream soon
I miss you so much
My good friend

☩ ☩ ☩

1992 is a couple of hours away
I'm staying in someone's house
I am almost thirty-one
All my stuff is in storage
I am single and plan on staying that way
To appeal to the more tender nature of a woman
Is a total waste of my time
What a joke
Meanest damn people I ever met
I am alone in the world and there's no changing that
My loneliness burns deep within
I don't mind because
I am one from none
My line has never been so clean cut
Death has stripped most of the words from my speech
Talk is a disease
Action is its cure
Death has been walking with me all year
Talking to me in the night
I answer with my insomnia
Paranoia has put a hard shine in my eyes
I mix humor with my fury
Efficiency with my alienation
Beauty with my rage

The rising sun is my silent battle cry
Exhaustion is my victory
Death is that which I measure myself by
I acknowledge no peer or ally
I understand death as master
And the definition of absolute power
My path is clear and laid out before me
The wind rushes past me
I dream of empty desert landscapes
And proceed forward

Now Watch Him Die

I am the aching negating Abyss
You can't talk to me for long without seeing it
You can't look into my eyes
Without being repelled by the desperate inferno that fuels me
A fire that burns itself, feeds on itself
Knows only its own needs
I pulled the air from the room when you came to visit
You must have thought I was pathetic
After you left I felt sick
Sick that I had filled the room with my emptiness
I didn't mean to let it out
I was going to try to fool you
I wanted you to think that I was cool
The Abyss came shining blackly through though didn't it
I don't know what I did to become this monster
Probably everything I possibly could

I stood over your dead cold body
And stared down
All your mother's relatives were standing outside
You were so damn still
Were you scared like I was Joe?
What were you thinking
Did you look into your killer's eyes?
When we came into the house
I knew that piece of shit was going to waste us both
But he only got you
I've been thinking a lot about hanging myself
It's always the same white extension cord
I think of the house and the shots
The pool of your blood boiling in the dirt
It's been two weeks and you haven't called

Dream 1.2.92: I'm shooting guns with Ice T. The gun I have shoots
bullets real fast.

I loved a dented, broken up woman
Ravaged, wrecked and crooked legged
She was tough as hell
But she was more alive than most
She was a walking mean streak
Wrapped in a sad accident
She couldn't help but hurt me
She did the same thing to herself
But she burned so brightly
That she burned everyone that she touched
At night when I'm alone and everything is quiet
I put my hands over the scars
They keep me warm
I pull a feather from the wing of Sorrow
Just to hear it scream
And waste time until I fall asleep

⚸ ⚸ ⚸

I am filled with horror
I can't talk to anyone up close
I'll only be able to be horrible
I'm cut off from the rest of the world
It's worse than depression
It's horror
Horror is in my blood
My silent partner
My cancer shadow

⚸ ⚸ ⚸

Dream 1.7.92 : I'm shooting a gun.

⚸ ⚸ ⚸

The only thing I'm afraid of is getting caught
I don't care about how much pain I might cause
The only thing I'm afraid of
Is doing hard time for shooting some piece of shit
You can do time even if you shoot a piece of shit
I'd like to make that guy shit his pants before I waste him

I'd like to make his eyes melt
I'd like to make him shake like he made me shake
And then I'd just like to shoot him in the face
Mess him up so the piece of shit that gave birth to him
Will puke when she sees him

⚘   ⚘   ⚘

Dream 1.14.92: I am staying at someone's house and somehow I
flood the place by leaving the tap on. I try to clean it up as the
people that own the place yell at me.

⚘   ⚘   ⚘

Melbourne Australia feels far away enough
It's late and I can breathe
550 people came to the show tonight
I'm back in the box
The moon is full tonight
I just came in from sitting outside
I closed my eyes and imagined Joe falling
Through the sky into me
I'll carry you brother
They won't hurt you anymore
You can't get too close to them Joe
They'll stay too long
Say too much
Drain every last drop
And then just hate your guts
You're invisible
I've got your strength
Those bullets shot you into me
I won't blow it
You'll see

⚘   ⚘   ⚘

I'll get the wrong idea
If you're kind to me
I'll start to make things up in my head
I'll think you'll want me

I'll hurt myself trying to please you
It won't be real
It will all be in my head
I won't be able to stop lying to myself
I will cut myself to pieces again and again
I won't feel it
You can watch

⚛ ⚛ ⚛

Living the boxed life again
Australia
Raining tonight
The room is hot, too hot
Still air and the smell of insecticide
I'm alone and far away from America
My life is now a chain of broken dream rooms
I like it that way
I can't go backwards
Death makes life easier somehow
Less choices
Less masks
Less of everything except grief
Lots of grief
Can't get far enough away

⚛ ⚛ ⚛

Joe. It's been hard since you've been gone. It's been hard on a lot of people. I'm in Australia right now and geographically it feels better than LA does but I still carry all my thoughts of you wherever I go.

I'm in a hotel room right now and I'm crying, thinking about you. I head back to LA in a few days. It's hard to go places there now because I know that just a few weeks ago you were walking on the same streets.

I have fucked up thoughts all the time, you know how you rethink things all the time like if they could have been different. I have gone through the last moments of your life so many times. I keep trying to change it so we could have tried to talk to them. But then I pull out of my thoughts and know that nothing will change the reality that you're dead. You were murdered Joe. Every time I put your name and that word together I start to sweat. I feel so dangerous these days. These people that talk to me have no idea what they are dealing with. I walk the streets now and stare through people. I feel like hurting people all the time. It's all I dream of these days. In my dreams I'm either shooting a gun or killing someone. The other night I had a dream where I killed a girl and chopped her in two pieces.

I'm doing all the same things that I usually do. Interviews and shows. The usual hustle. Only now it doesn't feel the same. I am so cut off from the world now that I don't mind working every night. I don't need nights off anymore save for rest for the throat. I just don't care about myself the way I used to. I feel like working and not stopping and going until all the parts fly off. I don't taste food. I don't think of any one person that I want to see when I feel lonely. I know that now that you're gone I'll never have anyone I can talk to. There's a lot of really great people out there but they're not you and they're not me. I find myself saying all of our jokes and one liners out loud because I have no one to say them to. I was doing it the other day in the back seat of a car on the way to a meeting and I started making myself laugh and the people I was with had no idea what I was going on about. Forget trying to explain it.

I've been out here for a couple of weeks I think. I don't know for sure, I don't look at the calendar anymore. I just find out what time and where the stage is and that's all I want to know. I don't talk to people. I just answer all their stupid fucked up questions like I'm a human answering machine. I don't care though. I think the whole year will be like this. I'll just keep going. I think if I stop I'll never get going again.

Thinking of you is hard. I have so many good memories but I know that it's all in the past. I wonder where they guy who murdered you is. I wonder what he's doing right now. I think of him all the time. People ask me if I want to kill him. You would love this Joe, I give them the rap about how the poor guy is just a victim of a fucked up system. Looks good in print. Like I really want to tell these fuck head journalists anything about you. I hope I get to deal with that piece of shit someday. I want to kill him with my hands. I would feel much better knowing he's dead. Not because it's better for society. Just because it would be good to kill the guy.

I know that it wouldn't bring you back but at this point it would be good to get some satisfaction. Fuck this.

My life will be different now. It will be different until I die. I don't care about it like I used to. I don't love it even though I tell other people that they should love theirs. It's like I'm half alive. The other half is dead and I can feel it.

⚕ ⚕ ⚕

Maybe I just need enough money
Buy a dark room and catch my breath
None of these people make sense to me
It's all just a lot of noise
Romance is out of the question
After what I've seen
I can't get rid of the horror

⚕ ⚕ ⚕

Dream 1.23.92: I kill a girl and someone I know cuts the body in two and loads the parts into two plastic garbage bags. I ask him if he got rid of the body and he says that he did but he thanked the plastic bag company on the back of his new record and thinks that maybe someone will find out. I see police with dogs going near my apartment and I know that they are onto me.

⚕ ⚕ ⚕

I feel free like I never have before
Cut off from all of them
There are certain things
That take time
But eventually they make sense
Hell is a private place where you re-live things
It's silent and hides from the light
It lives inside and keeps my mouth shut
I watch the sunrise over the highway of another motel
A girl is asleep next to me
Club trash
She only laughs when I forget her name for the third time
My life is full of horror and shadows
I only feel safe on the road
Sleeping next to the highway

Sex with strangers who have cars
Spitting out broken pieces of bloody life
The world is smashed and scarred as far as I can see
I am merely an abortion survivor
This place makes you think predator and prey
I used to want to be the predator
Now I want to be the prey
Wary and living in fast moving shadows
Always knowing that it could end in a finger snap

   ℣ ℣ ℣

I got my cord snapped off
I float through the blank hours
I now have the mind of a shark
I have never known a freedom like this
It's not cold
It's just seeing everything with rational calm
Seeing the sun set as it rises
Seeing the end all the time
Distracted in conversation by the Abyss
Realizing that the conversation is the distraction
I am almost 31 and I feel like I've retired
It's hard to talk to these interviewers
I look right through them and forget what I was trying to say
Life is over for me and I'm just riding
A lot of things that I thought were important
Aren't

   ℣ ℣ ℣

Loneliness has changed its face again
Cameras in my face
Lots of noise
Isolation
Lying awake
Sweating at 3:45 a.m.
Hotel room ceilings
I've got no words

No one to tell them to
Life is hollow
It allows you to fool yourself

⟁ ⟁ ⟁

I saw a picture of Joe's head all blown apart
I can see it now in the hotel room
I am beyond loneliness
I am an alien off a space ship
I want the rest of my life to be behind shades
I don't want friends
I want shadows
Darkness
Nowhere is far enough away
No one is anyone I can talk to
I define myself
I speak their language
It's a bad habit

⟁ ⟁ ⟁

After shows I go right to the bus
I don't talk to anyone
I've gotten good at disappearing
I don't sign wadded up pieces of paper
Answer questions or get thanked
If I stick around it gets weird
Last night some woman got into the back room
Kissed me twice and spoke in French
I escaped to the bus
At night I lie in the darkness on a bunk
The bus slams down some highway
I press my face to the ventilator
I try to forget and sleep
I think about imaginary women and Joe
Sex and death
From here on in it's all slow choking
The morning comes and I lie there for hours

It's dark and no one's there but me
I don't leave the bus until the afternoon
I talk to reporters and stand still for a camera
They have no idea what they're dealing with
I do though
Inside I silently scream
At this point I'm the most fucked up person I know
I don't know what to do except go crookedly onward
Nothing gets in the way of ascending plunge into the Abyss

   ⟁ ⟁ ⟁

I'm dead to the touch
Dead to the words spoken meaninglessly on streets
Dead to the eyes I look through
I see my reflection in cement

   ⟁ ⟁ ⟁

Wrap your skeleton around me
Weld your bones to mine
I need more than regular involvement
I need you to perform a miracle on me
Somehow still the horror inside
Please help me
I don't want to die screaming
I don't know if you can do it
Hold me in a violent grip
Outsmart me
I need something
A vacancy is growing inside me that I can't control
Fuck it
Don't even try
I'll just abuse you
It's all I know
I'm just afraid that I'll hurt you
More than I already have

   ⟁ ⟁ ⟁

It's pathetic
The spectacle I create
It's truly obscene
All this noise
All the bother
Sometimes it's more than I can live with
I disgust myself all the time
That's why I leave silently
I don't feel glory
I feel desperation and horror
What a lie
I think it's a life

  ⚴ ⚴ ⚴

I've been looking for a clean place to put my mind
I keep finding myself in exhaustion's ghetto
Another night I've eaten myself
I keep coming up with lean tissue
They talk to me
I always think they're talking to that other guy
Some version of me that I never met
The room is filling me again
Past one in the morning in Dublin
I can't escape the grey shadow
It follows me through these hushed frames of time
If I could only find the right way to puke
I think that everything would be alright

  ⚴ ⚴ ⚴

Dream 2.15.92: I am walking to Joe's house. I'm right at his front steps
and I hear a sound from behind me. I turn around and see the guy who
killed him. His eyes are huge and he's staring right at me.

  ⚴ ⚴ ⚴

I can't get away from myself enough
It all comes out sounding too close to the bone
Everything I say comes back and bites my marrow

I attack myself, even in my sleep
This planet is so lonely as far as I can tell
Maybe not but it is where I keep turning up
Could be I'm looking in the wrong places
Maybe I'm running out of steam
Maybe I'm doing it right and I'm burning out
I see through too much these days
Too cynical and paranoid
All I can think of is to keep moving and stay secretive
I feel a need to feel good for a little while every day
I don't want to be known
I don't want to be loved or understood
I want to disappear into the Abyss
I'm getting closer every day
That much I know for sure

⚭ ⚭ ⚭

I'm in a small plastic box in the ground
My father bought it for me
I'll be here forever
Nothing will happen to me
Their lives will go on and I'll never know
I reach up and touch the top
The plastic is smooth
In here it's total darkness
I wonder where Rollins is
I wonder how he's feeling
I wonder if he knows where this place is
Will I be able to know if he's standing above me?
Maybe he's dead too
Why am I here?
What did I do to get murdered?
Did I make a mistake
Did I say the wrong thing?
What happened?
I hate being dead

⚭ ⚭ ⚭

Dream 2.25.92: I'm fucking a young girl. I look down at my cock. It's made of glass. When I come it shoots all over the wall, the girl has disappeared.

⚶ ⚶ ⚶

I have become abusive because part of me has given up
I have become full of horror because I have written my own ending
I am afraid of nothing
Dulled by everything
The shark gets shot with a bang stick
And slowly spins to the ocean floor

⚶ ⚶ ⚶

Like a Samurai warrior
I'm walking dead
I don't care
I am ready to die
I pay homage to death with every waking moment
Nothing they say matters
Nothing they do gets to me
You can't fuck with a dead man
We just keep going
The shitheads can run in circles
Talk shit until they fall over
Nothing penetrates my dead skin
I was lucky back there
Only part of me was murdered
The other part of me survives
I will not be stopped until I am murdered
I know I will be murdered someday

⚶ ⚶ ⚶

Fuck you bitch
You should hear the shit fall from your mouth
You pathetic piece of stoner shit
I'd love to kick your ass
Just to see the look of shit panic on your face
Your bullshit weak self-serving righteousness

Filling the room with hash and your bullshit bitch complaints
I'm often ashamed to be in a band with you
It's embarrassing

   �; ⚛ ⚛

Dreams 3.1 - 3.12

I'm trying to fire my handgun but every time I pick it up it's a plastic one.

A series of dreams about an old girlfriend. She is with me and telling me about how she has to tell her boyfriend that she no longer wants to be with him. She lists different ways he's going to take the news.

I feel underneath a girl's shirt. She has her navel pierced. I remember that from the last time I was with her. I reach up her dress and feel that she has her vagina pierced as well. She says that she has that going for her now.

I'm talking with two girls and one is talking about sex. I don't want to let them know that I have fucked both of them. One starts laughing slightly and I remember that the last time I was with her I came on her leg or something, I hope she doesn't tell the other one.

I mouth off to a pig and he makes me plant a garden in his back yard. He says that when I finish putting the plants in the dirt I can leave town.

Something happens where a girl is trying to hurt me.

   ⚛ ⚛ ⚛

Mutilating you wouldn't be enough
Killing you wouldn't be enough either
Life and death isn't enough to hold me
Mass murder isn't enough to help
Even a good fuck isn't enough to live for
I am alive in the world of Horror

   ⚛ ⚛ ⚛

I imagine I know every beautiful woman I see on the street
In my mind I talk to them as I pass
I make up fake conversations
In these moments of illusion we understand each other
I can say what I feel
She doesn't look at me funny
She doesn't run away
I close my eyes for a moment to try to keep it in
I open my eyes and I'm standing in the middle of the sidewalk
New York City
Everywhere is the same
All strangers to me
I don't think of desert landscapes anymore
I don't think of burning sunsets and jungle floor
I am no longer choked with passion
It's now just rage and contempt for life
I lost somehow
I got murdered part way
A few bad turns
Now it's all real
There's blood and death wherever I go
No girls and stupid talk
Just tension and solitary corners
The smell of my sweat turning to ammonia
Darkness and silent horror

  ◡ ◡ ◡

So where are you tonight scar maker?
In some lit room making brain cells die?
Making some idiot lose his mind?
Have you ever seen a man tie his neck in a knot?
Have you ever seen someone kill themselves with a thought?
How are your eyes tonight self hate generator?
Cutting and advertising the last chance to breathe?
When I think of you the world gets dangerously huge
My heart beats once a year
I don't know when exactly to stop inhaling

I don't know where to get off
I don't know how to not feel
I wish I could get over you
I am dangerous to myself
All of this will end soon

⚜ ⚜ ⚜

Please come through the door tonight
It's so lonely and fucked up here
I'm confused and everything's strange
I wish I was just on something
You were the last woman that meant anything to me
I can't stop
I have no defense system
No attitude that sees me through
Sometimes I think that I keep getting up everyday
Because there's nothing else to do

⚜ ⚜ ⚜

Looking for answers to all the questions
I walk the cities of lies
I walk the floors of rage
I pace the hallways of Death
The words mean nothing
The ruined flesh that lies behind me
The stain on my eye
It all means nothing
Because I see where it all ends up
I got here a little too early I think
Now that I'm here I might as well make myself at home
Horror takes some getting used to

⚜ ⚜ ⚜

After life
Miles away
A life away
Up a long river

On a beach
Silent sun will watch over me
I will sleep peacefully at night
I will not hear gunshots
I will not regret
I will be free from horror
I will not have terror dreams
I will smile again and mean it
There is a place for me to breathe
It's somewhere I know it
1000 worlds beyond sickness and weakness
Unspoiled by city disease
Quietly in this room I wait
For the world to happen

⚭ ⚭ ⚭

There are bars on the windows of my room
The apartment is surrounded by locked gates
The front door is double locked
I have the lights low and I'm away from the windows
I crawled across the room to get here to write
There could be snipers out there
Paranoia, no such thing
Can't ever be too wired around here
Can't ever be too ready
I come out at night
Behind the locks and the bars and the gates
Like living in a shark cage
Want to sleep well?
Lock yourself in good
Put your money into security
Watch out for slow moving vehicles
Death squads
You don't think they exist?
Wake up or be dead
In the end, what an insult
To be executed by someone who can't even read

At night behind the bars and the locks
I think of you
My silent thoughts are good
They don't show up on their surveillance monitors
I like this room
I always keep a little music on
Messes with their wire taps
I run outside for supplies during the day
I make sure I'm inside well before dark
They're out there
They're everywhere but here

  ⚭   ⚭   ⚭

I want to meet a stranger
I want to tell her everything
I want to howl
I want her to make sense to me
I need someone
I need

  ⚭   ⚭   ⚭

I was with a woman last night
Same distance as always
What's the matter with me
Why am I so fucked up
What am I looking for
Is it that I can't get over
The last time my heart was broken?
I don't know
I sure am lonely these days

  ⚭   ⚭   ⚭

On the streets near my room
You might see pimps and whores
Rent boys and drug dealers
Guys who look like they would kill you quick
Wordlessly and without an emotional display

You might see danger and you might feel fear
You might see the neon and the rust of civilization
Reflected in the crime lights
Dried blood and sadness
I see sweeping eternal darkness
Enveloping doom and marrow drying sadness
All things leaning over to one side and giving up
People pushed until they act like what they fear to stay alive
To become human camouflage
My spine twitches underneath my skin
I wait for the bullet
I watch the small world wear itself down and die screaming
Alas

⟁ ⟁ ⟁

You see I did it
I made something out of myself
I am a slave to my parents
I am slave to my horror
I mutilate myself without their help
You can see it in major cities every year
I didn't blow it
I did good can't you see
I took the punishment out on the road
I don't need them to fuck me up
I can do it to myself real well now
I have it down to a science
I don't know how I'll end up
I don't want to know anymore
I'm afraid of the nightmares I've become
I live it sickly and darkly
My saliva is black

⟁ ⟁ ⟁

I don't know how to be anymore
When you called today and I was nasty
I didn't know how to be any other way

What a piece of work
When you said we should get together for coffee
And I told you I wanted to stab you in the face
I meant it
You said you were sorry about what happened
I was thinking
Fuck yourself you stupid bitch
I didn't say that though
You said I should call you sometime
I told you I wouldn't
I don't care about talking to people anymore
I'm not one of those people you can call and talk to
These days everything makes me sick
No more life
It's all horror walking
I wear a mask and have dreams of killing
The thought of brutal murder is the only thing that comforts me
When I walk down the street I feel safe
I'm not afraid to die
Someone without a gun would be
Fucking with the wrong guy
The wrongest guy
I mean really wrong
Oh man
You Hollywood danger boys
Move aside when I walk by
I have garbage thoughts
Of ripping your throats out
Breaking your wind pipes
I'm the ugliest person I know

⚌ ⚌ ⚌

It's late and I'm alone so I won't lie
If I could get through myself
And all the lies I use to protect myself
I could somehow talk to you
I could somehow listen

I could get out of my claustrophobic stranglehold
I would tell you everything
I wouldn't be so horrible
I would learn to communicate
I could maybe let someone else be strong
If I only had the guts

⚉ ⚉ ⚉

I want to be in love with a woman
One who loved me
One who could show me I could trust her
One who could show me
That I didn't have to be on my guard all the time

⚉ ⚉ ⚉

Been two weeks since the last show
Next tour starts in a few days
Relief
I could never deal with the room in one place for too long
Makes me feel like I'm choking
Touring makes me feel ok inside my skin
The last few nights have been depressing
I don't know what to do with myself
I'm pretty fucked up I guess

⚉ ⚉ ⚉

I wish I could meet a woman that could show me something
One who could make my blood stop screaming

⚉ ⚉ ⚉

Generic night
Another night in the room
It's past midnight
Waiting for sleep to take me out
All I can to do is write
I feel so wrong
Wrong planet
Wrong time

The whole thing
I am lonely and fucked up
Tomorrow another tour starts
My world will move again
I can get out of my mind for awhile
My dead friend follows me everywhere
I walk with grief and horror
I wish there was someone to talk to me
I have never felt such extinction
Loneliness, ripped away thoughts
I figure I'm allowed to write it if I don't talk
I'm ok if I keep writing and moving
I wonder if I'll ever meet someone I can be close to
Fuck it
I wouldn't know what to say
Like right now
I don't know what to say
Don't know the right thought to get me through
The streets around here
Man, they'll fuck you right up
You go out there for a little while
That's all you need
Heavy metal women
Whores and drug dealers
Police and filth
You know you're going to lose
Just by association

♠ ♠ ♠

I love you
I have no guide to help me
Nothing to protect me from your storm
I felt like an idiot sitting in your car
Your face was so beautiful
I didn't think I could love anyone
I love you
Wouldn't be great if you would love me
Maybe you would even trust me

I need you
Because life is not enough
I hadn't seen you in over a year
It all came back
With the force of depression
I still felt the same
I have been thinking of you all day
I feel as though I have nothing
I am alone on the planet
I know this and it hurts too much
Maybe with you it could be different
I can't ask you to want me
I'll just have to see
I don't like rolling the dice again
It's hard to load the gun with a picture of your face
Spin the cylinder and pull
All my life it's been the lonely click

⚘ ⚘ ⚘

4.10.92
It's Joe Cole's birthday
I'm in my room on a night off in LA
Too freaked out to leave the apartment
I figure the killer knows I want to go to mail some letters
He's out there waiting in the parking garage
I have spent the last few hours crying and writing
Nothing changes
I like the stillness of the night
In a few hours they'll all be up and making noise
I don't know how I do it sometimes
I have been back in the murder mind
I see the pieces of shit on the street
I want to go up and shoot them in the stomach
Walk away and say nothing
I hate the way they look at me
I must give them the vibe that they can take me
It's predator-prey
If they only knew

I'm only afraid of guns and numbers
The rest of it doesn't get in my way
I just don't give a fuck
The part that cared
Sits in a plastic box in Burbank
I keep saying goodbye
I keep getting a corpse on my porch
Every night is the same
I take it alone in silence
There really isn't any other way to handle it

   ⚸ ⚸ ⚸

One great night
I'm going to pack my belongings
And sneak out of this town
Won't tell anyone
The sun will come up and I'll be laughing
Thousands of miles away
Never to return
Not for any price
What a great plan
He never came back to California
Smart guy
He beat the game
Like you really want to die out here
Only losers finish out in California
I'll have to sneak out though
If they hear you're leaving
The killers line up to make sure you don't
Believe me
I've seen 'em
Shitheads on every corner
Looking like they own the whole game
They do out here
Kings of the shit house

   ⚸ ⚸ ⚸

I am thoughtless wordless
I walk down this wet night street
I am the desert and all its sand
I cannot hold onto a thought or memory
There's no need for heartbreak
Nervous breakdown or panic
Just go on and do what you will
Don't flinch or think about death
I can't tell you about romance
I cannot tell you how I feel
I don't feel, I'm slaughtered meat
I am the desert night and all its darkness
I'm not beyond life
Just next to it
Watching it slam down the rails
Some people need help
Some people just need
Some people know better

   △ △ △

I am alone tonight and it's a good thing too
I wouldn't want to try and talk the language tonight
I want to scream and fall into your arms
I know that will never work out
I feel like I should be vomiting right about now
Another tour starts

   △ △ △

It's night time in Ohio
I'm in a box but it's different this time
Some of them know where we are
It's not as safe as it used to be
We don't come into town as strangers
I get recognized even at night
Somewhere they know
They could come here any time
I feel safer on the bus

Rolling across the highway at night
Curled up in a black box
Alone with my pathetic thoughts
And terrifying nightmares
I lie awake in the black box
The road under my back
I think of her
I know she never thinks of me
It is pathetic
Tonight I'll sleep with some part of me awake
Wild eyed, scared and screaming

   ☙ ☙ ☙

He didn't do much
He just went from town to town
Did all the interviews
Shook all the hands
Said all the right things
Everybody got off but him
You don't want to know too much
If you get closer than an inch away
It's terribly ugly
I wouldn't lie to you

   ☙ ☙ ☙

My exhaustion is nervous
I don't know why I'm running
I'll vomit myself again tonight
I'll come up with another answer
When they come up with another question
Something about all that money
All this shiny stuff
They don't know that all I smell is blood and brains
That I want to die all the time
That I had a dream about killing myself last night
How much sense it made
That an hour before the show started

I was wrapped in a blanket sweating
They don't know, they'll never know
How much of a freak I think I am
I'll never be able to explain it
I'll just scream and fuck until I die
I think that's all there is besides truth

   ⚶ ⚶ ⚶

You can go see my friend's little piece of lawn
You can go for free
Doesn't mean shit to me
A nice place so the father can go
And feel better about himself
I have the horror memorial in my closet
A plastic container of the blood filled dirt
That remained after they scraped him off
809 Brooks Ave motherfucker
Right where his head fell
I had to take it before all the flies ate it
It sits right next to his phone
In case he needs to get in touch

   ⚶ ⚶ ⚶

All night blues
On the other hand fuck it
Fuck all of these late night desperation ideas
It's all self-serving bullshit
Like I could really love you
Like I could really love anything
I keep forgetting how fucked up I am
I get fooled by all the voices
I almost feel like I could fit
Then reality comes back and I know where I'm at
Stabbing you with my thoughts
Endlessly killing you
Mutilating you
The only thing that amazes me

Is how I can keep on being so fucking good all the time
I'll fuck but I won't love
I won't crawl again
I've seen life shortened by a shithead with a gun
Life's rope is too short for me
I can't be slowed by love's sick hand
There's only safety in the animal mind
Too many of these weaklings have guns now
All the time I'm looking over my shoulder
The shithead with the gun
I'm old fashioned
I miss the good old days
Punching the shit out of someone
Feeling about it
Like the other night
The piece of shit that cut in front of me in line
The only thing he had going for him
Was the fact that he might have been packing
That's the only thing that keeps me off your ass
One of these days I'm going to do the wrong thing
Not take shit from the wrong person
And get shot in a 7-11
That's how I'll go out
In a puddle of blood in a fucking convenience store
I fucking hate you all so much I can't even breathe
I'll find a way to hurt all of you

☖ ☖ ☖

4.30.92 Los Angeles California
Large buildings are on fire
The men who beat Rodney King are going to go free
Supermarkets are on fire
Pigs have shot 6, killed 1
Hospitals are overrun with injured
The news showed Westwood
A broken window
Three pigs on every corner

Outside you can smell the smoke
LA's burning
What the fuck did the pigs expect
What would they do if the shoe
Was on the other hoof
Some good may come of this
Some pigs might get killed
Every day is a good day for a pig to die

⚉ ⚉ ⚉

A super fantasy about the acquitted pigs going home
Getting ambushed and tortured to death
Me and Cole on the controls
Watching their kids burn
Getting their eyes pulled out
Getting fed their wives intestines
They need this

⚉ ⚉ ⚉

Another night is taking me through myself
I can smell the beast's flesh cooking again tonight
Down the streets they're looting
At first it was because of the pigs
Now it's just because humans like to fuck shit up
They're all the same
Here's what:
I see this one guy go up to a liquor store and throw a trash can through the front window. A few guys standing next to me start chasing him with sticks. People next to me were yelling, "Get him, he's getting away!" I didn't know who the biggest idiots were, the looter, the guys with the sticks or the people wanting to see the blood. I decided that they were all assholes and left. Fuck this place. Fuck this city. Los Angeles is for losers. I think I'll have to move soon. I don't want to live the rest of my fucking days in this decadent shithole. I don't want to die in this city. I have nothing left here anyway. I should get out of here before it gets me and kills me. But anyway, look at the shit we're in here in this fucked up place. I was leaving to go back to the room when the police came and

told us to get in our homes so we would be safe. I bet the pigs love it now
with the National Guard in town. I hate this place. It's getting too fucked
up to live here.
I think of desert
I think of a girl
I want to know a girl
It will make me have to work
I'll have to be bigger in my heart
I doubt if I can do it
I have pulled so far back from humans
I don't know if I can come back
I have dreams of a different reality
Waking up in an apartment in some city far from here
Walking outside and not getting recognized
Knowing why people want to know me
Not getting stared at all the time
Meeting someone that will make me listen
Fuck it
In the morning I'll come to my senses
I'll know that I feel this way because I'm not on the road
When I'm on the road nothing else matters
When I sit still I get soft
There really isn't any other life for me
I wouldn't last very long with a girl in a house

   ⚛ ⚛ ⚛

We'll get together soon you and I
As I sit here I can see it clearly
It will be pure
Animal
I'll pull your hair around my neck
We'll bite each other's flesh
We will understand each other
I'll understand that you're beautiful
Because you're alive
Maybe you'll be able to help me
I'm fucked up in the head

I'm a wounded animal
Staggering on the side of the road
Waiting for another car to hit me and leave
If you could make me cry
Make me feel something
Maybe I wouldn't want to tear my skin off
Maybe you could reach me
Please try to reach me
I think it's too late
I'm already dead pretty much
Hell with it
I'll shut up and we'll fuck
I'll leave and you'll call me weeks later
I'll be busy and have forgotten your name
I will have pulled into myself even further
You'll get a taste of how truly cold and black I am
You'll want to puke
When you think that I was inside you
From now on it's like this

⚜ ⚜ ⚜

Not alive
Not me
Not anymore
Say what you want
Leave any time
I don't even remember you
I'll never miss you
I'll never think about you
I'm so far past that shit
It's a joke to me, all of it
Stab your mother in the teeth
Stab mine
I don't care about anything
Except a night in the desert

⚜ ⚜ ⚜

At the end of all of this
I won't be wondering about shit
I won't be surprised by a fucking thing
Don't get me wrong
I'm not like you
I puke out memories
I want to hurt people
I'm negative and paranoid
I think that sex is always fucked up
A no-soul cock with a mind behind it is nothing
But a tool of cruelty
I collect them and hang them like teeth
Put them in a bag and keep moving
What the fuck do you expect from a stranger
I'll tell you the truth always
You're more alone than I think you know
You're never more alone
Than when you're with me
Because with me it's different
My touch fools you
It begs for understanding and then
Prepares itself to spit on you
When you reach out to me
You humiliate yourself
I mutilate myself in front of you
You think I'm being open
I'm not
I'm being fucked and cruel
It's all I know
Animal is as animal does
Hey look
I don't ever wonder why about shit

   ⚴ ⚴ ⚴

Deathstar CA: Do you want to die a few feet from your house? All you have to do is move here and it all can come true for you. Do you want to see a sea of dead eyes and toneless voices talk about bullshit? Do you want to see millions of people waste their time when they should just be wasting themselves? It's all right here. All the pigs and bullshit. Every time I come back here I always kick myself. What a bad place to be, evil place. Only a sucker would end up old in this city. Why do it when there's so many places on the planet. 31 isn't old is it?

⚐ ⚐ ⚐

Cab ride on the way to the airport
Riding down La Cienega
Looking at burned out hulls of stores
One said:
Looted, tenants upstairs
Other store fronts
With pictures of Martin Luther King
Like that's going to help
All this shit burned up on the streets
It was good to get out of all that dead cement
Fuck that dead city
It should have never stopped
The whole city should have burned to the ground
We were almost there

⚐ ⚐ ⚐

All the parts disconnected
All the parts broken down
Another room down my throat
Slack jawed paranoia
Thinking about killing them and myself
I can't.....
It all falls into a violent display
I fall in on myself
I don't wonder why about shit
I can't find a way to get the parts together
You ever seen a pile of parts
Walking by you
Yea, it's like that
Just fucked up and thinking about death

⚐ ⚐ ⚐

She calls me and wonders why I don't call her
I struggle silently to remember her name
I listen to the bullshit pour from her mouth
I don't listen and tell her that I'm hanging up
She demands that I don't
She keeps talking and I'm fighting the urge
I want to tell her to get the rubber out her tits
And stab herself in the face with an ice pick
I hang up and I go back to the room
There's a gunshot outside
I see myself emptying a 9 mm in the general direction
I've been here three days
This shit doesn't work for me
Fuck it
I'll kill myself if I stay here too long
It'll make too much fucking sense
Why?
Because fuck you

   ❧   ❧   ❧

Mother on the answering machine
Mother through the wires
I listen to the message and I start to burn
I want to start kicking holes in the wall
A rage I can't identify courses through my body
And I just want to explode and not exist
I think about the shrink I went to
Because I was so fucked up right?
Because she was so fucked up
And now I've got this rage and nowhere to go

   ❧   ❧   ❧

Alive without a head
Cursed with a little too much brains
Your sight is too clear to lie your way out of the night
Alone in your room
Some fucking city somewhere

Hear the idiots outside shooting guns
Yea it's come to this
You're right in it
Trying to separate yourself
Just like me
Trying to separate yourself
Balled up like some forgotten piece of paper
I'll go to the bottom with you
I'll stand on the edge with you
You always know where you are
I'll show you around these parts

⚐ ⚐ ⚐

Come into my room and check out some pathetic shit
Get a good seat and watch me
See me sit in here alone crying in this chair
As I go steadily deeper inside
Watching 2 a.m. turn into paranoia
Look in the closet
My friend's dried blood is in a plastic bowl
My life is pretty fucked up at this point
I re-live horror perfectly
I don't want to talk to anyone
Yet I am lonely and violent
I don't know what to do anymore

⚐ ⚐ ⚐

At night the scars of loneliness rip open and it hurts
You look into the wound and it's deep
Put there with feeling and conviction
It's no lie
It goes beyond words
You've tried to put it down
Some piece of paper
You got so frustrated
Fuck words
Sometimes they just don't work

You have a lump in your throat
You want to break something
You wish it was different
Life I mean
You know that this is a huge part of it
You can tell that there will be many nights like this
There will be
Look at the lines in the faces
They look just like yours
In the deep wounded night I am your friend

⟡ ⟡ ⟡

I love you and you'll never know
I could tell you and it wouldn't matter
You wouldn't get it and why should you
It hurts to know you'll never know
It hurts to sit here alone and really mean it
To feel it so deeply that my bones ache thinking of you
To imagine how the conversation would go
How you would stare with your blank eyes
Say nothing until
I think you're really a great guy....
And hope you could leave it at that and just leave
And of course I would watch you walk away
Knowing deep inside that no one
Is anything but totally alone
There are some like you
Who deal with it
There are some like myself
Who don't deal with it as well
The scars are easy to see

⟡ ⟡ ⟡

Fuck it
I walked away from the wreckage
Turned my back to the waste
Staggered into the desert

You can see it in my eyes
I'm not here
Sometimes I think
That someone should love me
They really should
But then I remember how I think
Stabbing and kicking
No explanation
I can't cry anymore
I'm all dried up
All I see is the Abyss
I just keep walking through shadows
The varying shades of blindness
I end up in these rooms alone
I understand how perfect all of this is

  ⚅ ⚅ ⚅

Time with you was perfect
Never boring
Never wasted
You were always the same
Intense and beautiful
Amazing
I would look at you as we sat in restaurants
You awed me with your sheer presence
When I was away from you I would stare at your picture
Endlessly
Something you never got a chance to find out
Something you'll never know
One fact:
I would have done anything for you
Knowing that it all could be used against me
I know what happens when you do that even a little
I have the scars
For you I would have pulled sunlight from thin air
And lifted the curses from your life
I loved you so

It's tragic at this point
Like an ongoing funeral
You're out there somewhere
Sometimes I can feel myself dying slow
You know how those barbed and clawed nights can pass
They rip the meat off your back
Send you into a corner
And leave you with enough of your senses to realize
That you'll live to see another hammering night alone

   ☧ ☧ ☧

It's hard for me to talk to you
I have a problem with my face
I got shot in my left cheek last December
You can see the hole in my head
I feel strange showing myself in day light
All the powder burns on my face from the gun
It looks like someone lit me on fire
I can't make my mouth work too well anymore
I have almost stopped talking altogether
I feel so crippled
All these people staring at me
They know my name everywhere I go
I wish I could show them the horror behind my eyes
Because this place doesn't care
You go looking for a hand out
I tell you man
You'll waste your life looking
You find holes in all your pockets
Nothing in your head
Except bitter memories and spent bullet casings
Be careful, so careful
Life has no meaning
The world is full of strangers
Love is a tightrope walk
The rope is made of inspiration
Intertwined with desperation

When you fall
You fall

   ♊ ♊ ♊

If I keep writing
Traveling all over
Pushing myself until I squeeze truth
From out of my pores
She will find me
It's worth it

   ♊ ♊ ♊

I wonder if you live in a happy world. If your sleep releases you, if you have a life that makes you look forward to life. I do not begrudge you your happy life if you have one. I wish I had one too. I wouldn't want you to see mine. I wouldn't want you to deal with it for a second. I sometimes wish I could get out of existence and not have to feel. It's been a series of small abortions, inhalation of glass shards and paranoia. Insomnia and horror. I wish I had a happy life. I don't see the merit in torment. It's to the point to where I can't tell if I'm awake or dreaming of being terrified all the time. I don't mean to carry on with this bad trip. I look into their eyes and I wish I could see what they see when they smile. Last night was bad, real bad. I was overwhelmed with panic. I was in front of a lot of people and they never knew that I was freaking out in front of them wishing there was someone on the planet I could talk to. Someone to relieve the horror. Today has been strange, hanging around silently waiting for the beating. I hope you have a happy life, maybe someday I'll have one too.

   ♊ ♊ ♊

6.11.92 Florence Italy: Night off tonight. We drove about 18 hours to get here. Been going since Amsterdam last night. This is a night off. Another lit box on the trail. People outside are talking loud and the traffic is whizzing by. It doesn't matter where we are tonight. I feel lost and found wherever I am these days. I don't know where I am but I know where I'm at all the time. I hang in moments. I think of other places and other times. Tonight while driving into town I thought of where I grew up and how I showed part of it to Joe and how he wrote about it in his book. I feel like dying a lot of the time now. I don't tell anyone about it because I don't want to get into a discussion about it. I don't want anyone trying to cheer me up. I don't want anyone to tell me anything. I am tired of hearing them talk. Last night there were these people waiting outside the door of the side of the building near the bus. These days people that want to meet me I automatically don't want to talk to. I know it's ridiculous but I see it as an insult. It's as if I didn't give enough of myself an hour ago on stage and they want more. I'm so tired at the end of the night that the luxury that I have is that I don't have to talk and to have to take compliments for ripping myself up every night. They came near me and I froze them out so fast that it even surprised me. Some girl wanted to give me some flowers and I stared at her so hard that she just held onto them and walked away. I figure that they shouldn't get close to people like me and I'm right.

⚜ ⚜ ⚜

Nice guys don't play good. Nice guys suck when they play. You can't be nice and be any good. The ones that make music that sticks and burns aren't nice. Charlie Parker wasn't nice. If he was nice he wouldn't be onstage with his horn on fire. These days people would rather have nice people playing music than the real thing that moves you. Music that kills the player. They'll never make me nice. Nothing will ever tame me. When these fucking journalists ask these stupid questions, I can tell that they're nice people who have no clue where the real heavy shit comes from. They wonder why the real heavy duty cats are greedy, mean assed, damaged, dangerous people that end up dying pathetically. I know why. No one has to tell me shit. Some people are born fucked up and a few of them make it onto stages. It's simple. The good ones sit in a room by themselves and hate the life that they were given because they see it as what it is, an affliction. A plague. Fuck this place.

⚜ ⚜ ⚜

I am typical and I'm thinking of her tonight
I met her months ago
Spent a few days with her
Called her on the phone several times
It was good to talk to her

Pretty good
When I saw her again a few weeks later
I couldn't see why I had talked to her at all
I had nothing to say to her
Had trouble remembering her name
Couldn't wait to leave her
Haven't talked to her since
Haven't thought of her until tonight
Does this happen on Earth all the time
Or is it just me being totally fucked up?
Sometimes I wish I was stupid
Because sometimes I want to be happy
You know how hard it gets to live here
Life puts you in these rooms alone at night
Time drags you out and turns you on yourself
I wonder if I hurt her feelings at all
I doubt it
She probably already knew I was a creep
But it's deeper than that and much worse
I know that I'll never meet anyone that I can be with
I have too much distance in my eyes
Too much damage to deal with
It hurts to live beside life
Never really knowing what it's like
Yet feeling so torn and confused by it
How do you explain that to someone
Have you tried and seen the blank stare too many times?
Yea me too

♤ ♤ ♤

The cleaning lady wouldn't leave the room. I told her that I didn't need anything. She kept apologizing and cleaning anyway. I had slept in the bed for less than an hour and she was trying to put new sheets on it and I kept telling her that it was alright, I didn't need anything. She said that she was sorry and she would only be another minute. She left the room and I thought I was clear of her and she came back in with all her gear and started to clean the bathroom which hadn't even been used yet. I told her that it was ok and she could split and she said it was not a worry and she started to clean it anyway. She said that a younger maid recognized me when I checked in a couple of hours ago. She told me that the younger maid was replacing her and that she herself was "one of the redundancy maids" and was going to be let go next week. I looked at this older woman who wouldn't make eye contact with me at all. She diverted her eyes like I was some kind of lord. She kept running around me cleaning up, straightening the clothes that I unpacked, folding newspapers, this went on for minutes. Finally she apologized for talking and wasting my time and then without another word she pulled out of the room with her buckets and sheets.

I imagine her at the end of the day. She lies down in the maid's closet with her coat as a blanket. She steals a biscuit from the tea service and makes it her meal. A few hours later she gets up and cleans rooms all day and returns to the closet. She cleans ten miles of rooms a day. One day she cleans and there's a man at the end of the hall and he opens the door and shows her another one hundred miles of hallway and tells her to clean every room and she says yes sir. She cleans the one hundred miles of rooms and she gets to the end a month later to see that at the end of the hall there is an open grave with headstone with her name on it. The man returns out of nowhere and tells her to jump in. She apologizes, says thank you and jumps.

⚭ ⚭ ⚭

They had just finished sex
He said that he was going "out there"
She asked him when he would be back
He said that she didn't want to know any more
That he was hollow
And that if she got any closer
He would damage her for the rest of her life
By telling her everything
He said goodbye, got up and walked away
He walked across a stretch of sand
He was met by an ocean made of fire
He turned, smiled and ducked under a wave of flame
He disappeared and the night started to scream

⚭ ⚭ ⚭

Cindy Crawford
I'm in this hotel room
Smelling the bug spray and watching you on TV
I'm listening to you talk
You're one of the most intense people I've ever seen
Fascinating
You must be so great in bed
Not

 ☙ ☙ ☙

I've been thinking about your Hollywood television actor ass today. I'm looking forward to getting one of your fucked up phone calls and listening to your voice and its reading off a script sound. "Joe was my son." Where's the music? What's your motivation in this scene? Too busy with your bimbos and AA meetings to notice your son until he gets shot in the head and all of a sudden you're out of your fuckhead world back into the real world where one take is all you get and that's it. Stepping into your role as dad. Remembering the moves, making sure you look good for the cameras. Real life you piece of shit. You're so fake. Why don't you just finish the job and blow your fucking brains out and make me respect you. Why couldn't it have been you instead.

 ☙ ☙ ☙

Two strangers lie in a hotel bed
Underneath the weight of the dark
They speak their truths in hushed tones
They wrap their arms round each other
And hold tight
Because
The world is so huge

 ☙ ☙ ☙

Dennis Miller Show after thought
I'm not running for office
I'm not trying to make you like me
I'm not trying to sell you anything
I'm not a comic

I just wanted to take a minute to remind you of something
Life isn't short, it goes on after you're gone
Time is not running out, time just goes
It's your life time that is short and running out all the time
So what are you doing taking drugs?
Why are you putting cigarette smoke in those beautiful lungs of
yours?
What are you drinking that poison for?
Weeks ago sections of this city burned to the ground
For nothing
Months ago my best friend was shot in the face and killed on my
front porch
For nothing
Life time's up for him
You're different
You're alive, you're breathing
I'd like to see you stay that way
Don't do anything for nothing
You're too important
This trip is all about you

   ⚘ ⚘ ⚘

They sit across from each other and wait for the food
Several minutes ago they were having intense sex
The sweat was running off their bodies
It was mutual need nothing more
Now they sit and talk about nothing
They both know that they're looking for something
Each know that the other isn't it
Yet they go on talking and fucking
Idly
Watching out not to get too deep
Neither has the energy
They couldn't if they wanted to
Both know that the other isn't concerned too much
In the mean time they're looking
That was me tonight
I don't know what I'm looking for

In someone else's eyes
I don't know if I'd know at this point
You can get so numb over the years
You'll work, pay taxes and lie to yourself
The whole nine yards to nowhere
My eyes drifted off to the street
The lights of the cars kicked at the corners of my eyes
I forgot to pretend to listen
I was filled with emptiness
I felt old and stupid
I could do nothing but breathe
Now I sit in my room alone and I feel better
Sometimes you're faking it
Sometimes you're a coward
Sometimes you just get tired of taking the beating

At band practice today I made up a song about you. It was about the scars in your eyes and how they alter your vision to where you think I'm one of the ones who is going to hurt you. I could never hurt you. I think of you all the time. I have no idea where you are but still I think of you and the way I could sometimes see a spark in your eyes like some diamond that didn't get crushed to powder under some man's fist. It would never last long, it would fall from sight behind a strip of scar tissue.

I thought I saw you the other day. It wasn't you but looking into the girl's eyes before I had to look away in total embarrassment made me remember you and how much I wanted to try to bring your eyes back to life. I would live for the way your eyes would come to life every once in a while. I miss you. Nothing much for me around here. My loneliness doesn't use subtle hints. It comes up and stabs me. You know how the nights are built to rip you apart. Right now Charlie Parker is soloing through mine. Outside, Los Angeles burns and rapes. The whores are a few blocks away getting in and out cars parked on the Blvd. This is unfinished because life is unfinished. Hot stabbing night. Past three in the morning. I am here, the pupil in the black eye.

Choices: Let's say you were a lonely man who once had a best friend. Months before, your best friend was murdered right next to you outside your house. Since your friend had died all of your days are full of pain. You sleep with horror and bad dreams. You can't understand why you were allowed to live and your friend was the one who had to die.

Life has lost its shine, it's not all that special anymore, you start to lose interest in things and life starts to pass you and you stop caring. Sometimes it's all you can do just to get through the day without breaking down and crying. It never seems to get better either. You realize that this will last you the rest of your life. You know deep down that you will never have another friend like that and even though you can accept that truth, you cannot find a way to deal with it. You have feelings that you are afraid to tell people about because you think that they will think you are crazy. You become withdrawn and isolated. It gets so bad that sometimes all you can do is sit in a dark room and try not to think. You feel that life is over for you and you're just waiting for it to end.

You have a dream one night. It goes like this: You are given a choice between two realities. The first choice is that nothing changes and you live the rest of your life the best you can. The second choice is that your friend will be brought back to life. The catch is that you will have to spend the rest of your life in solitary confinement in a prison. You will be shown a couple of pictures of your friend so you're sure that the deal went through. Otherwise you live alone with no contact with your friend or the outside world. The only consolation is that you know your friend is alive. He will have no memory of you or your friendship.

In a hotel room in the desert a woman asked me if I ever got lonely. I told her I was one of the loneliest people she ever met. Outside the desert wind threw sand against the glass. Middle of nowhere's nowhere. Walking the balance line between light and dark, always coming up odd. From now on life is transparent and insane. I know it too well so I know too much. I am an endless choked scream. Inside I claw myself and wait for nothing.

☸ ☸ ☸

Straight haired girls
With bleached brains
Walk up the Blvd

Strike poses at the corners
Trying to look like every man's fantasy
Bow legged and underfed
They look distant and hard
The street comes up to meet their rusted stare
And backs off
Hollywood

⚛ ⚛ ⚛

I'm not going to bother with you anymore
I don't need all the extra thought
I got enough right now as it is
Not going to wait for your phone calls
Not going to think about you
And what it would be like it were different
It's not different
It's like this
I won't think of you when I'm in some shithole
Or a rented room by a numbered highway off ramp
I will not bother to find stamps to send letters
It's living a lie
To pull myself through your studied indifference
Is to be insulted by pain
A pain that cannot teach or strengthen
Only a pain that messes with your guts
I'm throwing you out of my thoughts
You'll only hurt me anyway
I'll find better ways to hurt myself

⚛ ⚛ ⚛

I know what I want
I want you
Too bad I'm too fucked up to do anything about it
All I could do is hurt you
I am a wounded animal blinded by headlights
This could be the universal blues song

⚛ ⚛ ⚛

Don't think that you need me
Or that I hold any answers
Don't think of what it would be like to meet me
Believe me
I'll only let you down
You'll hate me
There's nothing I'll be able to say to make it any different
It's the oldest story
One filled with self hatred
Cannot do anything beneficial for others
When they get too close
I can't handle affection or friendship
Too fucked up and scarred
I wrote this girl a letter the other day
Two words: Don't bother
It's like talking to a dead body
Or a shark

♤ ♤ ♤

I keep telling myself:
You have to get this shit on your own
It's easy to die
People are wrong when they think they're hard to kill
Humans die easy and without much fight
If you listen to them for too long
They will sell you the fuck out
Pull back into your mind
Master yourself before someone else does
You are all you've got
You can make or break yourself any time
People measure themselves
Using the yardstick of others
Good for a while
I must maintain the One
Keep the number strong within me
It's the only number there is
People around me telling me things all the time

If I listened I wouldn't be here now
Look at them and see them
Not yourself in them
You are not them
Exhaustion level is extreme
Body pain all the time
Non stop schedule
It's my will power
Presence of mind and clarity that gets me through
If I listened to them I would fall apart
That's something they'll never understand
I fly alone in the thin air

🔺 🔺 🔺

Busted LA again
I must have forgotten
Been gone from here for so long this time out
A few hours in my room and it comes back to me
The traffic outside
The chopper blades hovering near the roof
You leave this town and you can forget
It all came back to me on the plane today
Listening to the male models call each other dude
Looking at their tinted hair pony tails
Wondering what they would do
If someone put a gun to their head
Broken lying city full of dead blood and cheap death
I daydream of leaving
I have to get back to the East Coast
Walk the streets that Coltrane, Monk and Parker walked
Listen to language that means something
Not this painted rubber killing field collection of catch phrases

🔺 🔺 🔺

Alien encounters single female earthling
The idea that I had met you and that you liked me
For the simple reason that you liked me

Was incredible
One of the single most validating things
That had ever happened to me
So when you left
I really noticed

⚅ ⚅ ⚅

Tripping on
Joe's
Dead
Body
By the time it got dead
It was no longer his
For a while it belonged to the state of California
Then it belonged to his father
Now it belongs to a graveyard
This cold slab of property
What a way to go out
Also
These people who say shit like
He's not dead
He'll always be alive in your heart
There was a reason, there's a reason for everything
This makes me want to say
See that guy over there?
Then walk over and shoot the guy in the face
And say
He's not dead
He'll always be with you
There was a reason
There's a reason for everything
And
Would you like to be next?

⚅ ⚅ ⚅

Dream sickness
She kissed me
I said it had been a long time since I had done that

She said that it had been a long time since she had wanted to
For a few moments I felt special
I existed for the first time in months
Now the hours are blank
And I feel normal again

⚘ ⚘ ⚘

My best friend got shot in the head
Murdered
A few feet away from me
I heard his shoes shift on the pavement seconds before
I have a perspective on things
I don't have to explain

⚘ ⚘ ⚘

I wish I could have understood you
I wish you would have needed me
It hurts to know I'll never be with you again
I think of you all the time
I have been with other women
I accidentally call them by your name
I can't help myself
These nights go by
Always different cities
But the same pain
I am becoming more familiar with myself
More strange to them
I wish I knew someone
I could talk to
I wish
I wish I didn't sound so struck, so pathetic
I should feel lucky to be alive
But I don't feel so lucky
Most of the time
I don't feel anything at all
My eyes hollow out
And the time passes unnoticed

⚘ ⚘ ⚘

Sitting in the box near 8 a.m. and all I can think of is playing and destroying shit. The drag is that I have to leave here in a few hours and talk to shitheads about all the little bullshit details. Press people don't get it and never will because they are press people. If they had a real life they wouldn't have to ask questions. Sometimes the guys in the band are weak and it's a drag to have to be around them. Not a warrior amongst them. That's why I spend so much time in the gym. I like being around people who are going for some pain. When I work out I don't have to listen to the bullshit and I don't have to deal with weak people. I can get off on myself and work out hard and not have apologize for the way I am. I fucking hate having to explain myself to people. I hate having to answer all these questions and be nice all the time. In the gym you go and slam the iron and everything makes sense. You pick shit up and you put it down and that's all there is to it. It's not an intellectual pursuit. It's pure animal and I can live with that.

☖ ☖ ☖

In a small room a man sits silently and tries to forget himself and all the things that have happened in his life. He ceased being outraged at how quickly life turned on him and left him alone and broken. At first it was incredible, every day felt like crawling out of a car wreck and staggering through the smoke past a small group of strange onlookers.

He lost touch with people immediately. At times he couldn't understand what they were saying even though they were right in front of him. It all changed on him so fast he thought that he had been transported to a different planet. Days went by like dreams. People would call and he would ask them not to call again and he meant it. He would listen as the words came out of his mouth and it was as if there was someone else living inside him saying these things. It was a relief that they stopped though. He found that talking to them only made things worse, made him more aware that he was alive. In the darkness of his room, if he sat still and concentrated only on the darkness sometimes he would forget himself.

Time went by and they stopped calling, they stopped writing. He didn't notice, all he could think about was the huge abyss inside him that was the color of the total absence of light. Soon he found himself inside this black void. He had become consumed. It was overwhelming.

☖ ☖ ☖

The sun is setting on 9-12-92
Gold Coast Australia
On the bank of an inlet
The blue Pacific to my right
Around this time
No matter where I am
The desperation closes in
And a scream lodges itself
Like a bullet
Caught in my spine

   ❧ ❧ ❧

I am a broken man
Washed ashore in humanity's
Low tide
Dislocated
I feel no kinship with humans
I do my best
To forget myself

   ❧ ❧ ❧

I know nothing else
Florescent bulb overhead
A few hours until show time
The opening band's boring talk
Seeps through the walls of this room
I always end up in these places
filled with wordless isolation
Even more these days
Sounds of traffic outside
Blends with the talk
The world is out there
I have no place here
I must keep moving
So they don't find out
That I'm dead

   ❧ ❧ ❧

Nothing behind the face
I move through cities
Mixing with silence and shadow
I'm too freaked out to remember
What life is like
Without exhaustion and paranoia
Nerved and heavily charged
I go through the hours
Waiting for dreams to start

☙ ☙ ☙

I have new eyes
They see less than the old ones
But what they see
They see clearly
Too clearly
It's all I see
All I know
I choke on myself
My thoughts are hushed and dull
A new lease of life has been inflicted on me
I stagger
I no longer speak their language
I cannot translate what my eyes see
I am alone at all times

☙ ☙ ☙

Hollow night
Tonight one of them sprayed Mace while we were playing
Aren't they a trip?
These fakes
Why do they bother coming
They could just stay home
Shoot themselves in the head
And spare me the drama
You can't get close to humans
Can't like them too much

Can't waste time making sense out of their emotions
All you'll do is waste yourself
Torment yourself with their image
What a cheap high
They'll either get killed
Or they'll spray mace
I don't want friends
I don't want a girlfriend
What a fucked up idea
Could you see me with a girlfriend
I remember once my father ran out of cigars at a restaurant and he
smoked one of my stepmother's cigarettes. He devoured it, the cigarette
looked so small in his mouth. He took it halfway to the filter in a couple
of drags like it was nothing. That's me and a girlfriend. A girl with her
arm around a human scream pain machine. Angry when her name is
forgotten a few times, angrier when she threatens to leave and gets no
response at all. Right down to the filter in no time.
What a joke
Knowing what I know
Makes it impossible to live the life I had before
Seeing what I've seen
Makes it impossible
To let it be anything but exactly what it is
A lie
A lie that never stops being true

  ♁ ♁ ♁

I'd rather have their money than their affection
After they spend the night spitting on me
Throwing shit and getting in the way
I look at my skin and see the scars
Cigarette and lighter burns
Chipped teeth
Stitches and concussions
If had a nickel for every piece of someone's spit
I've scraped off myself
I'd buy another planet to live on

I like knowing that I leave the hall
With some of their fucking money
I'm not one of those who thinks
That money can't buy everything
I live in the real world and I know it can
Money can buy any fucking thing you want
I don't live for the stuff
But I'd rather have a dollar
Than your phone number
Or the mouthfull of beer that you spit on me
I'd rather have some dough in the bank
Than my mother's fucked up guilt ridden love
Or my father's beer soaked respect
With money
I can buy some room
And some piece of shit to shoot you in the face
If you come in uninvited
I learned early on about getting the fuck out
It's all I wanted
To have a door to shut
I feel the scars on my skin and understand
That I can't depend on you for anything
But potential harm
I'd rather have money
Than any fucking thing you got
Friendship doesn't mean shit to me

  ♑ ♑ ♑

I was alone in bed with a woman last night
Wondering what the hell I was doing
I wasn't there for any of it
When I came I didn't feel anything
I knew it was time to sleep
I'm just a stupid animal
Affection and attention are wasted upon me
I didn't let on though, she was nice
I am the Hollow Man
It comes in and falls to the bottom

It all falls in and disappears
I am a waste of time
Imagine having sex with a mechanical shark

❧ ❧ ❧

The power of depression is undeniable
When I'm in its grip
I don't remember ever feeling any other way
It coils around my body and holds
The room turns into a suspension cell
Outside the neon roars and people walk at high speed
In here nothing moves
All thoughts are instruments of torture right now
I fell asleep an hour ago
I woke up thinking about my friend
I cannot shake the hounds of grief and guilt
They show their teeth and jump at my throat
I hear their jaws snap as they pass
I don't open myself to others anymore
These nights are all mine
The endless replay of events
Wishing I could tell one of these humans
That I'm sorry
I'm so sorry

❧ ❧ ❧

I see pictures of myself before my friend was shot
I try to see if there's anything different about the face
Nothing
No knowledge of what was to come
Today I wanted to crawl inside one
Live in a time when I didn't know what I do now
I don't mean to be selfish
It's that I got left behind
I'm alone on the planet
And I have to figure out
What to do with the remaining time

❧ ❧ ❧

I'm dead
Don't bother
I don't care about what you thought
About what I did
Dead people see through you
I watch you on the dance floor
I listen to the shit you insist on saying to each other
I don't wonder
I don't dream
I don't know anything
I am the Death Star

You have to watch out for people
I have found that they will fuck you up
If I stood too still
I wouldn't be here now
The world can fill you full of death
Imagine a man
Living in a dangerous city
And not wanting to leave
Because he's afraid of losing his edge

You were really hoping I would want to fuck you
It was painful to watch
You kept trying to keep me talking to you
There's only one thing worse than a desperate man...

Her mouth is a soft explosion of roses
A burst of raw animal definition
For a few moments I was mortal

Only an idiot would test his blood in the streets
There's better things to do
Than die begging for your life

There's better things to do
Than searching for a cheap ending
The night holds a knife to your throat
Stand to one side of the window
Listen to the extras in their cars
Only a fool would want to prove himself out there

⚭ ⚭ ⚭

I am a prisoner chained to myself
I don't know what I've done
Bars will scar the windows
Of every room I will live in for the rest of my life
There's no reason I can find for all this pain
Here in solitary I can't see
I wonder if the jailer is me
In this blackout cell
I crouch paralyzed
Stricken by my own horror

⚭ ⚭ ⚭

Hollowood: In the first perfect scene she finds him staring at the ground with his hands tightened into fists. She takes his face into her hands and kisses him. He takes his eyes up from the ground and looks into hers. She asks him what is the matter. Somehow he is able to tell her just what the matter is.

   Life falls flat when you lean too hard upon it. They should have put up warning signs on all the bus stop signs that life is hazardous to your health. So much time spent suppressing screams that have no origin that you can find. You are continually ripped apart and slammed back together. Look at them look at you. Extras, all of them extras.

   It is a small miracle. She holds him and he feels himself melting into her. He imagines their collarbones fusing together. He feels hot tears on his face. He is at once ashamed. She tells him that it's alright and he feels what she says. The screams of the beast inside him fade to nothing as the two of them stand motionlessly in the semi dark room. They are the only two people in the big lonely world that matter.

   I walk by the man. He pulls out a broken boom box out of a paper bag and shows it to me like I'm supposed to want to buy it. Instead of saying no thanks, I attack him for no apparent reason. That's how he sees it at least. I hit him in the face as hard as I can and when he falls to the ground I kick him in the head several times and then run away. Attack, attack. I no longer watch out for those filthy fuckers on the street and they can see it in my eyes that I am hoping that they'll start some shit so I can swarm them without words, pure action. Pure violence. I am someone that they have to look out for. If they have a gun they'll never get a chance to use it. It will be too far up their ass.

The man to the woman in the dream: If I could find you I would love you forever. If I could find you I would do anything for you. Nothing would be beyond me. This world wounds me and I have lost words, I have lost everything except the ability to feel and deliver pain.

When it ends, it ends and the pigs come and stand around your body and talk that mindless pig bullshit. If you shot the brains out of a pig, rats wouldn't even eat them. I think that humiliation will be unavoidable at this point. I would transcend with you but my feet are nailed to the concrete and I wouldn't go anywhere without my hammer.

⚙ ⚙ ⚙

Trick or treat: I can only write this behind a locked door for fear of the world coming down on top of my head. I was at a Wal Mart in Joplin, Missouri. I was standing in line with some shaving cream. All around me Halloween displays were up and Halloween candy was everywhere. I stood in a long line with all kinds of people. Most of them were holding bags of candy. Men coming home from work, tired eyed with slightly bent backs dressed in heavy clothing, standing in line with nothing in their hand but a bag of candy to give to little kids. I didn't think they did that anymore. I tried to imagine kids going door to door where I live. No way. Standing in line with the humans and their candy it made me feel like I came from a different planet full of bullet casings and dried blood. I am fucked up and sentimental I know. I remember how much I used to look forward to Halloween. 24 hours later I was at a hotel near the Greyhound station where drug dealers were working the parking lot. Some things are over with, really over with. Out.

⚙ ⚙ ⚙

I have spent so much of my life trying to get away
Throwing weight over the side of the basket

So the balloon could rise higher faster and escape
So real life could be lived before death sets in
And slows everything down
In seemingly accidental moments of clarity
I have thought that I had seen what it was
That I was trying to get away from
But when I tried to level the foe
I found myself on the move again
I can't stop moving

   ⚇ ⚇ ⚇

I will get away from the cameras and the questions
I will find my brain again
And when I do I'll try my best to handle it

   ⚇ ⚇ ⚇

When I fuck I feel like a rapist
I equate my sexual desire with pornography
I see sex and violence as the same thing
I would never hurt anyone in a sexual situation
I look at women and feel disgusting
Like some fucked up animal
I am so far from humanity
If a woman is attracted to me
I think she's fucked up
Some one should straighten her out
I shake so many hands
The idea of touch makes me sick
I never set out to be so fucked up
But I ended up fucked up

   ⚇ ⚇ ⚇

Movieline magazine asked me if any movies had influenced my work at all. I faxed them this: "It's easy to see from even the most casual glance over my total work span that Sylvester Stallone's staggering work in *Over the Top* and *Oscar*, not to mention *Rhinestone*, has had an immense and embarrassingly overshadowing effect on my life and my art. It's hard for me to admit all of this but you know, it feels good to come right out and say it. I agree with Sly when he said that if Mel Gibson could do Shakespeare, he could do Macbeth.

⚶ ⚶ ⚶

I fuck as an after thought
Like when I eat too much
An excess thought
A stock reflex

⚶ ⚶ ⚶

You always end up
Where all those bent, hit, bashed up people end up
Where ever the hell that is tonight
You'll be there
Even though you can't see me
I'll be there too
It's unbelievable how easy it is to end up there
Wherever the hell that is tonight
Do you know the times when you catch yourself falling?
Like when you freak out for a fraction of a second
You quickly recover and it's then
You realize how fucked up you are
All of a sudden it all makes sense
It's beyond words
It makes you look down at the floor for a long time
It's where you end up
At that moment you think that you need someone
Right then
Someone's eyes to somehow make it make sense
Make what make sense?
I don't know
That's the part where the holes get pounded into the walls
And life gets lived

⚶ ⚶ ⚶

I went out tonight to feed
It's really turned into something out there
I mean you really have to watch your ass

Hard neon reflector boys manning the corners
Blocking the sidewalk silently begging confrontation
I walk around and think about how good it would be to...
And how I would never be able to...
In the hamburger place they sit and stare
Unknowing soldiers with corn row hair
Staring under the florescent light
Outside the streets mercilessly scream
Everything out there is screaming
A whore gets into the car and they park in front of Thrifty's
All I do is watch my ass around here
I immediately size up any males coming towards me
Look for the one good shot
Get ready to take it
Walk on by
You stupid mortal easy to kill motherfucker
Walk on by

☖ ☖ ☖

Ian sent me a clipping from a newspaper
Mr. Klinger
My high school English teacher had died last week
November 13 1992
I was in Orlando and didn't feel a thing
The paper said liver cancer
Sometimes he would call me at night
From the student dorm where he lived
He would always be drunk
I never told any of the other students
I never told anyone
I used to think of how bad it would be if the headmaster knew
Mr. Klinger would get kicked out of there fast
He would be disgraced
I think he was the loneliest person I ever knew
Years after I graduated
I thought of contacting him
To tell him that I still remembered the things he taught me

He was so lonely
It was pathetic
I used to sit in class and wonder if anyone else saw it
You could see the pulling sadness in his eyes
I used to imagine him riding the school bus back to the dorm
Weekends drinking himself into a stupor
Thoughts of suicide and young boys
He taught there 22 years
It was his life
Some life
He was one of the only people in the whole place who liked me
He left no relatives
Not even me

⚭ ⚭ ⚭

Inert: Now the touring is over for the year. I'm sitting in a chair in my room and it's late and I'm tired but not the kind of tired that I like. It's not the exhaustion derived from a gig. I worked out hard tonight with the Iron but without the music I don't know. I really missed not playing tonight. The next few days will be hard to deal with because I have to talk to people. It takes me days to decompress and regain the ability to act human and not blow my fuse with them. I feel alien when I come back from the road. I have nothing that I can explain to them and I can't fake my discomfort. I feel like a weakling when I'm not on tour, I will have to deal with that as well. I just feel useless when I'm not out there. If I told that to someone they wouldn't know what the hell I was talking about. There's nowhere I can go with these feelings so I sit in the room and wait for the pressure to get to a manageable level. It's times like these where I wish I could open up to a woman and be with her. I imagine scenes where I am talking to a woman and I feel good and she somehow says things that make me not feel like exploding. Someone who could remove the distance I feel. It will never happen. I try to imagine opening myself up like that I know there's no way. Everything I do is geared for confrontation. When you tell someone that you work at extending your threshold of pain they look at you like you're crazy. Of course it sounds nuts to them. But what do they know about a reality different than theirs? Nothing, they'll never know. I'm over here and they're over there. When I try to hang out in their world it only brings me confusion and pain. My struggle is internal. When it comes out in their world it comes out violently and loudly. I isolate myself further with every breath I take. It must be what I want. It's evolution in a lifetime. Between tours I'm not alive. I am inert and I fall prey to all the bullshit. My life is only of use when I'm moving. Everything I do is geared for that world. When I'm here they all turn against me. My strength seems to attack me. To be able to keep a clear head I avoid them and their gatherings. Avoid the parties and the endless talk that they never get tired of. I must stay lean and hungry at all times. Otherwise all is lost.

⚰ ⚰ ⚰

Hack up the life and kick it from door to door
Didn't know that anyone would notice
Words fail me
Turn on me
Kick me in the mouth
I listen to the words of others
They take me hostage
I read their words
They shove me around
I wonder what life would be like
Without language
Would you still love?
Would you do anything that wasn't a pure survival move?
No smooth talkers taking the women away
From the big dick
Loud mouthed thick skull/muscle bulls
Could you think without words?
Just feel the basics?
Hunger, cold, fear, desire
I know enough to know that I know
Too much about that which matters
To people I don't know
And too little about what matters to me
They take that away from you at birth

They try to sell you their fucked up version
Why not
Their parents did it to them
And now it's their turn
I talk like he does
Same meter, tone and timber
It gets worse with age
Almost everything does

   ♠ ♠ ♠

I can't get away from myself
I have tried to crawl out of here several times
I always come crawling back
Staring at the closet with Joe's stuff still in it
I have convinced myself
That the closet smells like his death
Tonight I opened the door and the smell came out
Usually it makes me cold
Tonight it wrapped around me like a damp blanket
It felt ok
Like when I made friends
With the darkness of the basement
When my stepbrother used to lock me in
You just breathe in and know that this is it
It's your own little tragedy
A little closet full of shame
I ran all this year
Only to come back to this little room
To think about the same things that I always think about
I wonder if I'll ever do anything with my life
Except try to make it sorry it had the bad luck to fall into me

   ♠ ♠ ♠

Have you ever outsmarted yourself too many times to where you can no
longer pull the wool over your eyes when you really need to? Like when
you're alone and you're thinking about someone else because it makes
you feel not so all alone and your thoughts turn to some kind of feeling

if closeness with this person. You know how it is, you're alone in the safety of the number one. No one can read your thoughts. So no matter how embarrassing they are, no matter if it's stuff that you could never tell anyone for fear of them laughing in your face or being eternally uncomfortable in the same room with you, you really let yourself go. It's those thoughts that can really save you from one of those severe drops into hard slamming depression. The kind that doesn't fool around. The depression that makes you think you're some kind of diabolical genius because you could come up with something that you could inflict upon yourself that is totally and perfectly devastating. Sometimes the depression is so bad that you think that some government agency beamed it into your head because you would never level something that horrible at yourself. So have you ever gotten to the point to where you want to pull yourself out of the teeth of loneliness and you try to think of a perfect situation with one of those people out there and you are unable to do it? You keep looking at the wall and nothing happens. You just keep seeing the reality mixed with the sounds of traffic and the smell of your own skin. You see too clearly and you wish that you could soften the focus a bit so you could get a break. Yea it happens to me too. Like right now. I swear this room is the loneliest one on the planet. I don't know where you are or what you're going through but you're not here now and I'm all I've got in here and I can't go walking around my neighborhood at this time of night because the gangsters selling the drugs down the street make me freak out. So tonight I'm stuck in here looking out through the bars on my windows. Trying to think of nothing because tonight it all makes too much sense. I think right now all I can do is wait it out until I wear myself down. It's called sleep. I call it finally giving in. Sometimes it's good to get beaten.

   ♾   ♾   ♾

I am glad to be alone in this room but at the same time I am not. I am relieved that there will be no one in this box with me to accidentally hear something horrible come out of my mouth. I get angry at how far I have withdrawn. I know how much of a monster I am and it keeps me to myself. I find my mouth unable to open to answer the questions they ask now. I have trouble understanding what people are saying to me these days. They ask me things or tell me something and I'll just stand there and look at them and not know what to say. I find it hard to believe that they're even talking to me. I always think they're talking to some living person in my immediate proximity. I don't cry anymore or care about most things that I used to. I have become detached and withdrawn from the human experience. I wonder if they know that I'm stuffed with sawdust.

   ⚬ ⚬ ⚬

Alone in this room in Hollywood
I am afraid
I am afraid of falling apart
I am afraid of doing what I want to do
I want to be able to open myself up to a woman
Just one woman in a room
Without projecting all my pain onto that woman
Without lying
But I am afraid
I am afraid of unraveling and falling to pieces
And not being able to get up again
After a lot of years I have grown used to pain
I want to get rid of it but I know it's what makes me
When I'm cold I build fires and then don't come near them
I'm afraid of getting too warm
I harbor great conflict inside myself
I contradict myself constantly
I am addicted to pain
It is the only thing that ever told me the truth
The only thing that ever protected me
The only thing that ever forced me to move forward and survive
That's as honest as I can be right now

   ⚬ ⚬ ⚬

Makoto: I will be awake for several hours. It's as if I'm plagued. I tried to get to sleep early tonight to try to duck under the wave of depression that I knew was coming. I didn't make it. I was overcome with an overwhelming surge of depression. Power depressions, anxiety monster blues, I don't know what to call them. It got me out of bed. Here I am. Freaked out and alone.

It's early for me, only 12:50 a.m. I have been staying up until near five every morning writing, trying to get it out of me. Tonight I thought it was going to be different.

So now what do I do with myself? I know what I'll do. I'll be honest. The main thoughts that attack me in these bouts of depression are those of deep and terrible loneliness. During other times I can shrug off the idea of loneliness by being busy or by making tough jokes. I feel close to no one on the planet.

I have these thoughts of falling endlessly through blackness. Long trudges through deserts of night. Cold, poorly lit rooms. Arguments. The sound of my mother and father's voices. The smell of my father's car. The fear. People recognize me where I go almost every day now. I feel vulnerable all the time, it gets to me. I wonder about their lives as they stare blankly in recognition. What a strange disease life is. It gets thrust upon you and you have to deal with it as best you can. You are trained to have answers for everything and you're told you are to be able to fix yourself up when you break down. When you don't have the answers, you catch a lot of flack, or worse, you have to listen to someone else, you risk having to trust them. It would seem that everything can be explained. But it can't. Worse thing to do is walk through life thinking it owes you something. It doesn't even owe you an explanation, not even your parents can give you one. Life doesn't even owe you life, all it owes you is death.

I know that no amount of talking will make it any better. I've tried being with women. I've tried hanging out, spilling my guts with great abandon and I felt like a damn fool. I walked away feeling like some kind of criminal. I thought that would be the answer but it never is. When I'm with them it's even worse. When they touch me I feel like I'm choking. All I want to do is be alone. When I am alone for too long I start to wonder what it would be like to be able to be with someone else that didn't make me want to run away. I start to lie to myself and invent realities in the presence of others. They try to get me to talk and I can't find the right words. I can't find words to describe the abyss inside me. Words ambush me when they come out of my mouth. I know of nothing that makes it better except working at the ridiculous pace that I do. I know enough to know that it's nothing but escape. I don't see anything real to confront. When you confront the Abyss you play yourself and lose.

So what do I do with this loneliness, this hole? I feel like a marked man. Doomed to walk and have this gaping wound no one can see. The thing that makes me so frustrated is that I can't figure out what the fuck is wrong with me. The only thing I can think of is loneliness. But if that's what it is then what am I lonely for? What part of me is missing?

I have always kept moving. Thousands of miles and I have made friends through the years. Somehow motion keeps me breathing. I fear these still nights in the same room. I sleep better in hotels. It's a room I'm in because I'm on the move. I can deal with that much. The only way I have been able to get through life without spending all my time freaking out and hurting myself is movement and music. The fury of the music matches what I feel and I have a temporary world that I can exist in for two hours a day. Spending years on the road in search of this relief is beyond the comprehension of many. They ask me how I do it. I have no answer to that one. I amazed to survive sleep. Sleep is the state that I fear most. Insomnia and paranoia are two of my constant traveling companions. The road is the only thing I have found that keeps all the parts from flying off. It keeps the brains in my head. The idea of standing still for too long freaks me out. I wonder if I'm addicted to exhaustion.

I am afraid of losing control and killing myself or killing someone else. It's fucked up to say but I have noticed that all the stories I have read about serial killers say that they were terribly alienated from people, most all of them were loners. I was reading about the man who ripped up all those boys in Milwaukee. He was a study in depression and alienation. I feel some kind of affinity with people like that. I'm not trying to come off like I'm all shocking and shit. I'm not trying to say that I want to go kill a bunch of people tonight but I can dig the heavy choke of not being able to get along with people and having to do something to separate yourself from them all. When the man received his sentence and stood up in front of the parents and relatives of the boys that he had killed he told them all that he was terribly sorry. I believe him.

I can understand a drifter who wanders through America and kills men and women because he's lonely. He strangles a man that picked him up hitchhiking. He never even asked the driver's name. He throws the body off a cliff without feeling anything but deep and momentary relief. Crying and cursing, wishing the body was still there to kick and embrace because life is so fucked up and full of holes it makes you want to skin yourself alive. He screams through his tears and stomps the ground because he knows it will never be enough. It just makes him want to kill more. He is more lonely than he can remember. He gets in the man's car and drives off into the night. Sometime in the next 72 hours he kills again. His loneliness is an inferno.

Sometimes the only way to see any light is to get away from everyone and wait. That's all I can do sometimes, just wait it out. Keep to myself, tell no one. Tell anyone that asks me how I'm doing that I'm fine. Say as little as possible. Try not to have to explain the unexplainable. You wait for the sun to turn the sky that cold grey color and you think that it might be safe to finally close your eyes and hope that you won't dream.

In the middle of these silent nights I am alive in a small lit box somewhere on the planet. Trying to understand this deep pain that leaves me confused and scattered. Don't tell anyone.

⚶   ⚶   ⚶

Saturday night in this room. The sounds of traffic have slowed down to near silence now that the clubs have closed. My neighborhood used to be dirty and full of rock and rollers with fake hair. It was a drag but not dangerous. Now the corners have Crips that have come north from south central to sell drugs. You can't go anywhere without seeing those guys. In the room, against a wall, sit boxes of mail. Talking tape letter from a manic depressive, pictures sent by models with their phone numbers and "Use it! XXOO!!!" written at the bottom, faxes from rockstars, letters from convicts doing several years and youths in correctional facilities waiting to be released in the spring. Manuscripts, magazines, cards and hundreds of letters. In this hole I sit like a sniper without the gun. Bars on my windows, locks on the door. No one knows my street address. The phone doesn't ring, nothing moves. I am unreachable, untouchable, unknown. It is somehow a relief. I have not used my voice for hours. I have sat in this room for a long time tonight just staring and thinking. The air in the room is filled with the sound of the Arkestra's Interplanetary Music and the heater. No one can help you. No one can heal your wounds. I think you get better by keeping moving and learning to take the pain. My desperation is silent and moves to me with precision. I have boxes of pictures of myself. On the floor are several crates of tapes of our band's music and my speaking dates. Hundreds of hours of documentation of pounding blood into wood floors. In the closet is more than a decade of press articles about me from all over the world. Interviews, reviews, boxes stacked one on top of the other. Against another wall are crates of work in progress, notes, manuscripts, outlines. In piles are things left from tours that have been completed during the year. Receipts, foreign money, hotel stationery. On the door knob tour laminates hang like discarded pages of history. Then there's the dead people. In a coffee cup, leaves stained with the blood of a guy I knew who was shot to death by a policeman last summer. In an old Rolaids container a piece of brain wrapped in tin foil from a woman who shot herself in the head with a shotgun in Nebraska 8 years ago. A plastic container of dirt with parts of my best friend's head sits in the closet next to his telephone. There's letters from dead people, a ring a girl gave to me that her dying brother wanted me to have. So the room is filled with the forgotten, the past and the dead. I sleep in it, work in it and stare at its walls until the early hours of the morning. I don't know anyone and no one knows me. When I am not on the road I am here. When I am here I don't know what to do with myself except work and sleep. Sometimes I don't leave the place for days. I don't know how to deal with people. I avoid them by spending most of my time traveling and onstage. It's not the way anyone should end up.

⚛ ⚛ ⚛

Sunday night in this room. I did something that I should not have. A guy I tour with was here tonight. He's from another country. I asked him if he wanted to see a documentary on LA street gangs. He said yes so I played it. I hadn't seen it since Joe and I used to watch it a long time ago. It played itself much differently tonight. When the part came where these people were walking by a body at a funeral and the face of the corpse was shown, it had the same unmoving dead look as when I saw Joe in that room nearly a year ago. Watching the show brought a lot of the horror from that time back to me. Now I'm alone in the room dealing with it. Now I'm back in that same mortal bag again. It's easy for the fuckers to take it away from you. You can have a good enough life and then some piece of shit stranger can take it all away. The guy who killed Joe is out there somewhere tonight. He's breathing out in the world somewhere tonight, right now. Like me in this room. I feel like calling somebody but I don't know anyone to call. I wouldn't call anyone even if I did know anyone I felt comfortable talking to. You can say that you have cut yourself off from people and see it as a setback but that's only if you put a lot of value in having people around that you can dump on. If you're like me and know for sure that you're really alone in the world then thoughts like these are only fleeting. They get rapidly ripped apart by the reality that rules the domain of you mind. I sit here with one small light on. In semi darkness I think about my friend. In a few days it will be a year since his death. I remember when it was a week. I sat behind the desk of the office space I was living in and I was amazed at how unreal the entire week had been. I kept expecting to wake up from it like a dream. Now it's almost a year. 5 days away. Actually 4 days and some hours to go. I think about it every day now. I thought I had climbed a few steps out of the hole that I have spent most of the year in but now I find myself back down in it. In the last 12 months I have distanced myself from people. I will distance myself farther away from them as the years go on. I have had enough of them and their bullshit. You can call me anything you like. A walking contradiction, a bastard, a hypocrite. I am all those things and every other thing that you can think of. Now that we all know everything then there's nothing to complain about. All I know is that sometimes it's hard to leave this room knowing that there's people out there. I have no safety net because I don't lie. All that can happen to me is that I will die somehow. I've been through worse. I'm going through worse right now. The worst part about it is that I'm alive enough to be aware of everything around me. It's hard to give a fuck about a lot of things. Humanity, human values, the things they say. I walk in shadows. Nothing really gets to me anymore.

   ⚑ ⚑ ⚑

If I allowed myself to care about you
I would hang myself up again
Like I have done so many times before
When I lost my self control

I would like to think that I could control myself at all times
But it just isn't true
I catch myself slipping all the time
I laugh when I caught myself tonight
Wondering if you were going to call me
Like you said you would
When the clock went past two a.m. and you hadn't called
I knew I was in one of those situations
Where I could not attach myself to it
Or let it drag me down
So I let it go
And now I see that I did the right thing
By not giving a fuck about you and your life
What was I thinking anyway?
I'm a lot of terrible things
But at least I'm not a sucker anymore

⚠ ⚠ ⚠

I learned about loss by losing: It's getting close now. In a few days it will
be a year since Joe died. I am alone in a room in the middle of Los
Angeles. It's past midnight. I am so ashamed. I don't know why but I am.
I am embarrassed at how at this moment I have things that I want to
write but I am too ashamed to. All I know is there are situations where
you can lose parts of yourself and the hole the absence creates can never
be filled. That's what we do instinctively. We seek to fill the holes, shove
plaster into the cracks. We seek to replace what has been lost with
something else. Something that resembles what is gone or replaces the
way the departed thing made us feel. You know, like how someone
replaces heroin with methadone. It's one of the ways we resolve the
reality of loss. I've been trying to replace what cannot be replaced and
all my human tendencies are turning on me and tearing me up. Some
losses you can't make up for. You just have to get on with it. I know this.
I didn't before but I learned it by getting dragged through the last three
hundred and sixty some nights. I know I am not capable of telling
anyone what I feel and what fury and anguish courses through my veins
during almost every waking moment. Sometimes I feel like I am
suffocating inside my skin, like I should be ripping out of it. If I ripped

out of my skin, where the hell would I go. Right. I know that I just have to keep walking the trail. I hope my fury won't turn my bones to ash, even if it does, it won't change a thing.

I remember this one time I had my arms around her and I was thinking to myself that I would never let anyone hurt her ever. I could feel her chest against mine and her arms around me, holding on. To me. At that moment her arms were holding onto no one or nothing else on the planet except me. It seemed like the most perfect moment I had ever experienced. I've never felt that way with anyone else. I still think about her and I wonder where she is. I know that no one will ever love her as much as I do. It's been years but still I miss her so much. I think about her every day. After you leave messages and write letters and hear nothing back you finally figure out the fact that she obviously doesn't want to hear from you so you come to the conclusion that you have to move on up the trail and take it as it comes. I can sit in this room and think about her all I want but it won't change a thing.

⚶ ⚶ ⚶

I can't let too much show at once: I have to be careful when I walk down the streets in this neighborhood at night. I don't want the piece of shit drug dealers and scumbags to know that I only fear the fact that they might be packing a gun and that I could kill them with my bare hands and think nothing of it. When I see them look at me like I'm prey I wonder if they see it in my eyes that I know who the prey really is. That I could physically break their necks and jaw bones and there wouldn't be anything they could do about it, short of running for their lives. I am barely able to contain myself when they look at me on La Brea Ave. I feel an overwhelming urge to attack them savagely. Bite pieces of their faces off. I cover it well. I can't let them see too much. I hide my eyes from them on purpose. I don't want to get shot by a piece of shit. It's too easy these days. So many weak pieces of flesh out there.

⚶ ⚶ ⚶

Alive inside my atomic super heavy loaded brain tonight. She lives off the guy and fucks him so she can keep the cash flow going. He knows it too but he tries to forget it. It's easy to forget when he's with her, when she calls his name in a public place or puts her hand on his arm. He thinks to himself that she really likes him. He allows himself to believe that he belongs to her. It makes him feel good about getting up in the morning. In fact the more she treats him like dirt, the more it keeps him holding on. He believes. He needs it so bad. All she talks about with her friends besides the bills she runs up when she takes his credit cards shopping is all the guys she wants to fuck.

I want to hide from all of them, they make me sick. My atomic idea is active and flashing. They will never take me down like they take down all the others. They'll never get that close. One thing my parents taught me from making me sick to my guts at the thought of being alive was to reject them before they get too close. Before they can divorce you or scream into the phone while the child watches silently and stupidly from across the room. Fuck him up and scar him for life. Fuck me up and teach me what I need to know. Break my bones and let my scar tissue mind strengthen. Show me the power of the ability to maintain distance and take the pain year after year, beating after beating. They'll take bullets to your head, they'll spend your money and watch your pain and grow numb. They'll become pigs and arrest you. They'll murder the only life that matters and leave you in a cell of your own for the rest of your life to live the horror over and over again. You can do it too, you can grow old and never live once. And you can take it too, I know you can. I have proof. Some can fuck people up and others can be fucked up and take it. Take it over and over. You get good at taking the beating.

He sits in a house because he can. He doesn't know what else to do. She's weak and it makes him feel important from time to time. He learned how to be one that carries the weak from getting injections of guilt early on. Don't try talking to me because I'll only laugh in your face and if you get too close I'll mutilate you and the only thing that will save you is a gun or a pig. I'll show you rejection. I'll show you things that you can understand. I know how to threaten and ruin life because mine is threatened and ruined every day and I've learned by punishing myself how to turn it around and put it in any direction I want. I don't feel guilt, remorse, none of it. I used to but I overcame it by getting it shoved up my ass.

   ♨   ♨   ♨

The man said to the Storm: When life hands you a lemon you can squeeze it and make lemonade. The Storm said to the man: Some squeeze lemons and all they get is blood. They close their hand and the hand goes away and all they get for such troubled magic is a fist. There are some people you can't reason with because they aren't hung up in the wires like you are. The wires couldn't hold them and they fell through. They know that nothing will hold them and they never trust anything completely again. All they have to do is fall once and faith goes out the window. All they have to do is have a brief visit from pure animal panic and true horror and they come all the way back. They try to get back and part of them does get back but a large part gets stuck way back there with the fear and the horror. They see things differently. Their eyes aren't clouded like yours are and they can take one look at you and they can tell that you can't see it. That's why some people pick a rose off the bush and get a rose and others pick a rose off the bush and get a knife.

⚵ ⚵ ⚵

I'm in my box off Hollywood Blvd. In less than two hours it will be a year since Joe was killed. In the last couple of hours some strange things have tripped me out. I went to the store to get some food. I walked in and heard someone call my name out. I turned around and looked. It was a guy that was in a lot of Joe's video footage Modi and I had been looking at yesterday. Ron Frasca. I had never met him. I talked to him for a while. A guy with my sun tattoo painted on the back of his leather jacket walked by and watched us for second. After a few minutes I had been spotted and people were starting to come over to me. I told Ron that I would contact him later. I got my food and left.

I was almost back to the box. It was a hard walk back because no one had explained to Ron what exactly happened and I did in the store so I was thinking about it as I walked up the hill. I turned the corner and right in front of me was the Rat Sound truck parked outside a local club. The big Black Flag logo looking right at me. Joe and I rode in that truck so many hours it's not even funny. I stared at the door on the driver's side and thought about how Joe had opened that door so many times and now the same door is just sitting out there on Hollywood Blvd.

Joe's father took out some big back page ad in Variety magazine. He got a few facts wrong and thanked all his AA buddies. He had some of that typical full of shit sentiment "What price life?" Whoa. I wonder why he didn't mention me. I know he doesn't like me at all. Maybe it's because I was more tuned into his son than he was. The most humorous part was his spelling of the word "homicide" as "homocide". Anyone can make that mistake right? It's fitting that Mr. Cole would take out a full page to advertise his grief. Nice picture. Wonder if he'll get any work out of it.

It seems like all the progress that I made getting myself down the road from all the horror of what happened is slipping away tonight. I have been having to keep myself from breaking down a few times today.

What am supposed to feel on this night? Is it really any different than any other night? What is the difference if it's a year or a week. I guess I have a thing with years because of all the tours. I seem to take things a year at a time as far as measuring things.

   ♬ ♬ ♬

Moving the shit: I'm taking all the boxes out of the attic. Loading through a small hole and down a small ladder and through Joe's room and through the front door, over Joe's blood and all the flies and into the truck. Joe's small room is filled with his parents and their brothers and sisters and assorted relatives. Most of them I have never met. I feel like I am in a room full of strangers talking about someone that I know. The person they are talking about and the one that I know are two distinctly different people. They are dividing his possessions, going through boxes and pulling out pictures. I show them how he had all the letters he ever got all separated into envelopes with the name of the sender on the outside. I give them out to all the people that had one. They remark at how organized he was. I think to myself how I taught Joe to organize all of his stuff so he could find things whenever he needed to. As I'm distributing the assorted envelopes of mail I notice how closely he had his things organized just the way I do. I am loading things out of the attic and I'm trying not to bump into all these people as I move box after box. I have to step over Joe's dad who is now sitting on the front steps. Sorry Mr. Cole, someone got killed here and we're moving all the stuff out as quick as we can. I have to step around him, over the blood and into the truck. I make trip after trip. The family has now parted into two factions. Joe's father only has a friend talk to the other side and to me. The mother talks to me. I am the go between for the mother and father. I am keeping busy moving all the things in the house on no sleep and no food and only the fact that a few hours ago I was walking with this guy down the same sidewalk and two guys with guns came out of the bushes and now Joe is dead and last time I ever saw him alive was when he was face down on the sidewalk with a gun at the back of his head. I remember the things I was thinking at the time. I remember looking down at him and thinking how scared he must be. I felt lucky, the guy on me only made me get on my knees.

I'm moving box after box. The neighborhood is spitting me out. It killed my best friend and now it's making me get the hell out. I look at all the people across the street watching me load box after box into the truck. Later they would fill up three detective's notebooks telling about what a bad person I was and how Joe and I bought drugs and used the local hookers. Hold on, the phone is ringing.

11:43 Don calls and we talk for about eight minutes and I tell him about the things that happened at the store and about seeing the Rat truck. He thinks they're good signs. He says he's been sitting in his place in SF thinking about what Joe and I were doing at this time a year ago. I guess that we were just finishing a ten mile bike ride on the beach. At this point Joe had about 45 minutes left on the planet and neither of us knew. There was nothing different in the wind at the beach or anything. We didn't know it was coming. Joe's death is much more important than JFK's. I tell Don that we're in for a long night. I tell him that I'll call him later. Somehow, the fact that it's not 12:30 yet makes me feel good. Like he's still out there somehow. I know what it is though, it's the same form of denial as when I didn't sleep for a long time right after it happened thinking that if somehow I stayed up, there was a chance that he might not be dead.

These pieces of shit were kicking me out of their fucked up neighborhood. They stared at me blankly as I loaded in the boxes. I looked at them and tried to make them look away but they just stared seeming neither interested nor bored. Excuse me Mr. Cole, I have to move these boxes out of the house because someone got murdered here last night and I can't stay. Don't bother to help or anything, just keep talking like you're reading off a script. Only this time it's real.

I am the go between and as the days pass I have to be put through the ups and downs of a family that I don't want to know. That was a year ago.

Joe has a few minutes left here. I wonder if there's anything special I should be doing. Do I dare open the closet and look at the plastic container that holds dirt with his blood. Will his phone that sits next to it ring. We were in the market right now. Getting some food before we were going to watch a movie back at the house. We are probably right near the checkout now. He couldn't afford juice so I was buying some for him. He had a bag of popcorn and that was it. I remember I ate it the next day as I was unloading the truck into the storage place realizing that I had not eaten all day and was almost falling over.

For a few weeks I would go to the storage place and sit inside the room full of boxes of my old life. I felt like I was in the basement of some huge government building looking at pieces recovered from some disaster in history. I stood next to my old life as I silently inspected the boxes piled against the wall.

I remember running. I remember when I hit the back door to pull the door slightly up to get the bolt to turn. I remembered to do that. As I ran across the back yard I looked at the chain link fence thinking how the hell to get over it. Before I had finished the thought I had gone over it and was running east up the alley towards Lincoln.

I think by now Joe's history, gotta be by now, if it's not now it's within a few minutes of right now, It really doesn't matter. His ashes don't think about it. Yesterday I was watching one of his videos of interviews. I randomly pulled one out and the first thing on it was a girl telling Joe about looking at her father's ashes.

It doesn't feel like a year. It feels like I have been frozen in time until tonight. I can remember the event better than what I did yesterday.

I wonder if the guy who killed Joe is thinking of Joe right now. He's gotta be thinking about the fact that it's been a year and he got away with murder in America.

So I'm through the first year. It's my own New Year's party here in my box. It's year one in Colefornia. Nothing's different. Nothing happened. He didn't call the phone, I just looked in at it. It hasn't moved from the place I put it when I called his old number on his birthday and said hello. I don't have the strength to call him now. There's no one to call, he's dead.

Now it's 1:23 a.m. It's bit better now somehow. I think the worst part was going through the walk from the store to the house. Now that it's been almost an hour, I feel like life has come back to normal. I have a feeling that this time every year will have some kind of meaning.

So now I'll just do what I usually do at this time. Write and listen to music. I feel better. It's as if running into Ron was a life time ago.

3:09 p.m.: I fell asleep at some point hours ago and woke up at around noon. I had this bad dream that was good to be able to wake up from. It was me and this girl in a room. I knew that I loved her and I knew that she was going to fuck me up. I knew that I was in a no win situation and I knew that I was pathetic, but for some reason I kept on. I don't remember all of the conversation but I was begging her not to leave me and she was just smiling and talking on the phone and pretending that I wasn't there. After she hung up she told me that the new guy was on his way over and that they were going to be busy and that I shouldn't bother them. In the dream it felt like the world had ended or something. It was good to wake up and find out that I was still here. Can you imagine that, begging a woman not to leave you. I'll never put myself in that position. Fuck that. To have to beg. By the end of all of this, I will have mastered myself. That is my goal, to master myself. It's the highest form I can aspire to.

⚤ ⚤ ⚤

Sometimes I wish there was someone I could write a letter to
I look at the piles of mail on the floor
They have someone to write to
I bet it's not a bad feeling
To be able to reach out
And believe in your heart that someone will be there
I wish I could believe that too
Isolation shoots me in the knees
Makes it impossible for anyone to believe
That all my intentions
Are good

⚤ ⚤ ⚤

The last few days have been silent
I have been choked into forced silence
I don't want to get myself too knotted

I went out there again
I had run out of food
Some guy at the intersection
Waves me over at a red light
Hey how about a signature?
Like I'm supposed to walk across Hollywood Blvd.
And serve it up
Slaves at the money machine
Blood drying on Mecca
The men that live in the cardboard boxes
Move before the club opens
The bouncers have fun kicking them down the stairs
Humanity grows dim in these parts
I don't want to test my speed
With the neon flesh reflector boys
Bullets run faster than my fear
And then there's always the pigs
The box has been good
Day after day, right here after right here
Listening to 1992 shake the bars in front of my windows
Waiting for the year to die
There's no one I miss or think about
Nothing on my mind
Without confrontation I am nothing
But this thing that breathes and waits

    ⚭   ⚭   ⚭

It's hard to be close to one of them after the first time it blows up in your face: I don't let them get too close to me. I have learned that it only leads to heartache and self destruction. People will slow you down all the time. The more you need them the more you'll get fucked up when they do something to you. I got used to people not being dependable. I learned it from my parents. The more friends you have the more you have to miss when they're gone. I light fire to a square block of houses in Hollywood. All the people in the houses are now out in the street holding a few things that they were able to salvage from the fire. They are crying, thinking about all the things that they lost, all the things that took them all those years to get. The local bums stand there and laugh. Their shit got burned up as well, some rags, a pair of shoes, a blanket. They never had cars and pianos to lose. Nothing devastates them. I don't want to love someone. It puts me in a sucker's position. There I am waiting to get ripped apart. It happened to me a couple of times and to this day I regret ever having made the contact in the first place. I must have been bored or crazy. I keep my distance. I get more done and I don't get played like a fool.

⚉ ⚉ ⚉

At this point it would just sound like a confession
Some man talking with his eyes glued to the ground
Not knowing what to do with his hands
Barely able to get the words out of his mouth
Never feeling right where he should be anywhere
Only stopping to prove myself for no reason
I'm no fucking musician
I stand next to music and watch it while I scream
When they talk to me
They don't talk to me
From now on it's going to get deeper and more painful
I'm going for the bone
I have no protection left
I am stripped to the truth
Rage, fury and death
The rest doesn't figure in anymore
I have freed myself from my illusions
Straightened myself out from all the bullshit
I was desperately clinging to
I am not interested in impressing anyone
What a waste of time
I am heading to the Abyss once more
And this time I'm not going to miss

⚉ ⚉ ⚉

The cartoon version is probably better anyway:
I can see someone looking at me

Saying to his friend:
Let's cut him

⚘ ⚘ ⚘

Cast iron body suit
Think about a fish
Swimming around near the surface of the water
Swimming weakly and slowly
Pulled slightly off center
Because the leech attached its side
Is filled with blood
Think about your life
Your compromised vision

⚘ ⚘ ⚘

Go for the Visa card, the car, the works:
Set him up slow
You might have to put out a little but it's worth it
Talk to him and make him feel good
Make him think that you look up to him
Validate his stupidity
Ask his advice on almost everything
Feign astonishment when he tells his stupid stories
Let him flex worldly knowledge he got
Through all that abuse and violence based experience
Widen your eyes in amazement
Play him like a deck of cards
You got him where you want him right?
Because he's stupid, right?
Because he wants the same thing they all want right?
Who cares about loneliness and pain
You got your place in the sun
He's breathing easy
You hate him so much now you can barely stand it
Ok, quickly now
Take him down

Listen to the lines as they fall out of her mouth
How many times have you heard this
You wish she could be a little more creative
You need what you need
Life is short
So you say the things you should
Pretend to eat the bait on the hook
Swell up with false bravado
Put on a good show
Run a good con on the con artist
Take it to the limit
I mean really take it to the limit
Get what you need
Malice makes it even better
Then start laughing as you turn your real face to her
Throw a few crumpled bills at her face
And tell her not to call you again
Fuck these people
Some of them
Beg to be ruined

Night time in the box
Same thing always happens
I'm right about to fall asleep
I start thinking about Joe
Standing paralyzed in the living room
Hands in the air
A bag of food on the floor
Thinking desperately what to do
If we go to the back room we're dead
What can I give them
All of this in the space of a few seconds
Listening to the gunshots behind me
My eyes snap open
I'm awake and alone in the world
It's dark and it's 1992

I close my eyes and I'm in the room with Joe's body
He doesn't move
I've never seen anything in the world so still
I look at the hole in the left side of his face
Mortician's clay packed into the hole
Dotted with ink to resemble beard stubble
Straightening his hair with my hands
Touching his cold face
Half afraid he's going to jump up
I open my eyes again and I can't sleep
Afraid that if I do
I'll wake up and it will be longer since he died
That he'll be even more dead
I lie on my side
I wonder how much pain and horror can be contained
In one human mind
I turn on the light
All I can think about is going somewhere
I feel like a target
I feel aged and no one can tell me anything
I feel hard, jaded and partially dead
Then my eyes start to ache and get moist
There's nothing I can do to change what happened
Sometime later near dawn I fall asleep
I get up and go out there
Go through the motions
Trying to look like someone
Who's alive
Inside I'm screaming all the time
Every day dealing with the many shades of horror
There's nothing anyone can say to me
Nothing anyone can do
I am that which survives
You know that quote about that which does not kill you
You don't want to be made stronger like this
It's all I can do to control myself

Ripping someone apart
Myself or someone else
At this point it doesn't matter
It's all life and death to me

⚇ ⚇ ⚇

1993 go
I will continue to pull the muscle from the bone
I will find out more
I will grow stronger
There's nothing else to do
No other place to go
I am in Detroit
Getting ready to go out and see the Beastie Boys play
1993 is a few hours away
I can't wait to put this year and its faux, hollow glory behind me
All the facts, stats, numbers
Want to dump it
Too heavy to carry
Four trips to Europe
Two to Australia
First tour of Japan and Singapore
182 shows
400 + interviews
I shook 1992 by the neck
The road shot into me
Now there's only 1993
Don't attach
Hit hard
Disappear into the treeline
Keep moving
It gets harder to get up in the morning
Lines on my face
It should start getting interesting right about now

⚇ ⚇ ⚇

CITIES

January

17 Sydney Australia: Five in the morning LA time when I walk onstage. Eyes hurt and I want to puke. There's a dead friend in my thoughts. He'll be waiting for me in my room if I ever get through this gig. They yell and I can smell the beer coming up through the rug. Earlier today it was interviews and heat. Small hotel room and loneliness. It's what I know. It's all there is.

18 Sydney Australia: The room smells me. The room knows me. It doesn't wonder why I don't go outside. The room knows that I don't want to talk, don't want to know. I talk to interviewers. I feel dead. I know I am and I'm amazed they can't tell. I figured that when my hand turned black and fell off the one guy was going to say something. The lady interviewer shifted in her seat when I shot myself in the head. These rooms always smell like insecticide. I share the room with hundreds of dead insects and one dead man.

19 Melbourne Australia: I stood up there and told them what I knew to be true. If I think about it too much I want to scream and run away. I throw myself out like the trash in cities all over the world. The cities don't care. They don't even notice if you live there, leave there or die there. They really don't care, they really don't. Don't let the world break your heart too many times.

20 Melbourne Australia: Sometimes I feel like that guy at the end of the movie *Runaway Train*. You know the part where he's standing on top of the train and the train is going into the side of the mountain and you know he's going to get crushed. That's how I feel up there. Standing there with lights on me and my guts flying into the Abyss. The Abyss laughing at me the whole time. Laughing at me, laughing with me, laughing every step of the way. Look at the idiot up there ripping himself to pieces. He comes so easily. What a good dog. He's satisfied with so little. After the gut dump was over I came back to the box here and inhaled the bug spray and thought about you Joe. I thought about you and kept right on dying. Invisibly bleeding and reliving it. Sat outside for a while and looked into the sky and thought about you Joe and I felt huge and empty. I felt enormous and desolate. I am living inside my skin. I am next to life but no longer in it. I walk beside it staring in silent stretched horror and shock.

21 Adelaide Australia: I skipped this town with the band last time we were here because of the bullshit that went down. We were playing James Brown and Parliament and people in the crowd were telling us not to play "that nigger music." Really great. I wonder what the show will be like tonight. I'm in the bug spray smelling hotel room looking at footage of a man digging up his parents in Hungary. They were executed. This room is cold and it's raining outside. The last few days have been hard. I wonder if the rest of my life will be like this. The last month has been unreal. Like walking through a dream. Later: I'm back in the box. The show was really cool actually. More people showed up than when the band played here. They were a good bunch as well. I told them why the band didn't come to Adelaide the last time we toured Australia. I told them story about when I met Dion and he told me about touring the South with Sam Cooke. So now I'm back in the box and will be going to Sydney in the morning. I'm glad no one is here right now. I have a feeling that I will be spending a lot more time alone now.

24 Brisbane Australia: Been back and forth from Melbourne and Sydney. In the hotel room. The opening guy is sharing a room with me but he's gone out to drink with his friends so I moved out into the front room so I don't have to listen or smell. I am the one who's a fool. I got no life. I should get one sometime. Sick of answering drunk's questions. The road and the cities will conspire to kill you. They'll get you and they'll always win. I could barely contain myself around them tonight. Question after question. I wish I could have vomited as hard as I felt like so they could get an idea of how I feel. I kept tripping over his body onstage tonight. They watched and talked and called out. I'm a million miles away from them, they'll never know. No matter how I try to make it different, they'll never know. Maybe I'm wrong. Maybe it all waits for me in the next city. I have nowhere else to go.

26 Sydney Australia: Last talking show in Australia. Soon I leave and the entire year starts kind of. I don't know. Everything feels new in a strange way. Joe has been all I think about. I talk at these people. I do interviews. I stare at the ceiling in my box at night and it's all the same. Inside I'm screaming. No one will hear me or see the difference. Perhaps something strange or unsettling in the eyes will give me away. Other than that, it's all in my head. I see them from ten miles back in my skull.

February

01 Trenton NJ: Tonight was good and one of the only times I've ever felt a bit nervous about going on a stage. There was more people there tonight than when the band plays. About seven hundred. I told them everything I knew. I really like the Trenton crowd. I have been doing talking shows on that stage since 1987. After the show death overcame me again. People were around me all talking to me at once I did my best to hear them all and talk to all of them. It's hard after spilling your guts out for over two hours. After that, useless sex in a roadside motel somewhere on Highway 1. These nights hammer me. I wonder why I don't wake up with blood on my pillow. I figure my brain will break some day. I guess I am hanging in here because I am into self torture. I will not allow myself to burn out. The ones who burn out are the lucky ones. Then there are the others who hang in for the long haul and get really chewed up. I know something about this.

02 New York NY: It was hard. Sitting at the bar waiting to do the thing knowing pretty much what was going to come out of my mouth because right now there's nothing else on my mind and there's no way I can stop it and there's no way I'm going to be able to deal with it very well. Also knowing that when I'm done I will return to a room next to the road and wait for the next thing to happen. I sit at the end of the bar and watch the place fill up. A while later I'm up there talking away. It's pretty amazing what you can take and still keep going. I see now how much of life is auto pilot. You can get by with a lot of your controls down. The last few days have been walking through the cold getting to the right place by smell, by taste, by memory derived through repetition. After the show I was trying to get out of there and deal with people who were being really nice to me. It seemed that the nicer they were the worse I felt. I am often taken aback at how kind people can be. I don't see this kind of thing in myself so when I see it in others I am startled. I said thank you a lot and tried to be cool but inside I was confused and dying.

11 Rotterdam Holland: I just want to hurt them as much as I can tonight. I look at the press and the way people hang around and I want to freak them out and destroy them with sweat and pain. I workout in the dressing room. I can feel the pain in my arms. Sixty minutes until we play. I love opening sets. Something about them makes me play like a motherfucker. We open for the Chili Peppers for the next few weeks. I have trained for this and I want to bum out their fans. I want to be a clean annihilating force. First band show of the year and I couldn't be happier to be anywhere else at any time. Did a few days of press and all that did was piss me off and make me wish for this night and all the nights to come. It's not even about music to me. It's about rage and feeling it. Fuck them.

12 Hamburg Germany: First of two nights in this place. The Peppers soundcheck with a Stooges song and it makes me mad. I'll just have to wipe myself all over their nice little fans and bum them out. Finished the set. It hurt and the lights were hot. They just watched. It will destroy you if you try to make it mean anything to anyone but yourself.

13 Hamburg Germany: Second night in this place. Played better than last night. Got taken out to dinner by people from the record company. Ate with a bunch of drunk Germans that were really cool and that was it. The only thing on my mind is playing well. I love opening. I can't wait to hit the Peppers fans again, they're so nice. Fuck this shit. Let's be honest. The Peppers are cool people and they kick the hard jams, but all I want to do is blow their asses off stage every night and that's the only reason I'm on the this fucking tour. Wish I could see more of Hamburg but there's no time of course. Doesn't matter. All I'm good for is playing doing interviews and sleeping in my black box.

14 Gronningen Holland: A show on our own without the Peppers. I don't know how many times we've played this place now. Always the same people who work here show up. Pretty cool place they have here. Trying to play hard and have a life. I think of my friend. He was in this place in 1987. Everything has changed for me. The way I do everything is different. I don't know if I'm better or worse or what. I wonder if people notice anything different about me. Place was hot tonight. I don't know if they liked the gig or not. I never know in this place. I like playing on our own better than playing a short set opening for the Peppers fans. Some times all I want to do is kill.

15 Deinze Belgium: Woke up in the bus in some parking lot. Staggered in and watched the crew build the stage for the night's show. Did interviews all day long. I am an enemy of my brain because I know at this point it hates me for putting it through all the questions. Made sure I played hard as fuck tonight. I tried to pack a full show in the six songs that we played. All I want to do is pound the audience, damage them, show them something that's not nice, fuck them up with a feeling. Later the Peppers went on and it was so loud that even behind the stage it was painful. I can't see how they can take it onstage. Soon I will go into my black box bunk. I will do my best not to think of anything so I can get some sleep. Try as I might I know that I will soon be thinking of murder and loss. We go to Paris next.

16 Paris France: Woke up in my box. Parked on the side of the road near the faceless huge venue we played in tonight. Interviews all day. I played hard as I could tonight. Opening for the Peppers is a constant inspiration. I see their backdrop and all the people with their Peppers shirts on and I feel like Tyson coming out of the corner after the bell in the first round. Just wreck the fuckers. Destroy them with music and a sheer love of animal pain. After the show no one knows us. We pass through the halls invisibly. Nothing exists except the Peppers. We are the faceless opening band. I sit in the back room and sweat onto the floor. Hit and keep hitting. I'm not expecting anything to happen. I'm not looking for success. I get what I need every night. Animal pain. The rest I don't need. Imagine me in a stage costume.

17 Amsterdam Holland: I woke up in the morning in the black box. I got out and found that we were parked at a rest stop. I went and got some coffee. When I came out I found that the bus had taken off without me. Luckily I had some money. I took a cab to Breda and caught a train to Amsterdam from there. I had enough to spare to get a hamburger on the way to the club which I happened to know the location of. When I got there the bus was there and the others were sitting on there, no problem. I was right in time for soundcheck. The gig went well though. I don't like playing that place usually. The stage is hard to hear on and the staff is pretty lazy. Most of the Dutch people at clubs are pretty fucking lazy. The people at this place make me want to randomly smack them. It's hard for me to help myself at this place. They piss me off and I react poorly. I usually regret it later but I can't help myself.

18 Nijemagen Holland: I think if you give people too much sunshine and clean air and remove a large percentage of the violence and crime from the streets then the people get bored from not having to watch their ass. That's my opinion anyway. Like Greg Ginn once said between bowls of pot: "In the absence of intimidation, creativity will flourish." You can see how it flourishes here in Holland. How the crowds just stand there in their silly pants and dumbass hair cuts and tell you what songs they want to hear. Little do they know that the singer would like to randomly smack them when they tell him what to do. They never get to find this fact out. That's why shitty music comes out of this country. There's no tension on the streets, there's no angst, nothing. The fact that the Urban Dance Squad comes from Holland is a miracle. Yea, we played and they watched like they always do. I liked it better many years ago when Black Flag played this same hall in '83. There were fights and people throwing shit, it kept us on our toes. Shoot pigs in the face.

19 Munster Germany: Another show in Germany. I wonder what they think of us here. I can't always understand Germans. I like this country because the people leave you alone when you're on the street. Pretty dead crowd tonight. I played right through them, right over them. I play for myself. They have no idea how heavy this trip is. They just smoke and look on. I used to get mad at this but as long as they don't get in my way then I don't care what they do. I have been seeing things differently these days. You do everything for yourself, even when you're doing something for someone else, you're doing it for yourself. So now I just play from the bone marrow out and not bother with the rest. I think that will make me play better. Now when people yell at me I don't have to let that matter. I know now that the music does not care about attitude. The music is pure and the more attitude you throw at it, the more it will become clouded. You have to approach the music with a strong thought, with a clear mind. Music will tolerate no shit. It will always throw itself back in your face and show you out for the fool you are. If you serve it then you will be rewarded by the lesson of strength that it endlessly provides.

20 Kassel Germany: Same as last night. I get up and play. They watch and talk and drink and smoke. I wonder sometimes if I have ever lived in real life at all. I go through all these towns and I don't notice the years pass by unless I am told how many times I have played in a certain place. I could get lost in the countries of Europe. Never come back to America's killing machine again. I've seen what it can do. I've seen it and I can still see it. It sells you out and leaves you on the sidewalk so a bunch of pigs can stand over your body and talk a bunch of pig bullshit. I am covered with blood and they can't see it. I am full of screams from a horror show and they'll never know. Best thing to do is to keep on playing and pulling in the pain. Maybe someday I'll just explode up there and then they'll see something.

21 Hannover Germany: A guy got up onstage tonight with a sun tattoo on his back that was bigger than the one I have. It had all kinds of fucked up colors in it. Green, put on all crooked. Sometimes this shit trips me out to the point where I can't get myself out the door. A lot of people at the gig and they were onstage all night. I wonder how much sweat comes out of me a year. When they talk shit about me in magazines that's what I think about. I think about all the sweat coming out of my skin and landing on the floor. They'll never know anything. Moving across borders totally unknown. I feel like I am on tour with Joe's dead body. I keep expecting to see the corpse on my bunk in the bus. I drag it with me from town to town. It's been hard doing all the press and getting asked about him all the time. I think the whole year will be like this. I don't know how I will get through it.

22 Saarbrucken Germany: Woke up on a deserted road in the middle of nowhere but now I find out it's Saarbrucken. I walked to a gas station and got some food. Peanuts and orange juice. I came back and found that some of the other bus dwellers had gone into a local bar and were getting some coffee. The place was already full of old guys drinking and arguing. So hours later we played and they watched and that's it. I managed to play hard enough so that I thought my bones were burning afterwards. I took a shower in the backstage place and it was cold. Now I'm on the bus listening to people knock on the windows calling my name. I am playing a tape of Miles Davis. Waiting to leave down this dark road. I have some shitty food that I got in the dressing room. It's good enough. My body feels like it has been beaten by strangers. It's me though, always me. The emptiness after playing is huge. The vacancy inside is enormous. I try to describe it so I can somehow deal with it better than I do now but perhaps it's just what happens with this trip. I have stopped questioning a lot of things. You can do almost any damn thing you want. You can play your ass off and you can get shot in the head. People think that everyone else gives a fuck about them. I know different.

23 Zurich Switzerland: Cold out tonight. I was outside the bus working out with dumbbells for as long as I could without getting frozen. Interviews most of the day down the road at the BMG office. They wheel in one after the other and we have a fake talk. They stand still tonight like I have never seen them stand still before. Tonight is the thirteenth show straight. I feel good. I walked off stage and minutes later I didn't remember playing the show at all. All the faces fell away as I watched the sweat run off my legs and felt the pain and chill bite into my ribs. What a strange way to live out a life time. If the music doesn't mean everything to you then you lose because you're just doing it for them, handing your guts out to strangers without getting to take a bite before you pass the steaming entrails on to those who walk over them and never know.

25 Munich Germany: I work out all the way up until the doors open. I feel like a coiled spring. Sometimes I find it hard to control myself. It's a good thing that there's the music to pound into. I have headlined in this place a couple of times before. It's strange to open for the Peppers here. A gig is a gig. I'll take it. I don't care who it's with, same thing happens every time anyway. As we played I wanted to bite them in half, to squeeze their collective necks. To savage them into impotency.

26 Munich Germany: Night two felt better than last night. I watch the Peppers guitar player stumble around in a pot and wine stupor. I could do a lot better things with the money. Flea and Sim do Monk's Bemsha Swing at soundcheck. Other than that it's a lot of playing. I only know myself through playing shows and traveling. I couldn't tell if I was being distant to someone, or rude or even hostile. I only know a good night and a bad night. I know that I remember the bad night longer than the good night. Touring is more important than love. If I didn't know people than I wouldn't have to feel anything when they get murdered a few feet away from me. As it is now I play and get back in the bus. On this tour I am learning because I know that the Peppers audience doesn't give a fuck about us. I get off only on the music. That's all there is for me. The crowd is just a distraction, an expanse of flesh that throws cups and ice. They were lucky tonight. There was a barrier to keep me away from them as I know that I could casually release short controlled bursts of body damaging violence to strangers without raising my blood pressure one bit.

27 Frankfurt Germany: The Marines up front made it hard to play tonight. They look at you and tell you to "kick ass" and that "None of these assholes know shit man!" Too bad they don't get it. There's always a few of those guys at our shows in Germany. They figure that since they're fellow Americans that we're going to be all buddy buddy with them. I don't know if they have any idea how sad they are. They were the security for the show for some strange reason so there was no way to get away from them. It was a good gig anyway. I went to catering afterwards and ate and went to the bus. This is the biggest place we've ever played in Frankfurt. I've been here so many times at this point. I was sorry that we didn't get to stay over night in our usual dingy hotel by the train station where you can find any drug or trade you want.

28 Innsbruck Austria: I did a talking show here in this place before. In the bus today Chris played a tape that Joe made him of himself talking. It was strange hearing Joe's voice. It was hard to take. He was being funny as hell and that made it worse. I sat there kind of laughing and kind of bleeding out the side. I listen to dead people on records all the time. It's not hard to take when I listen to Coltrane or someone like that but it's different with Joe. Eventually he took the tape off. I sat in the backstage area and stretched and waited to play and wondered if the crowd was going to be the same bored looking bunch that always seems to go to our shows in Austria. We played hard and they watched and that was about it. Went back on the bus and waited to leave. The mountains were beautiful today. I cannot imagine living in a place like this, having a view like that everyday. I wonder what that does to your mind if you were born and raised in clean air and streets that were not violent. I wonder what they think of people like me who come in from a different world.

29 Vienna Austria: We played in this club in 1987. It's small and it's pretty much just a disco. Better than an night off. The Peppers have a night off so we're playing this club that we played in about five years ago on our first tour here. The show is over and it was alright. Sometimes it seems like the Austrians are not even at the show. They just stand there and talk. Like last night. I don't know what gets them off. The place will be packed and I don't know if they like us or what. Doesn't really matter. We just play right through'em every night. Getting used to opening for other bands, it's good training for what I don't know but I'm sure it's good training for something. It's a good test.

March

01 Milan Italy: I'm glad this is a Peppers show and not one of ours. I don't have to worry about the bullshit of "Fuck we're in Italy nothing works and the crew are the laziest pieces of shit known to rock and roll."

I can just go out and play and not think about the fact that every other time I've ever played here it's always been such a load of bullshit just to get onstage. I had to do a press conference. I counted the tape recorders, there was fifteen of them in all. Some others were just writing shit down on paper. Whatever. What the hell are they going to use it for anyway? I would be surprised if they can get the printing presses to work. I watch the Peppers crew agonize with the local crew people who are dropping delicate equipment and thank my good luck that I'm only in the opening band. A security guard tries to stop me on the way into the back of the hall. I laugh in his face and walk past him. It reminds me of the scene in Saturday Night Live when the crew comes on the set of Star Trek and takes down all the props and Chevy Chase tries to put the Vulcan Death Grip on a guy and the guy just laughs at him and says, "Back off joker." How can you take them seriously when they barely have any shit together? They make this huge arena right next to a church. The nuns won't allow much noise so you have to run the sound at way below normal level. How typically Italian. I heard that and laughed. Perfect. Hours later we play and it's a great time. I sit on the bus wait to go and eventually have to leave and wait in the parking lot because there's so much pot smoke that I fear getting contact weakness by being around people who are so weak they have to smoke it in the first place. At least it's a nice night to look up at the stars.

02 Lyon France: This was a show that the Peppers were supposed to do but for some reason they didn't do it. We did it anyway. They moved us into a smaller hall and we played in front of about two hundred people. It was a good time. For some reason there was a television crew there filming us. Of course Andrew had to fuck up things by not bothering to play and pose out in front of the cameras so much that I had to ask them to stop so we could get through the songs. No matter what, Andrew will always sell you out. I feel like beating the shit out of him all the time. He waits all day to act like a dick onstage. I wish he could get it out of the way in the morning in his bunk or at lunch but no! He has to wait until we're trying to play. He always talks about how he's always into playing. He's so full of shit. I came right here to the bus after we played because I didn't want to talk to anyone. I was hanging out in the dressing room but there were these drunk assholes who somehow got themselves in and were getting themselves groomed for an ass kicking by someone who won't tolerate the hazy out of focus world of the alcoholic. There were people out by the bus and I did my best to be nice because they don't know the black box that sits on my head and the death and horror in my brain. Soon I will get into my little black box and dream the same dreams and feel the same tears go down my face.

04 Birmingham England: We have to be good tonight. We're in Sabbath's home town. Walking the same streets as Geezer Butler, Ozzy Osbourne, Tony Iommi and Bill Ward. The mightiest band there ever was. Later: We played hard as hell. I don't know what the Peppers are going to do. The place is so hot that the walls in the dressing room two flights up are sweating. The stage temp has got to be insane. As soon as I went on I knew we were in for a hot one. People were cool and seemed to like us. I was afraid that people on this tour would be giving us shit because they were only into the Peppers but they seem to be into us enough to tolerate us. You can tell the girls are bored and wish we were out of the way but what the fuck. I could feel the day off kicking my ass. It's a good lesson in how fast the body forgets all the training that you put into it. if I don't stretch for a couple of days, all the flexibility I had goes away. It's like I never stretched once in my life. A few songs in the pain starts. It comes as a stranger every night. It's like I have never felt it before but then a few songs later it feels like I have been that way all my life and then I really start kicking it. It's like my little secret. I don't know anyone who plays with pain. I never heard anyone in a band talk about it. It keeps me at a distance with people. They don't understand why I am in a bad mood before shows. They don't know that I am trying to get my mind ready to take on a high level of pain. I snuck out of the hall through the hello Cleveland route and got to the street without having to sign any autographs. I feel good when I can play hard and walk out and not have to talk to anyone or get thanked or shake anyone's hand. I am trying to feel better about everything and have a life. I'm really trying. I am feeling a little better as we go down the line with these shows.

05 Liverpool England: The Peppers production guy tapes up a sheet every day in the dressing room telling stage times, after show travel plans, etc. Today's said that the "punters are mental" here in Liverpool. The hall is freezing. I am told that even in summer the place is cold. It's got to be at least two thousand years old. Looking forward to playing. Later. The crowd was really cool. Easily one of the best crowds I've been in front of since I've been coming to the UK. Being in the opening spot is a good way to start a long tour. It's good to get out in front of an audience that is not there to see you. Tonight was one of those shows that you do and then walk away from. Sometimes the opening slot leaves me a bit unsatisfied. You never get to really expend yourself. I finish and sit in the dressing room wishing there was another gig across town. The shower room was in the front office for some reason. This shit doesn't matter. I see how tunneled out I can be. I wonder what I would be like in the real world.

06 Dublin Ireland: I spent the day doing interviews and had to go to Windmill studios to do something, I think it was MTV. It's the studio that U2 bought and their idiot fans have made the place some kind of mecca. Every square inch of wall space on the entire street is taken up with messages from fans to the band. "We traveled all the way from Sydney Australia because seeing you eleven times there wasn't enough. We love you always." Shit like that. It was pretty intense. I hope the camera got all the footage of me spitting all over the walls and kicking them. I hate that band. What a drag that they own Windmill. It's where Thin Lizzy recorded some of their albums. Much later I'm at the gig. I didn't know what to expect. They ended up being one of the greatest crowds I've ever been in front of. I laid into Bono and crew almost immediately to see if that would get a rise out of them and they were laughing immediately. The rest of the gig was good. I told them about Joe. It was a good show. Another night of leaving entrails on the floor. Nearly got into a thing with some piece of shit outside the place. He told me that he was the guy that threw a beer mug onstage when I did this show in San Francisco once. It missed me and broke on the floor and exploded and sent glass all over these girls who were sitting on the stage next to me. I told him to walk away before he got hurt. He told me that he wasn't aiming for me, he was trying to get me excited so I would do a good show. He also said that the glass didn't break. He wouldn't stop talking to me and I kept trying to get away from him because I don't want to get arrested for fucking up one of the pieces of shit. He eventually went away. I was relieved. I am now back in the cold small box. I am waiting for sleep to come.

07 Dublin Ireland: I did an instore experience today. The people were really cool but the whole thing was unnerving. I eventually had to slip through the people and leave. After an hour in a tiny store with people all around you it gets to be a bit much. The show was real good tonight. People really like the Peppers here, it was pretty insane when they came on. I like those guys ok. They're easy to tour with. All the people in their crew are great and the guys in the band are cool as well. The high point of the night was meeting up with a man named Smiley. Smiley was one of the Thin Lizzy road crew. Apparently he worked with Phil and Co. for quite some time. He told me some cool stories. He said that Phil was a great guy, really big hearted but in a lot of pain. It's kind of what I got from listening to Thin Lizzy records. I listen to Thin Lizzy almost every day. I never get tired of them. Phil had it right. That song "Running Back" from the *Jailbreak* album is a perfect song, that's a great album to have out on the road. Smiley said that I could come by his place the next time I'm in town and see some stuff he has from his years on the road with the band. Now I'm in the tiny hotel room that will house three of us tonight. Me and Chris are here and we are giving the floor to a friend of ours that has come from England to see us. I am trying get out of the hall as soon as I can after I play. I find that the more I'm alone, the better I feel. I am trying to deal with the dull haze that I find myself in almost every day. It's like I have a lead cloud over me all the time.

08 Belfast Ireland: Most intense border crossing I can remember. I was sitting up in the front seat with Tim the driver. He told me to be cool and always show my hands. We were met at the gate by a terrified teenager holding a rifle aimed at our faces. We told him that we were in a rock band and that we were playing with the Peppers. He immediately put the rifle down and asked, "You're in a band?" Right then all these teenagers in fatigues came out of several hiding places all over the roadside. We had been in front of half a dozen guns the entire time.

They came on the bus and we gave them shirts. They told us that they would love nothing more than to be at the show tonight but they had to be here. There was a sign up that apologized for the wait at the gate but said it was because of the terrorists. It's no joke there. We get to the gig and it so happens it's right near the place where some bombs went off as couple of weeks before. Finally we get to play. The crowd was tense and wild at the same time. Got hit with some spit. I didn't think they did that shit anymore. We were so far from the crowd and the stage was so high, I don't know what they saw of us. The bouncers had this system of grabbing kids. One would get the kid in a head lock and the other one would put two fingers into the kid's mouth and pull his cheek back and the two of them would take the kid out real hard, then they would come back and laugh about it. All of this was going on the whole time right below me. It was hard to take. I sat in the dressing room until it was time to go. I didn't want to be in the bus if it got fire bombed or some shit. They have security out there guarding the tour busses because they were afraid that someone might put a bomb underneath one of them. It will be good to get out of here.

09 Glasgow Scotland: The band has a night off and I have a talking show. The first thing I did was tell them the reason why I haven't been back to Scotland for eight years. I walked out in front of a bunch of people that were there to see a spoken word show and one of the first lines that came out of my mouth was "I think you all are fucked." I think they liked me after that. A night off from the band in Scotland and I find a way to make trouble for myself by not being able to say no to a gig. I must like what I'm doing. The only thing that was troubling was the young man that came up crying and hugged me and wouldn't let go for what seemed like an eternity. He has no idea how much it freaked me out to have someone touch me like that. I am a haunted house. I am a freak show. I am all the police line ups. I am good at being a witness. I am good at being a victim. It's in my DNA. I was always good at watching them do everything and me doing nothing. I was always good at letting the world do what it wanted to me. I learned to take it from my mother and father and the people they fucked. I am trouble, big trouble. I can't control myself like I used to. This is a strange time. I have been cut loose to swing in the darkness of the Abyss. I do interviews all day long talking shit to people I don't know. It's like a fast fuck. Always business, never personal. I don't know anyone and I know too much because no one can tell me anything.

10 Glasgow Scotland: I was figuring that were going to get pelted, spat on and all the rest. It was a great gig instead. The place is a famous venue called the Barrowlands. Real good sounding hall. The load in is a drag because there's several long flights of stairs and no elevator. The loaders are famous for getting gear up and down the stairs in no time flat. Since most of them are psychotic biker motherfuckers, you stay out of their way. I watched the Peppers play tonight. I have never seen anything like that. The place was packed to capacity of course, and everyone there was jumping up and down at the same time like the whole thing had been choreographed. I thought the floor was going to break. Now I'm in the dressing room which is cold and smells and the shower only gives out cold water. I'm not lonely because I'm not human. I am this thing that plays shows and gets it going on every night. No matter what happens to me, the music and the road don't care. The road is always waiting for me to throw up my hands and walk off. It's always trying to tell me that I never really had it, never really meant it. You have to keep rising to the occasion, that's what it's all about, you have to be ready to go without to get to it. That's why I don't hang around for the talk and adulation fests. I know better. The road watches and laughs thinking that it's going to take me out. You stick around and get congratulated and patted on the back, then you lose your edge. That's what these bands don't understand. In order to give it up you have to be pure. The impurities are what wear these rockstars down. Most of these people with guitars are so lightweight. So fake. They don't rise to the occasion. The road chews them up and spits them out. They complain about the road being hard. It is hard so you have to be hard. It's so simple. Either you go for it all the way or you pose out.

12 London England: Did two shows today. I did a talking show at a club for press and record people. I talked about Joe, what else is there. I don't know if I bummed them out too much. I felt strange talking to these people in the middle of the afternoon and then going on to do interviews and another gig. The crowd tonight at the band show was limp. I didn't understand what the deal with them was. I would look up and they were just standing there. We had to take breaks between songs because drum mics kept falling off and that kind of thing always fucks us up. Nick Cave was at the show tonight. It's strange, he always seems to come to shows that I don't like as much as the one before when he wasn't there. It was cool to see him anyway. It's cold out and of course it's raining. We have two more shows here in the UK and then we're out. Nothing much on my mind tonight. I am burned out from the interviews and the fact that I did two shows today. I guess I'm doing good because if at the end of the day I'm so tired that I can't think then I must have given all I could. I am unable to protect myself. I don't have any shields up anymore. I just take as best I can. I don't know what else to do except play.

13 Brixton England: Just got back from the first of the two shows at the Brixton venue. I think we played well. I got a workout in before we went on and that was a good help to me. I like it when I can hit the weights before I go on. I feel better about myself. I feel like a slob when I don't work out. While I was hitting the weights, Andrew sat on his ass and smoked hash. Typical. If Joe saw that he would have laughed so hard he would have fallen over. Like Joe used to say, "Andrew smokes dope and cigarettes, drinks, kicks back and complains." He plays bass sometimes. I want to get a different player in the band. I'm tired of this lazy piece of shit. He wants to have a meeting with me and Gail tomorrow. I hope he wants to quit. I know he'll be complaining about something, he always does, nothing's good enough for him. I really don't care at this point, after what I've been through, bullshit is nothing to me. It's not like he's getting his head blown off on my front porch or anything. I did press for hours today. I did radio, television, an instore at Tower. The press was hard to do. I was at it all day right into soundcheck. Right after that I worked out and went to play. Now I'm back. I think nothing of it. I don't care. I'm still standing. I can still work.

14 Brixton England: Last night with the Peppers. All the Beastie Boys showed up. Now that was something. One of the only bands that matter. The Peppers guitar player walked into our dressing room and mumbled something about it being a beautiful experience playing with us. I guess he was stoned. Seems like a nice enough guy. I never said a word to him the whole tour except a hello in passing. Andrew is all bent out of shape about all kinds of stuff and asked to meet with me and Gail and when I said ok let's talk he has nothing to say. It's always the same bullshit with him, he never confronts. Fuck it, I played hard as hell and gave it up. This has been a good tour I think. It was hard to look at all the Beasties in the room hanging out and not think of Joe and how much he would be getting off on all of this. I have to go to New York and do press for the next few days. Night after night and I'm still here. You have to keep coming back and hitting year after year. You need to be unbelievable. That's the part that a slob like Andrew will never be able to get to. You have to have a great deal of straight up pride in what you do and realize that it matters more than sleep, more than anything. I have Samurai in my blood. The hall here in Brixton is cold and the rooms smell. Some guy that we remotely know from London came in here and started to fuck the place up and I had to throw him out. Drunks are so pathetic. I can't take them. If I know someone and they get drunk and get in my face I no longer respect them. Somehow I can tolerate when someone in the band gets drunk because they never do it onstage but I can never respect someone that drinks and gets drunk as much as I could someone that is straight. If you really want to destroy then you are straight all the time and you get it done. Otherwise you're just talking shit.

April

01 Fullerton CA: We played outside today at Cal State Fullerton. It was good. A few songs in it started to rain. We kept on playing. It really started coming down. But we kept playing. I fully expected to get shocked and killed. There was a girl up front grabbing me and she had on all this lipstick so I wiped it all over her face and wiped it onto mine and went for the scene with Frank Booth in Blue Velvet where he's kissing Jeffrey. I was telling her that I was going to send her straight to hell fucker. We finished the gig and like rockstars left the equipment behind for the road crew and went to the Dennis Miller show where there was more gear waiting for us and we soundchecked and then played "Tearing" on the program. I hung out with Dennis on the talk show scene for a few minutes and it was better this time then the last time. I feel ok, nothing really on my mind. We go to San Diego in the morning for two shows. Strange day. One set outside with people watching from all sides, no walls, the music just flying into the trees and into the air and then a television show, all in one day. Now I'm in my box waiting for the road to begin.

02 San Diego CA: First night here in San Diego. The opening band was crap. It had the old singer from TSOL. I think his name is Jack. He's the same bullshit as he always was but now he's overweight. Whatever. These punk legends are hilarious to me. Punk rock! Anyway they sucked and were quickly blown offstage. I remember I was here a few months ago doing spoken word with Don. As far as the gig, the only stand out thing besides playing our asses off was some large punker guy insisting that he jump off stage and squash people and then tell them that it was better in eighty something. Thanks Punk! Don once told me that the nights in San Diego are the best in the world. It's great outside tonight. I wish I wasn't so tired. It was hot onstage tonight, the heat beats the hell out of me every year. I always wonder why my tattoos don't melt off my body. After shows I am filled with emptiness. I have no idea how the will to play comes back every day. Strange how at the end of the day all I can think about is getting to the stage and playing. I figured I would get tired of this trip after a few years and now I know nothing else, for me there is nothing else.

03 San Diego CA: Played hard tonight. The sun is coming up and I am writing. A girl I met is sleeping in my bed. It was a good night of playing. A band from the old LA scene opened tonight. Actually, it was two bands that have taken members from both and made a band. One band was The Controllers and the other band was The Skulls. They have a band called Skull Control. I think they were a little surprised that I knew their old records. I have all of them from both bands. I thought they were cool. If I see their name in the paper I will go check them out. I don't know if the crowd could get to them but it was great to see them go for it. I did nine interviews. Sometimes I amaze myself at how I can do that shit and still play, I don't know how long I can keep that up. With the schedule that's up for this year I'll get a chance to find out.

04 Los Angeles CA: Instead of a night off we are playing at the Palladium as part of the Magic Johnson AIDS Benefit. Should be cool. I'm riding my bike down to the gig. That will be a first for me. Later: Had a good time with the whole thing. Hung out with the singer in Fish Bone and did some pictures. Did some interview stuff with MTV and radio. Porno for Pyros played tonight. I think it was their first gig. I'm not too sure but that was what I heard. I thought they were cool. It was hard to watch them from out front because people kept coming up and talking to me. I had to tell some people to leave me the fuck alone. I really wanted to see Perry do his thing. I think they will be better when they get some more shows under their belt. When Perry hit stage the crowd went off. People really get off on that guy. It was like there was some kind of magnet at the front of the stage. We played after that and it was ok. I have a problem with short sets where I tend to come out of the gate too fast and blow my pace a little. I tried to cool it before I went on but I was so fired up I was punching the wall and hitting myself in the head but I pulled off the set ok. After that I hung out for a while and then spilt. I can't stay around the LA scene thing for too long without feeling like I am getting drained. It's bad for you to stick around and listen to that band bullshit and even start talking about it. The more you talk to others, the more you become like them. You don't want to get on topics of "common ground", the best thing to do is to do your number and get the fuck out into the night and disappear. The only thing I should be thinking about after a show is the next one.

05 San Francisco CA: MTV is filming a couple of our shows. Luckily for us they are cool people so I see there being no problems. It's hard to be in the hotel that we're in because it looks out across the street to the apartment building of a girl I used to go out with up here. She doesn't live there anymore. I can see the window that I used to look out of though and it's a drag. The gig is hours away. Later: We played a good one I thought. The place is the same place where I do the talking shows up here. I gave it all I had and it was a great time. Last time I was here

Joe was videoing me right to my right side. Before the show we were talking to these girls doing one of our typical good guy bad guy routines. They didn't recognize either of us and we were asking them how they got here and what they were expecting and we told them that we knew that Rollins guy and that he was pretty fucked up and that he had killed a bunch of people and no one knew about it and that they should keep it a secret as well. Andrew's brother played percussion with us tonight and Morgan played violin too. We went for a Sabbath sounding jam that felt good. Now I'm back here in the room. Soon I will go into another room and have sex with this girl whose name keeps escaping me until the last moment. It will be meaningless in typical Californian style. I will become more hollow. My eyes will fill with the local night. Syringes, hookers, garbage on the streets. The old words from the place across the street. Ghosts and gunshots, horror and dried blood.

06 San Francisco CA: We played with Morgan and Andrew's brother again. Another great night in SF. After the show was over I was walking Morgan back to her car and this guy came out of nowhere, he had a poncho on and I couldn't see his hands. He came up and said hello and I was getting ready to see the gun come out and ready to be held up again. His left hand came out of the poncho first and I figured that the other was going to come out with the gun. The other hand came out and there was nothing in it. I had an overwhelming urge to attack him and take him out before he could do anything to me. Do it to him before he could do it to me. Eliminate him without asking any questions. He turned out to be some street guy looking for change and he was very cool. He had no idea how close I came to attacking him. Like a shark, like a pitbull. Like the most terrified man on the face of the earth. It's all I know. I know panic and hotel hideouts. Sometimes I really think that I could rip the flesh off my bones. I get a few seconds out of every few minutes. I watch the time go by in strangled increments. I meet people that call my name and it all sounds like screams and terror to me. Compliments sound like threats, like the great send off going away party to the Abyss. The music makes me more berserk. You shouldn't talk to me tonight because there's not much I care about and a whole lot I don't give a fuck about.

07 Los Angeles CA: In LA the blood dries at night. The streets never cool down. The sound of helicopters fills the ears and sends knee jerk shots of panic, paranoia and animal savagery through the veins of the shuffled extras too numbed by glamour overload to notice that there's not a single intersection in the entire city where you can stand and not be an animal waiting to see your own intestines slide down your leg from a stray bullet. In this city they kill for the fuck of it, fuck for the hell of it and live for no reason. If I could have a nickel for every siren I've heard go screaming into the distance to some scene, I'd still be here, still be looking out the window of my room, still laughing at the fact that I can't get my window open very far because the security bars get in the way. Every window in the apartment has iron bars across them to keep me safe. I don't feel safe. I don't feel safe anywhere. I don't feel safe and I'll attack you because I'm scared and full of fear like the next guy. Like the next dead guy. Like the next guy who knows he's nothing, nothing but a piece of meat waiting for something to come around and charge him double and scar him for life. I played tonight and challenged my muscles and pain threshold and I won again. I think about a sword and its brutal simplicity. I temper myself in the furnace of these hot boxes all over the world. I come out stronger and stronger. I will outlive the fear, the spent bullet casings and the ravaging heartbreak of this city. Any city. Every city.

08 Los Angeles CA: Got back here a little while ago. Another good night at the Whisky. I had a good time playing. We had Chad and Flea from the Peppers and Steve Perkins from Jane's Addiction out there as well. Two bass players and three drummers at once, it was really cool. It totally worked. Last night was cool as well Perry came out and did vocals with me on "Obscene." It was great to share a stage with him. I did an instore today. It was a drag. The people were really great as they usually are but there were so many of them. I was there for nearly two hours. I don't think I'll let them put me in that position again after the ones I promised I'd do are over with. I don't like making people stand in line to talk to me. I can't take it. I wanted to bolt out of there a few times today. It's hard because the people are so cool and they like you and I want to give them everything. I don't know why I'm like that. I hate myself when I think that I left anyone out. I could never hurt their feelings. The pigs called me today and asked if I wanted to see more line up shots. I told them that I would do what I could. So far they have no leads that they would tell me about. Just talking to them put me back in that pig frame of mind. I have a day off tomorrow. I'll get in a good workout. Looking forward to that. Looking forward to getting left alone as well. I will do the best I can to get my mind to myself. It's hard with the pigs bearing down on me all the time. I feel like hiding out and protecting my thoughts from all these people that seem to be so interested in all the pathetic little details of my shallow, blasted life.

11 Phoenix AZ: Played at this outdoor radio get down with all these bands that would never play together if it wasn't for this. Imagine us with Social Distortion and the Sugar Cubes. We didn't get to use any of our own equipment and it was a drag for the rest of the guys. It didn't help that no one really knew what was going on. Our dressing room became the designated area for all these coked out DJ types who think we're really impressed and don't realize that we don't give a fuck about anything but playing the gig. So we get to play and we gave it up as best we could. Hilarious, I wouldn't want to have been Social Distortion going on after us because they got their asses blown off stage so hard their socks landed in LA. Now I'm in the hotel box. Some girl slid pictures of herself under my door and she'll be over in a few minutes. Sometimes you get a break.

12 Dallas TX: At the instore I stood next to a table with a pen in my hand watching the line not end. I looked ahead of me. There were people with posters in their hands and they were looking at me and I was signing this stuff the best I could and I was trying to be cool but it was hard because the line never stopped. It's a great way to spend an afternoon if you want to learn to hate your own guts worse than you do at present. Nearly two hours of it and I felt like asking to get my hands chopped off. The PA blew up during the last song so there was nothing we could do about it and the coolest part was that the audience understood. Sometimes it's hard to tell an audience that the PA that's in the club is not so hot and it blew up and it's not the band's fault and there is nothing we would rather be doing than playing. Sometimes they flat out don't believe you, like you tried to blow it up or something. Hot place tonight. Sold out and people all over the place nonstop. Just another night on tour. Was stressed out after the instore thing and started running a fever after soundcheck. Managed to fall asleep in the bunk for a little while. I woke up in sweat. Outside people were lined up to get in. When you get out of the bus they stare at you like you're coming out of a spaceship. No matter how low key you try to get out of the bus it looks like some bullshit grand entrance and I'm sure that people start hating your guts before they even get a chance to find out what a fucked up, dented, tragic wreck you really are. I wish there could be something amazing that could happen every night on tour. Something to make me remember the name of the town we're in. So many nights are the same. I pull in, get taken away to do interviews with people who don't know me from spit and do the soundcheck and then you hang out and then you get ready and then you play. The playing is the total reason for living but then there's the emptiness that keeps me up until near dawn. The only thing that makes it better is the chance to rise to the occasion again and again. To challenge the pain threshold nightly. It's a heavy way to get off. I'm confused and tired, is it showing? All I know is that I feel empty all the time. In the last two weeks I've been with some great women and it never seems to make me feel any better. I always feel the same distance. I never felt that with the girl that dumped me. I bet I was just fooling myself though. But the other night I was in a hotel room with a girl and for a little while I felt somewhat close to her. It wasn't for long though. It would be cool to meet someone that I could identify with. Fuck it. I'm a loner all the way. I don't understand why I keep trying to deny it and get out of it. I always end up alone. I always end up insulting them and pissing them off. I'm better off alone.

14 Cincinnati OH: I think tonight was the first show where we broke a thousand paid in America as a headliner. I don't know if that's important but it put some shit into perspective one way or the other. I thought we played good tonight. It was a trip leaving the place. I walked out into the cold only thinking about getting on the bus and getting some sleep and there were all these people out there waiting to get their stuff signed and all. There was a lot of them too. I did the best I could. I'm standing there shivering with my wet shorts and the rest of my shit on the ground between my feet and I'm telling them that I'm really cold and I have to get on the bus and they just stand there unmoving. I don't know if they hear me or not. They just stand there with their stuff in their hands and they're not going anywhere. I did the best I could and then I finally got on the bus and I felt like throwing up. I am not the rockstar type. I don't want to bum any of these people out. How can you <u>not</u> like them? They like you, they came to your gig. It's hard for me to not like young people and it's hard not to like someone who likes you, even a little, even if they're strangers. That's my problem. I can't help but like these people, even though I don't know them. I think that's the part that's the hardest. I don't like myself as much as they like me. They have no idea how fucked up I am these days. How hung up I am with Joe and everything else. Some nights when I'm standing there like a cardboard cutout, I have to wonder who they're talking to.

15 Chicago IL: I am in one of those ruts where I can't think of anything to think of. I played all the way tonight and left my mind on the stage. I don't know how I do it night after night. I figure that at some point my head will explode or I'll have a heart attack. I think people in this town are cool. I always have a great time playing here. Tonight was no exception. I feel like I have been hit on the head with something. I think a lot of bullshit during the day like if I could meet a woman that could help me take my mind off of Joe. Not that I want to forget him at all, it's just that it's wearing me out. I'm never very far from losing it. It's become very hard to find inspiration. I used to think I was pretty unstoppable. Now I see that I was wrong. People are stoppable as hell. It doesn't take much. I'm a walking laugh riot I know. I feel different than I used to. I somehow feel like I live right next door to life. I think I have enough death in me to disqualify me from the status of the living. I just don't feel like I have anything in common with anyone alive. The world has shrunk around my neck. Become a small and lonely place not suited for disturbed loners anymore. I'm going to keep playing and see where the hell it ends up. I've got nowhere else to go.

16 Chicago IL: The guy walked up to the whore and stared at her. He walked around her and put his face within an inch of hers. I thought he was going to inhale her. He pulled back and said, "I don't wanna fuck <u>you</u>." She told him to come back but he had already gone across the street and was headed for another girl in high leather boots. Before that we played at Medusa. I like Chicago. Me and Joe were talking about moving here a few days before he got killed. We figured that we should be out of LA by the spring before the place really got to us. Some timing.

17 Detroit MI: Over twelve hundred people at the instore. Eight hundred got in. My intestines were on the table. Can I hug you? I held their flesh, held their babies. Outside the bus they wait for me to sign something. Thirty minutes until we play. I don't remember getting up. After the show my belongings are scattered and mixed with flowers, phone numbers and pictures. I'm afraid of vomiting in my sleep. The restaurant makes me feel like my eyes are resting on desert crust. Some guy asks me how many times I have found myself in a diner in the middle of nowhere after two in the morning. Over a decade. I think of one girl in particular. Please be with me for a little while. You don't have to do anything, just let me be next to you. A second later I'm one hundred miles past loneliness sitting in a moonlit desert, alone and breathing. I snap back at the sound of my name being called. Some guy wants an autograph.

18 Toronto: They'll drink themselves to death like their fathers did. They'll end up like their hammered old men fathers before they know what life is all about. They'll do their time in jail and lose their fear of it before they even get a taste for the hard stuff and when they finally do it's all over. They'll never get out, they'll just end up. I end up with one of the rare ones in a single bed late in the night. She tells me about death and how long it takes to get over it. She kisses me and I know she's right. She is one of the rare ones. I am too dead to fully notice. I fall into her breasts and nearly pass out from the sheer weight of the bliss. Death on the road, safe in hotels. Spitting out pieces of glass and million year old cigarette smoke. I fall through everything. You get a taste of the Abyss and nothing gets in your way after that.

19 Toronto: To do something that will reduce me to a bag of flesh that wants nothing more than cold water. Might be the act of a fool. That was me tonight. On the last song of the encore I wanted nothing more in the world than a large container of cold water. I know what I am. I am animal. They'll never take it away from me. I'll keep it in my teeth and shake it to pieces before they get it from me. Fuck it, they'll have to kill me.

20 Washington DC: Parked the bus in front of the bank I walked past for years on my way to school and work. The hotel is in my old neighborhood. My home town. Walked down my old strip of Wisconsin Ave. Most of the places I grew up around are now gone. I feel old and homeless. I am homeless. I don't know any of these buildings. I didn't know the old ones either. It's all a damage report. I don't want to be a casualty. How many hours sleeping on the bus from Toronto? Will I ever love a woman again? The spring air reminds me of growing up and spending time outside on these streets. I cannot smell the blood on my hands. I can feel my mother on these streets. I can sense her heat. I bet I could cough pure car exhaust if I wanted.

21 Washington DC: The line at the instore never ends. Girls there since the place opened so they could be the first in line and they didn't make it. I sign stuff and shake their hands and look into their cameras. It's all I am these days. I know nothing else. The heat at the show cannot be translated. At some point I stop being hot and become heat and then I can play. It's getting to that point that hurts so much. I made up a song during a jam. I wished you loved me, why don't you love me. It worked itself out right there. It's raining outside and I am thinking about how I made my escape tonight in a friend's car. At some point I have to just walk away from all the voices and questions and hope they understand. Out here is endless. They don't know me and I don't know them and that's all the space I need. Tonight my mother hovered in the dressing room. I left and sat shivering on the stairs. I don't want to know anyone, the very idea that I know anyone at all is a lie that I will not take.

24 New York: First night in NYC down. I had a great time playing. Vernon Reid came down to soundcheck to play with us. He brought a riff with him and we played it later on that night. The place was packed and there wasn't a great deal of air up there but we played well anyway. The encore with Vernon was great. It's so cool to play with him. He's a real good guy. Earlier in the day I did an instore at Tower. I stupidly said yes to doing these and I have several more ahead of me. It's a drag to stand there like a stuffed human xerox machine signing stuff. The people there were great and real nice to me and all but it's hard to stand there and smile and say thank you. I feel like a dick for being something that you can stand in line and see, something that you have to stand in line to see. After I do the ones I have agreed to I will never do them again. I like the people that come to them but I don't want to meet them like this. It's degrading to them and myself. It makes me feel gross. Other than that it's good to be playing well every night. It's good to be alone in this room and not have to see anyone. It's scary to deal with the thoughts that go through my head all the time now. It's somehow better to be alone even when everything in me wants to be with someone.

25 New York: The boy in the room next door has been screaming for the last hour. I've slept a few hours and some press people will be here soon. It's Saturday and I'll be doing press until soundcheck. I don't have a life. I've totaled eight hours sleep in the last two days. I can feel my eyes ache. I want to kill someone. I hate the way this shit makes me feel. My throat is coming off. The boy is screaming at his mother. A lot of people live in this hotel full time. It's all bug spray and bad heating. Too much breathing in this place will kill you. Hours later I am finished playing. The place was hot and packed tonight. Had a good time playing. I remember melting onstage and looking out at all the maniacs. Vernon Reid jammed with us tonight on the encore again and that was great. Iggy Pop and Alan Vega showed up a well. At one point they were standing together talking and I wish I had a picture of that, two of the greatest singers ever. I am exhausted and brain dead from the interviews and playing. I have to get up in a few hours to shoot a video for the song "Tearing". It's going to be live in front of an audience. It's going to be raw playing all day on no sleep. Just thinking about it makes me want to puke.

26 New York: Shot video all day on ninety minutes of sleep. Want to throw up. Sitting on a monitor between "takes" talking to the "audience" that was "invited" to the gig. Played the one song over and over live and synched until I could no longer remember the words. We were onstage for about ten hours today. The room waited for me until I got back. I cannot translate the language of exhaustion. I feel alone but I'm not lonely. The walls understand me better. I don't know anything. The more they want to know the less I know. Words make me forget all I know.

27 Atlanta GA: I fall asleep on the chair in the hotel room before I do anything else. The phone rings and it's time to go to some radio station and talk shit. I don't have a life. I listen to the bullshit come out of the DJ's mouth. She asks questions that amount to nothing. I notice that her hands are shaking. Everything in me wants to sleep and vomit. The pigs are trying to shut down the place we're playing. Too bad because the people who run it seem like good folks. I don't remember how the last shows have been. I am beyond loneliness. All I want is sleep.

28 Atlanta GA: My legs won't get loose. I do the best I can at the instore, they give me things and I promise to do the best I can to read, listen and use it all. If they only knew the language that I use in my brain. The language that screams with clearly formed words yet will not come out of my mouth. I stand there like some guy waiting to get smacked. I wonder if I'll ever get shot at one of these things. I hear these girls say ohmigod it's him. I realize that they're talking about me and I want to hand them my lungs and make a getaway out the back of the store. Tonight I'll play harder than I did last night. I remember the other times we played in this town. They just stood there and watched. This time they know all the words and they move and they even sent one of their women onstage to touch the wounded animal.

May

04 Menomonie WI: The sky is huge and filled with dark clouds. The hotel is in the middle of nowhere. I like it. They find me still. Call me in the room and ask to come over. I dodge them as best I can. I feel watched. I sit in the diner across the road and listen to the low rumbling of the truckers over in the smoking section. Better than the fire filled streets I left behind in LA. The only break is that I get to keep moving. Have to move like I have to breathe. To those who don't feel this, no amount of explanation will make them understand. I love the big sky country. The night air is fresh. Tonight's theater was packed. I told them the truth. I pulled out my guts and we watched them steam in the lights. I throw out my entrails and pull them back in at the end of the night. I go back to the room and wait to move to the next city. This is fine with me. Nowhere I'd rather be than on the way to the next city. How many of their fathers blew their brains out? How many sons came back to this town from some steaming jungle with an American flag over their remains? How many rapes, how many heartbreaks? What happens in a town this size when someone is murdered? I am in a lit box with a parking lot outside the window. Across the road are fast food places and small time desperation.

05 Chicago IL: You can hear the L train thunder by every so often. I stood and sweated in front of them. The lights peered into me. Afterwards they looked at me and spoke to me and shook my hand and I did the best I could. This city passes quickly. Not enough time to see any of it or remember any of the moves. It's just another room, like so many boxed nights on this trail. It's near one in the morning. Wish I had the energy to do something like think. Times like these make me think that someday I'll get it together to where at the end of the night I can have a brain to use instead of this hollow shell I keep going to bed with. The L runs echoes through me. My head is full of nothing, crammed full of their nothing, all their words and sounds. Laughter and clapping and words, so many words. Words piled on top of each other. Stranger's words escaping from their mouths, seeking refuge in my brain. What they don't know is that I hear it all the time and they got here too late. The sidewalks take the taste out of my mouth.

06 Cleveland OH: Flat and the dirt clings. Been here so many times. Stayed in one girl's house while her boyfriend who hated me shot junk in the other room. Another city gets stuck in my throat. Another flesh wave stands in front of my face. Heat. I sweat through my clothes. I shake their hands. The city waits outside the doors of the venue. Another night on the trail. Another city in the life. I don't want to know them like they want to know me. It never works out. I sleep off heartbreak like you wouldn't believe. I can't translate.

07 Denver CO: Empty streets except for hippies and homeless. Nazi stronghold here. Trees and streams, skiing and nazis. Old hippie people named Dale and Dinah. AA, NA, health food. Nothing moves. It's hard to breathe. When I'm here I can't wait to leave. I fear places that don't move. The creepy conservatism, racism. They're hiding and even the young can't escape the bullshit of these earth shoe wearing motherfuckers.

08 Salt Lake City UT: Spaced out on too much wide open and sunlight. They simmer in their own self righteousness. I see the sky so huge and the mountains so high and yet I feel stifled and freaked out. They look at me strange when I get coffee in the local diner. They really don't know what they're fucking with this time. The mountains scream. I've never felt at home anywhere. A city looks best to me when I'm leaving it. Dry heat and a show tonight. Two boys in heavy metal shirts tell me it's great to have me here. After them a group of boys comes over to the traffic light and tell me the same thing. It's good at least to be able to be something that someone looks forward to. I wonder about living a whole life in a place like this. Not my life —someone else's.

28 Los Angeles CA: I imagine watching myself from the back of the hall. I see a man with a bucket of his guts throwing pieces out to an audience. The bucket seems bottomless. The entrails never seem to stop coming. I feel sorry for the guy because I know that when the seemingly bottomless bucket is empty and he walks off stage to the basement and listens to the feet of the audience above as they walk out of the theater he will look down and see that there's blood all over his shoes. He'll look under his shirt and find that he has no more guts left. Confusedly he'll shake the hands of people who are for some strange reason in the room with him. He'll feel nothing for these people because he has no feeling in him whatsoever. He has no feeling of himself, for himself. He speaks thoughtlessly. The words fall out of him as he tries desperately to make these people who are saying things to his hollow frame feel at ease thinking that it will somehow make himself feel something. Soon they are gone and he stands in the room alone. He is as alone as he was several minutes before when he was in front of so many. He leaves the theater and walks unrecognized past people that are waiting to meet him. They imagine he is so much bigger than the average height and build human that quickly walks by them, a broken machine on two legs. He returns to a small room and waits for sleep. The phone rings. It's someone he doesn't know who got his number. The stranger tells him that he was at the show. He asks the stranger, this person out there somewhere on the end of a curled black cord, "Was I good?" The stranger says yes. He hangs up and unplugs the phone. He feels like the only person in the world, so remote, so horribly singular. He knows that all the pain and bloodletting in the world won't get it out. He'll wake up a few hours later and he'll be full of venom and guts and poison and he'll have to find another place to get it out before the pressure becomes too much.

31 Berlin Germany: Sitting outside a coffee place looking at what's left of Check Point Charlie. Some sections of the wall are still standing. Looks stupid now, like you wonder what took them so long to tear the damn thing down in the first place and you know why, but still. Small painted versions of the wall stand in gift shops. The sun sets and she and I talk about getting out of America alive. She lives here now and has no reason to go back. I think of America and it becomes a horror filled murdering plane. Blood, glass and needles. Lies and sorrow. Larger than death, so much larger. Seems too big to go back to, like it's the last thing you would want to do. The sun disappears and the night hovers above us. It's one of those great nights that happens around here all the time. I hear about her roommate who was from the East. Her brother engineered wire taps on her to turn her in for the state. You have to wonder about the ones who know how to use a title to their best advantage. Like he'll never sell you out, he's your brother. Sure he will. Your brother's human. So's your mother. What about a place where you could go and pay a small amount of money and sit in a room with someone and trust them completely and then after the time was up you would leave feeling like there really is someone out there that you can depend on. You would feel good about it because you had paid for it. I don't trust anyone and I don't ask anything from anyone I don't pay. Do you? What a mess we're in this time.

June

03 Dusseldorf Germany: My skull exploded onstage last night. I wonder if anyone in the crowd saw it. I saw bright lights and smoke. I felt my heart scream and die. It was so hot and the weight of the music was heavy. It occurred to me that there could be music that was so heavy that it destroys the people that play it. An honor to be destroyed by music. Build the body up to withstand the music that you took part in creating. Music doesn't care. Music will rip your guts out and laugh in your face. The heat made me a visionary. I heard the dead of Vietnam scream and I answered them with my own. No one would believe me if I told them. I looked up into the lights and felt so alone.

04 Stuttgart Germany: I don't know, all I've seen is the parking lot of the venue. I don't remember when we got here. I don't know the name of the city that we're playing tomorrow night. I didn't even know we were playing here until I asked someone this morning when we were pulling in. I have no context. All there is in the world is this hall and the show that we'll play in a few hours. I know nothing else. I have been thinking too much. All last night during the show I was screaming I want to die. I did. In the last few weeks things have become too much. I have been having a hard time handling. I don't know what to do. I am dealing with shit that's too strong for me. Cities will pull the brains right out of your head. I don't want to know so much all the time. I hate my loneliness and sorrow. It cuts deep into me. It defines me. They can't see it. I do these interviews and scream underneath my skin as I give them some kind of answer. I need something badly and I hate to think about it. Some things that don't give a fuck about you: cities, money, numbers, roads, time, life, death. I can inhale shared breath and exhale a naked vision of the Nile, pyramids and stars. I can wrap my arms around a stranger but the horror will never leave. I don't know whether it's patience or tenacity that keeps it near. I don't understand what my next move is. All the lessons I learned in the past fall flat and watch themselves bleed to death.

05 Bielefeld Germany: Saw a little bit of the city when we were coming in. Don't remember leaving the last town we were in. I fell asleep in the same parking lot I woke up in that morning. Another grind with a twist at the end. Walk into the place, wait for the coffee to come out. Drink it out of habit, not for any other reason. Walk around the venue and try to pass time. I feel stupid and dull. I am looking forward to playing. I don't remember what it feels like even though we played last night. It's coma to coma. We go to Eindhoven after this. I am dislocated from myself. I don't know what the lady was asking me today during the interview interrogation session. I looked at her and wondered what she thought of this guy she didn't know anything about who looked through her and talked about horror and death. I'm a silent crisis center.

06 Eindhoven Holland: I finished the show. Gave it all I had. I don't know these people and the stupid shit that comes out of their mouths just makes me meaner. Some guy comes up to me tells me that a woman that works at his favorite bar told him that the band I'm in sucks and women are just into me because of my body. Like I really have to hear this shit. I looked at some woman that was standing there and said that I was heartbroken because I thought that women liked me for my mind. Then I said that I should start stabbing common bitches in the face. She bummed out because I was staring at her when I said it. What the fuck do these people expect from me? Do they think that I'm some nice guy who they can talk shit to? Fuck these people. I don't care what some woman wants me for. Mind, body, who gives a fuck what someone wants. Remind me to not give a fucking woman the time of day for a few years. I think that more people should start getting stabbed in the face with screwdrivers. Fuck all of you. I hope you all get raped and murdered, fucked in the ass and slaughtered. I left out the back door and didn't have to say shit to anyone. I looked at the signs for the highway as I walked. I have played almost every city that was listed. People fuck with me too much. I am good for a few things. I am good at being that thing that you can throw peanuts at. Other than that, you don't want to know me.

07 Rotterdam Holland: Waiting to play I get bored. A few hours to wait until we hit. The wait makes me crazy. Finally we get to go and it's a relief. Been walking around the outside the club for what seems to be forever. Nothing to look at. Blank faced people. Another show, it could be anywhere. They don't come to the show for the same reasons that I do. I don't connect with them because I know the truth. I know how fucked up I am. I feel the cage. I wanted to wound them. Afterwards I walked around and looked for food. I sat in some cheap lit place and stared at a table full of people until they looked at the floor. I don't know whether dragging my life through these cities is the cure or the problem. It's the process of examination. It destroys me and I know the truth so I don't care.

08 Brussels Belgium: I will not lower myself to lust anymore. I don't want to love anyone. I don't even want to fuck anyone anymore. I don't want to kill them. I don't want to know them either. I don't think there is a more honorable way to go. All the talk is just time wasting. I was thinking about it on the way to this city. The jazzmen knew. That's why their music killed them. They went deep inside and explored and the truth that they pulled out killed them. Ate them alive, destroyed them piece by piece. I was thinking about the weight of this and then the non-weight of trying to talk to a woman and how the sound of the horn is more beautiful than a woman could ever be and maybe that's why those guys played the damn thing in the first place. Where they got to was a better place. It was so good that it killed them.

09 Paris France: I'm looking through the skylight of the bus as traffic on both sides roars by. The moon is almost full. Miles is playing on the stereo. I think of all the greats that saw Paris at night. I think of Monk and Coltrane, Art Blakey, Parker, Miller. I wonder what made Miller stay here for so many years. I don't know the people. The ones that came to the show tonight make me wonder why they bothered showing up. It's hard to know where others get off. After the show the backstage was filled with people that I didn't know so I came out here to be with the night. There was an old man sitting in the park near the venue today. He watched a young couple walk by and he called them over. They came and he gave them a piece of plastic jewelry. At first they didn't want to take it but the man insisted and they finally did. He smiled and waved at them until they crossed the street and then he looked down at his feet and shook his head. I wonder if he saw himself in the young man's eyes. Maybe he had taken a walk with a young girl on the very same path decades ago.

10 Amsterdam Holland: I'm sitting in the basement of the Paradiso. I look over to the corner and can remember seeing D. Boon standing there from when I played here in February 1983. I walked along the streets here this morning. I looked at the girls and they looked good but I don't lower myself to common lust anymore. We were here at this club a few months ago. I wonder if anyone will show up. We woke up in the parking lot of the club again like we have been doing for the last several days. I walked into the city and tried to think straight but was in such a bad mood from the dreams that I had that all I could do was trip. I have found a good way to deal with the loneliness that always follows me on the roads through these cities year after year. I knew I would come to some kind of answer and in the past I had thought I already had but it was not true. I always thought the answer was in some kind of hardlined tough guy bullshit but I have found that not to be true for me. I now see it as a relief of sorts. When I let it go a little, it lets me go a little and so I get to breathe a little easier. I don't have to thicken my outer shell as much as I have to understand myself better. Some people are not going to fit into the world as others do. There's nothing wrong with this as long as you can deal with it if this happens to be your reality. I know it's mine. It took my friend dying to see what really being alone in the world is all about. You don't know loneliness unless you're around a lot of people. You can pass them in a hallway or stand with them on the bus and you'll feel it. People are the root of loneliness. When I am by myself for long periods of time I feel better about people than when I spend long periods of time amongst them. I know what I want to do with myself until I die and it took me a while to find it out and it doesn't involve me dealing closely with many people. I have to re-learn all the things I've taught myself and I have to re-evaluate all the things I've seen. It will take me a long time to learn how to not slow myself down. Other's expectations will kill you and waste your time every time. You have to learn to fly alone if you want to get a lot of things done.

12 Florence Italy: Shit doesn't work and you know you must be in Italy. Didn't see much of the city, didn't want to. Something about this country pisses me off. Maybe because no one ever seems to have their shit together. They get mad if you get mad at that fact. For me I don't care. I'm good at lying awake in that bunk compartment re-living death trips over and over. Making up bullshit conversations with women that don't exist. Thinking of ways to try to fool myself into wanting to live. I like it in there in that hole, that dark box. I don't have to see anyone and I can breathe easy. I have become an enemy of language. When people talk to me I hate them for using the language that brings me pain. I don't want to talk. I want to get away from anyone who wants to know me. When someone tries to talk to me I only feel the emptiness of the language, the desperation of words. The hunger of the need to communicate. I know my truth in that I know I'll never be able to say anything back to them that isn't coming from the dark room that is my mind. All I know is horror and ugliness. I'd rather keep most of it to myself. It's like diving on hand grenades. I went out earlier and tried talking to the guy selling the horrible bootleg shirts outside the show. It was a great conversation. I told him he was a fucking thief. He smiled and shrugged. I told him to get the fuck out and he said he couldn't, he already bought the shirts. I told him he was fucking with our trip. He told me that he was sorry but this was his job. I told him I was going to beat the shit out of him. He begged me not to. I took a big pile of shirts and threw them to people in the street. He ran around trying to get them back and I grabbed him and wouldn't let him take them away from people. I told him to look and see how happy we were making people by giving them free shirts. There was really nothing I could do to persuade this guy to leave and I really didn't hate him, he seemed like too nice a guy to get mad at. In the end I don't really give a fuck but the shirts are so bad. I feel sorry for anyone who bought one of them.

13 Fribourg Switzerland: They are drunk against the Alps. They stand complacently against the clear blue sky. I feel nothing. I sit in the room and look out the window and wait to play. Dead time. The opening band is playing and I'm waiting through dead time to get to play. I'm hoping the music will somehow cure me of the pain that keeps my eyes to the floor and makes me so fucked up. I feel far away from everything. Nothing reaches me. I try all the normal things to get myself out of the haze but nothing works. I am an experiment. I no longer feel like I'm part of life. I am walking along beside it. I wonder if they can tell that I'm half dead. Finally we play. They watch and talk and it all seems to bore them and then you realize that they can't identify with any of it because they don't come from a polluted crime ridden land where paranoia is the landscape. It's not America that I'm speaking about. It's my mind. They have no clue. I am a different species and that makes it alright because for the evening they can hang out with an alien.

15 Sheffield England: Fucked up buildings. Every other block looks like it just got shelled. The people on the street look depressed and mutated. If I lived here I would get the fuck out or start killing people. All the restaurants smell like grease. The air stinks. The bands suck. The place is like a leech. It drains me every second I stand here. The shows at night are the only release. Waiting for them to happen is the drag. Nothing works, it's always fucked up every year. Like a sucker I keep returning to test myself against this bullshit machine. I can't help but hate all the shit around me. If I don't hate it then it gets too close to me and I go down. Fuck this slump backed shit. Fuck this leeching bullshit polite backstabbing population. I'll ignore it and play right through the fuckers. You can't let them grind you down. They won't care if you die in right front of them. If you're looking for someone to care about you then get the fuck out of music. When you let that idea go then it lets you go and you can really let it rip. I see no other way to go.

16 Newcastle England: The Beastie Boys soundcheck inside. I am in a cold trailer out back. I wish there was something on my mind. I hate the times when the brain is cold and dead. I avoided walking around the city. I don't need my mind polluted. There's nothing that I want to see in this city at all except the stage. I don't want to meet any of its inhabitants and I don't want to talk to anyone if I don't have to. I just remain inert until playing time. It's the only time that matters these days. I am going to learn to live with less and less as the years go on. I want nothing to hang onto me. I want no one to hang onto me. I think that's the thing that keeps people fucked up all the time. I want to empty myself of all filler.

17 Glasgow Scotland: I went from the bus to the venue. I have not seen any of Scotland. I don't want to know anything about it. I just want to play and leave. The poison thought is that I will be playing several more shows this year. If I look at the schedule it will kill me. So many nights of getting ripped apart by the music. The music never misses ever. It will always try to kill you. The music is pure and it exposes all that isn't in you. The music takes me out every night and beats the shit out of me. Trying to help me out. I know what there is for me now. I can't fight the music. I was fighting it without realizing it. Music is one thing that never cares about your bullshit. It will beat the shit out of you with your own arms if you lie to it. Doesn't matter what city it is. If you look too much at the scenery, it will ruin your day. Too many moving scenes over the years make the mind insane. I can't talk. I can no longer speak in a language that I can use to talk to people with. I fake it and use their language instead. It makes me lonely for other planets, other deserts. Sometimes I'd rather just howl.

18 Birmingham England: Couldn't sleep last night because I was too busy planning how I'll kill myself very soon. Spent the morning in the dark box not knowing that we were parked in the hotel lot. I Thought of a girl while still in half sleep. I think I was begging her to stay with me. All my money disappeared from my pants pockets tonight backstage. Lost, stolen, I don't know. I am choking inside myself. I don't exist. I breathe. I went and signed bullshit in a record store today. Everywhere I went I was asked to sign shit. I had to talk to employees in record stores while I looked at records, they wouldn't stop talking and I wanted them to die because all I wanted to do was look at the fucking records. They have no idea who they're talking to. They don't know that I'm not listening, that I'm screaming inside at them to leave me the fuck alone. They can't smell the animal that's standing next to them. I don't want to know these people who take my money and fill the world with talk. I'm sitting in the hallway of the hotel. The man in the room across from my feet is vomiting violently. I can hear him as he lets go over and over. No more autographs, no more contact. They take money from me, they should stay away. The shithead couple that got backstage and wasted my time. The man has no idea how close he came to getting maimed. Fuck this country and all the begging pathetic little thieves who occupy it. I am filled with horror and don't want to know anyone.

19 Manchester England: Don't hold onto time. Just let it go. Don't even look back unless you want to scare the shit out of yourself. I don't look back over the calendar these days. I don't want to remember night after night. I was there and that's good enough for now. Time will kill you. Standing next to the bus in a gas station on some highway on the way out of Manchester feels good. No one knows where I am and those who do don't care. I hope my brain doesn't leak out of my head. Manchester was a stage to play on and a small fucked up room to wait in. That's all I know. I woke up in the parking lot and didn't ask. I don't want to know anything about England. I could count how many times I've been to this country but I won't. I don't want to let time own me more than it does already. We drive tonight and wake up in London. After that we go back to America. It's all the same to me. I play and it doesn't matter where anymore. If you want it to matter then wake me up, get me out of this suffocation mind. It has all run together and no one touches me. I lie in that bunk and make up stories about suicide and mixing with the earthlings that talk to me. It's possible to be dead and still be filled with horror. This is what I have found.

20 London England: I don't know how long we were out here in Europe. Doesn't matter. We leave London tomorrow. Just back from the only food place open around here. Men staggering drunk. Three ugly limey shit bags try to talk up a whore in front of the kebab place. A man who can barely stand up urinates in a doorway. The show was a lot of steam and sweat. I don't know if it was any good. I gave it all I had. Did interviews today. Don't remember what I said. It doesn't matter. I get up in a few hours to go to the airport to fly to New York where I will have my only day off. I have nothing on my mind. Back sore, elbow smashed, face a mess. Stressed out and a long string of lit boxes are just up the road. Bury me.

21 New York City: It seems like I have a lot of friends in this city. Every block or so someone comes running up to talk to me. It's scary. I walked the streets for hours looking at the people. I wish I could share the city with someone. I see people walking together and I wonder what they're talking about, what they're thinking. I wish I knew someone here, someone to make the city seem smaller and more understandable. It doesn't matter does it? Tomorrow I'll be in an office a few blocks from this insecticide smelling room talking to strangers on the phone about bullshit so it really doesn't matter about this fucking city and the size of it and finding someone to share it with.

24 Los Angeles CA: This place is so dead except for the murderers. Whores on the corners, pigs everywhere. Burned out buildings. Piles of rubble. Men working in the hulls of huge structures with smoke marks all over. Friend in the hospital. The city is killing another one. My room smells of death. I can smell him in the closet. I can smell the blood. I can smell the brains. I leave soon. This city starves me for real life. It's a heartbreaker and all the inhabitants will die horrible deaths. I will not be one of them. I am a road man and get out whenever I can. You stand around here long enough and you'll get murder one done to you. Believe me, they're all scum.

26 Houston TX: I wouldn't want to die here, live here or anything else. Texas has always been one of those places that I'm glad to leave. I remember all the fights I've been in here, the heat and the bullshit. The redneck motherfuckers and the pigs telling us to take our van and get the hell out of town. Desert sprawl. I don't see how they do it year after year. Where the hell can you go? I wonder what someone from here would think of a place like Chicago. Instore. They want you to sign this thing and then stand still for the picture. I do it and I feel like I want to crawl away. If they knew me they would never come as close as they do.

27 Dallas TX: A lot of people look and talk. The heat is something you can see and touch, the heat is so much a part of things here that it has its own phone number and tax bracket. I find a way to look through them and sign pieces of paper. I mutter and try to disappear. The more they like me the more I want to break things. I hung out with a girl afterwards and it was no good, I was still locked up inside myself. It was good to leave. I wonder if there's a way to get though life without hating it all the time.

28 Austin TX: I'm talking to Selby on the phone long distance. He's in the hospital. I listen to his voice, it sounds far away and tired and beat. It's hard to take. He plays it off like it's nothing and asks if there's an opening in the band for a trumpet player. I think of the one partially collapsed lung he's breathing out of and it hurts. I want to give him one of mine. I can tell how hard it is for him to talk. Every word seems like an effort. I am getting upset having to stand in this abandoned strip mall and listen to this fading voice. I start crying while talking to him. A guy is standing next to me trying to get my attention so I can sign some picture. He and his friend both have cameras and they're taking pictures of me on the phone. I want to beat the shit out of these guys. I tell Selby that I have to go to soundcheck and that I'll call him tomorrow. I get off the phone and they're on me. I want to tell them that I was just on the phone with someone close to me and ask them how could they stand around me like that and can't they get lives of their own? Instead I just sign the fucking pieces of paper and stand for photographs. Later on the show proves to be one of the hottest onstage temps that I have ever dealt with. The Butthole Surfers come out and play with us, it's amazing. After the show I have to hide from the people because they want to talk and I want to kill. Gibby wants to have a boxing match with me for charity. He needs three years to train and he says he knows he'll take me out because he has an eighty inch reach on me. I listen and laugh and wish Joe could be here listening and laughing too. We get on the bus and leave.

29 Oklahoma City OK: Tonight was definitely a rock experience. A girl got onstage and we were making out like it was some movie. The whole gig was like a movie. A ninety minute MTV video. People all over the stage, flying through the air. It was hard to get any playing done because it was just all I could do to keep out of the way of the people running into me. So many nights now turn into the mere execution of the set list because of the amount of people getting in the way of the band. They really have no idea how much it fucks us up. It's the worst thing to take a night out of your life. A night you'll never get back and have to throw it away because people won't let you go all the way. I don't think they have any idea what it's like to walk off stage and feel totally ripped off. They wouldn't ever think that the band might feel ripped off for not getting to play hard. I'm not going to stand up there like some asshole telling them what and what not to do. I didn't get into this shit to be a cop. There were people all over the place in the parking lot when we pulled in for soundcheck and it went from there. After the show some young teenage girl was hitting on me enough times to where I had to walk away and stand on the other side of the bus. I think she may have struck a deal for the exchange of fluids with another member of the band. Of course this could all be a bunch of smoke. I mean I don't know for sure and at the end of the day who gives a fuck? I don't see what it is about bands that make people who have lives of their own stand around in a parking lot and stare nervously at you for half an hour and then go home.

30 Columbia MO: Everyone makes me crazy and mad. They more they talk, the more I get twisted inside. I sit by myself and they keep coming up with words. I wish I wasn't so fucked up so I could talk to them but I'm fucked up and I can't talk to them. I play an hour later and I don't know how it is for them. I know that they can't be getting the same thing that we get. If they did, they wouldn't get on stage and fuck us up. After the show I'm sitting in a place eating and a woman sits down and tells me that she likes what I do but the only thing she didn't like was what I said about pigs. She's a pig herself and she says that she's an individual. I tell the pig cunt that when she puts a uniform on that she loses all individuality. I told her that I party down when I hear that a pig has gotten wasted. I hope she goes out and gets shot in the knees by some low rent motherfucker who laughs in her face. She really thought that she was a human being. I don't know how they brainwash these shitheads into being so self righteous about being a bag of shit that should be taken out and shot in the face. Fuck these people. You never know when they are pigs in disguise. Fuck you, you stupid pig bitch. I hope you get Magic Johnson disease and die in some ward. I wonder how long I have left with this shit.

July

01 ST Louis MO: I had sex with a girl in the club shower. It was good. Then we played. I think we played well. It's hard to tell when they don't let you play as hard as you can. They get onstage and they fuck your shit up. We finished the show and I sat and waited for them to leave. It was hard as usual to deal with them after the show. I can't talk and they just make me mad. After they left me and the girl went back into the bathroom and had sex again. It was good again. She said that she was sorry that my friend had passed away. I told her that he didn't pass away, he was murdered. Whatever. The flies ate the blood anyway. I went to the back door to get to the bus and saw all these people waiting by the door of the bus. I pulled back in and snuck around to the front of the club and the bus picked me up and we got out of there. I don't know what they get out of the music. I think about it more and more seeing how many of them get onstage and stomp on people's heads. Now I'm vacant and waiting for sleep to take me out. The sex get off was mutual. I had to wipe my cum off the floor so no one else would slip when they came in. Another page of life has been ripped out of the book.

02 Lawrence KS: A girl got raped at the show tonight. She was taken into one of the toilets and raped and had cigarettes put out on her flesh. She does not know whether she will press charges or not. In bullshit land I woke up in the bus and was told to go to a room in a hotel and do interviews on the phone. I talked and slept in the minutes between calls. I am in the bus and numb from playing as hard as I could. I stink and I don't know how many shows I have done so far on this trip. I worked out in some community gym today with the hayseeds. Ghosts. There were ghosts at the restaurant this morning. I looked out the window to the parking lot where in 1986 the Rat Sound truck was parked waiting for the band to eat a late meal. Joe and I sat in cab and played Mississippi Fred McDowell and waited for them. I looked at the place where the truck had been and thought back to a few weeks ago when I saw the Rat truck in the back of a hall I was doing a talking show at. I looked into the cab and looked at the big fucked up seat and remembered all the times in 1986 that Joe and I sat in there and drove down the road. So many thousands of miles we drove together in that truck. So now I don't want to know about their lives. It hurts too much sometimes. I have invented a new kind of loneliness for myself. It is an animal that lives inside me. I must stay away from people because they only make it mad.

03 Omaha NE: When people like us that much I always think it's the prelude for them hating our guts that much as well. Hard to get through the set tonight. People onstage all the time. They wait outside the door of the bus, the dressing room, the side of the stage, they're all over the place. They came early to hang out in the parking lot. I was as nice as I could be. I like these people. I can't help but like them, there's nothing not to like about them. She asks if she can hug me and I tell her that I freak out if people touch me. It's true. I don't like it when they want to touch me like that. I waited in the room for them to go home and go to sleep. I waited for a long time. When I left, they were out there. One had a tape recorder on and read aloud everything I wrote on their ticket stubs and other assorted things. I hate autographs. I hate compliments. They'll never know how fucked up I am. That the only reason I do what I do is because I'm damaged. Still I like them. I get exhausted after playing. They have no idea what the entire day has been like, what the horror dreams of the night before were about. They don't know shit about me. It's a lonely gig.

05 Denver CO: Thin air for us tonight. Hot lights and sweat. I sat in an alley after working out. A few of them came and stared and asked meaningless questions. After that they left as silently as they came. We drive tonight. I am not thinking. I am not knowing. I don't remember how to feel. I thought of nothing all day. I don't remember anything except some panic stricken man on the phone wondering why I didn't know about some interview. My life is bullshit sometimes. We go tonight to Salt Lake City. That's all I know.

06 Salt Lake City UT: Something about this place I don't like. It's the Mormons. Fucked up conservatives. The promoter's boyfriend is one of these pieces of shit. I know that they're both fakes, brainwashed, uncreative and hypocritical. We played our asses off and I don't know what they thought of it and I don't care. I have the intellect of a shark and that's good. I don't want to take all of their bullshit onstage or anywhere else. I have to keep away from their words. I have to leave them all over there so I can get on with the real thing. They talk too much about nothing. I sit outside and I listen to them talk about getting fucked up and how much they are drinking tonight. I can't talk to someone like that. There's nothing we have in common. I don't have any energy to do anything. I get up in a few hours to go talk bullshit to interviewers.

08 Seattle WA: Joe's book came out today. I pulled a copy out of the box here in Seattle. It's great and horrible at the same time. I almost don't want to see it. It's a great book but I would like to be able to give him a copy and show him that he made it happen. It hurts to know that he'll never see it. I sat in the box and read the foreword that I had written for the book on his birthday, April 10. It hurts so much. I looked at the back cover at the two of us looking like we knew everything. Life is so different. I looked at the book and all I could think of was not wanting to live anymore. I can't explain to anyone how hard it's been to live. I feel like I'm going to explode sometimes. I know that everyone feels like that all the time but it's hard to do all this stuff and think of Joe. Tonight it's hard to read his book and laugh at the great stories and realize that he died thinking that he was a failure. I was hoping that this book was going to be the first of many things that we were going to do together to get Joe going. I know he would have been so thrilled to see the book. He would have wanted to send it to people and he would have gotten great mail and he would see that he could do many things he didn't think possible. I promised him that I would publish his book and I did it. The show was ok. I talked to the singer from Pearl Jam after the show and he's a really good guy. Saw one of the Soundgarden guys as well, they are good folks. They like to play and they're not into the bullshit. Now I'm in this box with my brain. I miss my friend and it's hard for me to be strong. I guess I'll have to lift more weights and play harder and wear myself out and fall over. End.

09 Portland OR: They never stopped getting on the stage and jumping off. I don't know if the show was good or not. The audience seemed to like it. It was hard to get into it knowing that no one cared about the music —they just cared about getting on stage and jumping off. I guess the music doesn't matter to them like it does to us. It's hard to talk to them after the show because I can't take them seriously at all. We come from such different worlds. She said that I had influenced her whole life and that she had read all of my books and that she knew everything that I thought. She was drunk and kept shaking my hand every few minutes and telling me the same things over and over again. She would get mad at me when I would have nothing to say the third time around the same thing. Finally she told me to fuck off and staggered away. After that I now know that I don't want to know any of these people. I play my guts out and tell the truth and then get told to fuck off. I need that like I need more bills. I'll do my thing and avoid them. I won't be able to go out before shows like I want to. I won't be able to warm up on the sidewalk like I usually do anymore. Things have changed. Next stop is California.

11 Sacramento CA: The pigs shut the PA off a few songs from the end of the set. Too bad the place was near the pig station. I was getting shocked for the last few songs. The pigs turned the lights on and freaked people out. It's a drag to be back in the police state of California. I will move from this state if it's the last thing I do. I will not live in this motherfucker. I was careful to stay away from people this time remembering the girl in Portland. They frisked people at the door. I can feel the laid back paranoia with every set of eyes that flash in front of me. I like them but I don't know who's packing. And then there's the pigs. They're all over the place and they know that everyone hates them and they love it and can't wait for one of these punk ass motherfuckers to step out of line so they can give it to them like their fathers did in their nightmares. I made an exit to the side door after the set and nearly got some people hurt because I started a crush of people trying to get to me. I made it outside and some vacant girls tried to fill me with hopeless night almost dead words. Party conversation. I knew I was back in California. The land of the paranoid and almost dead.

12 San Francisco CA: Over a thousand people in the place tonight. Gave them all we had. San Francisco doesn't count on the California is fucked up scale. For some reason this city escapes that. I'm in a hotel room that looks out at the apartment that used to house a girl I was too stuck on. Today I looked at the window and remembered all the great times I had with her there. I am sorry that these things can run too deep. I fall too far and hit the bottom too hard. I thought about her all day today. Nothing I want to admit to. Makes me feel too exposed, like anyone could come by and cut me if they wanted to. All there is to do is lift and play and tell the truth. We go to Santa Clara tomorrow. Who the hell knows what that will be like. I bet the audience looks like the cast of River's Edge. Doing shows in California isn't like being on tour. You just try to get through it without getting any on you.

13 Santa Clara CA: After the show she comes up to tell me how her brother saved her life and died doing so. She was getting raped by a man when her brother stepped in to protect her. His throat was slashed and he died. She wanted to give me his ring that he was going to give me the first chance he got. I sat with the ring and looked at it and listened to this girl talk. It was hard to take. He was only fifteen years old. She feels guilty and the pigs have been asking her all the stupid questions that only pigs can. They're so good at that. I left the hall totally empty. The heat was incredible. I was kicked in the shoulder at one point. I can't understand what they see in what we do. Thinking of them leaves me in a darkness of my own.

14 Santa Cruz CA: It's the place you want to plow under and then move into. Some of the staffers cannot hide their cocaine habits and contradict themselves. An hour at the venue makes me wonder how we're going to pull off the show having to work with people like this. The sun is shining and the palm trees are green and it would be better if it were a slum so these hippies would have to die of all known diseases. The audience. When they weren't fighting, they were making stupid comments and wasting our time. The most shallow people I have ever been in front of. A waste of a night. We played and I don't remember any of it. After the show they wanted to talk to me and I wouldn't do it because I felt like they should go die instead of wasting my time further with their vacant no brain no soul white trash bullshit. Be back soon? Never.

15 Los Angeles CA: Night off in LA. Got here this morning. I don't think it was a good idea for me to come here for this one day. I feel weak being off the road. It takes so much compression to get through the sets that when I'm not near it feeling the pressure so much that I stop feeling it, I fall apart. That's how I am tonight. Sitting here in my room wondering if I'll be able to do it tomorrow night. Knowing that I have to. I was with a woman tonight. I don't think it was a good idea as good as it felt to be with her. It fucked my head up to where all I can feel is the exhaustion that makes my bones ache from the marrow out. All I can feel is the need for my body and mind to get away from this for a little while. I also know it's greatness calling, seeing if I have what it takes. Greatness is seeing if it can weed me out. My room is the siren song calling out to me to stop what I'm doing. Trying to separate the eagles from the birds. To do this you have fly in the thin air. One cannot surround oneself with friends and feel that fake support. It only breeds a false sense of security. The only thing that will get you through this shit is to pull inward and harden and move forward. The less friends and words you exchange, the better. I have at least fifty to sixty more shows to do this year. If I don't do it just right, I'll wind up in the hospital with a nervous breakdown. This is my hardest year yet. A lot of things are going against me. It's greatness calling.

16 Phoenix AZ: In the middle of the first song a guy jumps off stage and smacks his head on the floor and we sit it out and wait for the ambulance. We eventually come out and finish playing. People are being thrown out left and right. I spend some time with a girl at the hotel. Didn't sleep until near six in the morning. Had to get up at eight to leave. I talked to her. I don't know if she knows that I told her things that I never tell anyone, you can do that with strangers. She probably thinks I'm some maniac. I will never see her again so it's just another human experience. All these words they mean nothing, they mean everything. It would have been the time where the brains blow out of the side of the head. She would be sleeping and be awakened by a gunshot in the bathroom. There I'd be, all over the walls. No note just a freak out. She would get treatment. Possible one word notes to leave when you kill yourself: Broken. Mother. Finished. Sorry. No.

17 Santa Barbara CA: The P.A. shorts out and the audience is kept waiting for nearly an hour as the sound team desperately tries to fix the system. People are packed in and pissed off. Finally we play. They never stop getting onstage even after they are asked. They don't care. They don't take the music seriously so I don't think about them at all. I find a place near the drum riser so I can do my thing and get off and not have to think about them. Before the set I hid from them. When they call me dude I want to hide. Nothing's more depressing than the trash that falls out of the mouths of guys who call you dude. I wait a long time to leave after the show so I can leave without having to sign autographs. They are in the parking lot waiting. I try to be cool but something comes over me and all I can do is run through them to a waiting car. They must think I am a total asshole. I think about this as the miles go by the window. I don't want to be like that but at the end of the night there's nothing left to give them and they'll never understand.

18 Tijuana Mexico: Knocked to the floor in the second song. Smacked in the head. I remember trying to get up. Everything moved slow and I heard people in the audience telling me to get up. The rest of the night was a balancing act of trying to sing and not puke. I kept it all in. Later on in the set some guy got onstage and tried to tackle me but only knocked me into the drums. My head was ringing all the way through the set. After the set I just sat and waited for them to leave. I had been called dude all day and it made it worse. California is a disease. Due to getting smacked in the head I don't know if anything else happened.

21 Los Angeles CA: Hot onstage. I actually felt pressure tonight. Something about the size of the place and all, I was wondering if we were going to get swallowed up in there. Body Count was in the house. Played hard but I don't know how it went. Dave Navarro came out for the encore jam. What a great guy, good to see him again. Looking forward to getting back on the road. Something about playing in California doesn't seem real to me. So many people, they come out of the cracks, they spill over the edges, they are everywhere. I like them more than they will ever know. I don't know if I'll be able to tell them the way I want to.

23 Anaheim CA: Live shoot for television. I don't remember much of it. Felt like band practice with people standing all the way at the back of the room. Had a good time though. I hid from the autograph guys as best I could but they found me anyway. We leave in a few days for a long time. It was strange being in LA this time around. The place alienates me. Looking forward to getting out to Florida and wherever else we're going this year. Nothing here but loneliness and sorrow. Dried blood and shallow breath.

27 St. Petersburg FL: Outdoor gig. Lights went off a few times. I don't know if they even heard us. They felt so far away, more concerned with beating the shit out of each other than anything else it seemed. I shouldn't be near people after I play. The farther we go the worse it gets for me. Sitting slumped over in a chair smelling the sweat turn to ammonia, catching breath for the first time in two hours. Listening to the ringing roar thundering in both ears, louder in the right. Feeling an immense emptiness. All of a sudden there is a poke in the ribs. A pen is being shoved into my side. Could I sign this piece of paper? I should be put in a cage and rolled out because all I want to do is kill this piece of shit. I can barely get out the words. I sign the paper. The guy looks at it and says "That's all you're going to write?" This is the point where a punch to the throat is the only thing that I can think of doing to help this guy out. Like I said I should be put in a fucking cage and hauled out because I can't deal with these people.

28 Miami FL: The best line all night was the guy who told me that I would be soon out of a job because I told the stage divers to cool it. Some skinhead asshole telling me that I'm going to be out of a job because I want to play music instead of getting out of the way of punkers all night. He should get his own television show. I like Miami. It seems like you could killed here real easy. Haven't been here to play with the band for years. After the show there were record company people with their pictures to sign, some terrified radio guy apologizing for all kinds of shit he isn't responsible for. I was so angry that I could barely make words come out. I said hello a little above a whisper and they took the hint and left. Some people will not give up and will stay there and wait until hell freezes over to meet someone. They came in and got their books signed. I tried to be as nice as I could be. I couldn't wait to leave. I talked to a girl outside the hall for awhile. I don't know her name. Now I'm inside the bus waiting to go to another city and I don't even know which one it is.

29 Gainesville FL: It's hard. It's hard to get the music out when they're stepping all over you. It's hard to make it matter to anyone if you can't make it matter to yourself. No matter where you go they will grab you, shove the mic into your teeth and smack you in the head. Sometimes I hate them. I hate their fucking guts and I can't believe I'm stupid enough to put myself in a situation where I can get picked at like a piece of meat in a field of crows. There's no way I will ever be able to explain myself to them. I now avoid them and their questions and compliments and small talk. It's hard to like them when one of them uses you to climb onstage and knee you in the balls. It's hard to see individuality when one of them swings at your head. The more they compliment the more sick it makes me. I saw them coming after the show. I was in the dark in the back looking at the stars, thinking about how good it was that I decided to let go of the idea that I will ever be close to someone. I was feeling good in my thoughts. I figured after playing over two hours of music that people should leave me alone. I saw them coming and I ran and hid. One guy came after me to tell me every time he saw me and he was in the process of telling me all the times I was on some television show and I asked him to stop talking. I told him that compliments make me want to tear my face off. Near two in the morning and they're still out there knocking on the window. They have no idea how fucked up I am, no idea at all.

30 Pensacola FL: Hottest show I can remember. It was like breathing your own flesh. All I could do was try to stand. I hid from them tonight knowing that I was in no shape to even shake anyone's hand. I woke up in the parking lot of a hotel with interviews starting soon after I walked into the room. I worked out too hard. Losing weight. Nothing but that. Didn't talk to anyone. Came here and played and now I'm leaving. I don't know if the people at the show have any idea what we're about but they seemed to like us ok. I am pounded flat and totally useless.

31 New Orleans LA: They never got off the stage except when we played a real slow one. I don't know if it was respect, reverence or boredom. I don't remember anything about today except waking up and walking into the phone. Interview with some stupid bitch who wanted to know if I hated some rockstar. I think I will have to start doing less interviews. They are getting to me. A guy asked me about Joe today and I told him that I didn't want to talk about him. I think that's good. It does no good to talk about him anymore. I don't want to wear out the memory by talking about him too much. I was thinking about seeing him dead while I was in my black box bunk last night. Thinking about it now it seems too incredible to be real. Just seeing him there like that. Tonight I sang about him. About living in the form of ash in a small plastic box.

I think we go to Tennessee tomorrow. I don't think it matters anymore where I go. I just go. I am unattached and falling forward. Nothing stops me anymore. Not to say that I'm unstoppable, it's just that I have thrown out a lot of my thoughts. What a thought that is.

August

01 Nashville TN: We played and they stepped all over us. What does it matter to play when all that happens is your ass gets knocked around all night? It was a waste of time. I only got to play two songs all night. The rest was just going through the motions of playing, looking out for the guys who have to get onstage every three seconds. Trying to get the words right and trying to find a place where they aren't. That's all that happened all night. Got in a workout that was more meaningful. Next is Minneapolis where there will be some air to breathe and maybe we'll even get to play some. What they don't know, what they'll never know is that they push me away with every word, every autograph, with every handshake I fall further away from them all.

03 Minneapolis MN: Eighteen hundred people in the big room. More than Black Flag ever had in there. I watched the equipment come in and all I could think about was loading the gear into the small room a few years ago. Taking shit from the one hundred and thirty-five in attendance as they got shitfaced. Tonight we played hard and it felt good to be set free from bullshit thought. Throw out thoughts that you don't need, what a great idea, what a time waste eliminating lifesaver. Went to a thing to meet people from BMG. Not my kind of thing. Standing around saying thank you. Thank you, I'm glad you like the way I'm fucked up. I'm not good for much but what I'm good for, I'm really good for and that's all that matters. The rest is just bullshit.

04 Racine WI: Watched some people get the shit beaten out of them as we played. People jumping on other people's heads and then getting hit in the head and then people seeing it and hitting them in the head. Same guys getting on top of everyone and rolling over their heads. I wonder what goes on in the minds of these people. What would you talk about with someone like that. I wonder if they have shit for brains.

05 Grand Rapids MI: We played hard as hell and no one got in our way. It was a good day and a good night so nothing must have happened. In a hotel tonight. I have thrown out so many thoughts in the last few weeks that all I think about is playing and death.

06 Pontiac MI: Played outside to over two thousand people. They were all over the place. He has been waiting for three hours by the gate to talk to me. His father left him when he was five and now he lives down the street and won't return his phone calls. As he tells me this stuff, other people are listening to the conversation. I feel sorry for him and respect his guts. I don't know what to say to him though. Hours later we finally get to play. The only reason I'm in this city at all is to play, the rest means nothing to me. I don't think it's necessary to talk to anyone, shake anyone's hand. Not every fucking person is suited for the ritual bullshit of civilization. Some people just want to play and get on with it and not talk about it. Sharks don't talk about ripping someone's guts out for lunch, they just rip. After the show they wait endlessly outside the tent. I walk outside and tell that I'm not signing shit and it's late. I leave and go to the bus. I hate myself when I have to be like this. At this point it's just survival. I can't give them anymore. There's nothing. What they don't know is that I couldn't talk to someone to save my life. I can't talk to people I know. I don't return phone calls unless it's business. I don't like compliments. I don't think I'm above anyone, that's what makes it so hard to listen to them. There's so much bullshit out there.

07 Cleveland OH: Sometimes I think that I don't have long for this shit. When the music becomes a secondary issue to the bullshit I think it's time to move. Watching the youths beat the shit out of each other. Having to endure the ego mood trips of the bass player, whatever. Tonight was a lost night. Having to watch out for them, it seems incredible to me that I have to look out for them. So it was a night that I will soon forget. We played, so what? I tried to be nice to all the people that were waiting at the bus. All I could do was look at the ground and sign their pieces of paper with silent submission. I hate it when they beat my spirit down like that. They won tonight.

08 Columbus OH: Played as well as I could. The monitors were not so hot. I worked out and went to soundcheck. We sold out the place that Black Flag never could. Nothing happened tonight besides a great storm. I am exhausted and blank. I don't remember what I ate today, what I said, what I did besides the show and the workout. I am boring and hulled out. I miss no one, I think of no one.

09 Pittsburgh PA: It's a shame to have to put up with the bass player's infantile shit night to night. It would be great to haul off and bust this bitch in the face but I can't do that because we have to do the dates. Otherwise it was a good show. It's all I remember of the day. Got here too late to work out so I was on edge before I went on. My head is exploding from a headache. I feel like I got kicked in the head. I played as hard as I could, trying to get the bad blood out of me. Trying to get my mother out of my system, trying to kick my father's bad blood out of my veins. On good nights I get a drop or two out. The rest of the time I hemorrhage and get thanked for it either way.

10 Buffalo NY: Played as well as I could. A lot of people onstage tonight. Somehow they were cool about getting onstage over and over. I don't know why they didn't piss me off like they usually do. After the show some girl tried to pick up on me, not a good start asking me if I was in the opening band. I didn't talk to her much because I didn't want to know a damn thing about her. Some woman told me a few times that her infant loves me. She was amazed that I had not much to say about it. I am amazed at how my face freezes when someone wants to talk to me. The worst is when someone wants to kiss or hug me. I feel like a human stone. Got in a good workout and that makes the day easier to handle. Otherwise nothing happens these days. Tomorrow there is a day off in Canada. I am feeling pretty good about being alive tonight but I don't know why.

12 Toronto Canada: Woke up in a woman's bed after a day off. Back into harness once again, felt strange to be out of the zone for 24 entire hours. Did a small press conference and then went to the venue, to a gym and then back to the venue. Phone interviews with Australia after soundcheck. Short sleep and then got ready to play. Twenty-one hundred tickets sold out show. By the time we went on the walls were sweating. There were no moments when the stage was clear of people. Tonight I tried a different tack. I stood in the middle of them and got kicked around for two hours. Sitting in the bus with no liquid left in my body. Sometimes the days turn into non-events. A day like today leading into a night like tonight where you get up and stagger around until soundcheck and then wander onto the stage, do your trip and wander off again. I stayed inside the venue until they all left. When I emerged from the hall no one was on the streets, it was as if the whole thing never happened.

13 Ottawa Canada: Tonight was like trying to run through water. Every song fought me. I looked into the blank faces of the audience and remembered the last time we played in this town to about one tenth as many people, it was the same. It's like the town that time forgot. After the show I avoided people as well as I could knowing that I wouldn't be able to deal with their questions very well. One guy came up and told me that the fact that one of our CD's is only one track for over seventy minutes is a "spit in the face" to the fans. I told him that spit in his face is a lot different than his CD and would he like to find out about that? He went away. After the show my entire body started to ache from the bottom of my feet up. Now I'm waiting for sleep. Beep.

14 Montreal Canada: Better show than last night. Did interviews most of the day and then went to the gym for a bad workout. Walked the whore filled streets near the venue looking at the ugly women for sale. One looked at me like she thought I wanted to fuck her. I looked at her and tried to imagine sex with her ugly junkie ass. Later on we play. It was good and we gave it everything. After the show I walked around some more and watched the freaks. I know that it's all about death and that's all it's about. Nothing occurs to me at this point. Playing empties me out all the way. Fatigue has set in and I am now a product of all its traits. I'm looking forward to getting back to America. Canada has too many of those long dead punks that still breathe. There's a day off coming soon, night after next. I don't look forward to the days off like I used to. I would just as soon play. Sometimes this is a boring trip I know. The last few days have been dull and have embalmed me.

15 Providence RI: Back in club land again. Nothing works, no food, same old shit. Played this place a year ago or so and the only thing different is that the place has gotten dirtier and more fucked up. Got to the place and went to the gym and then to soundcheck. Mitch Bury showed up so we had a star guest for the evening. Nothing happened that I'm aware of. We played and that was it. I think people liked it. I went into this thing about tough guys and how they aren't tougher than a 9mm bullet in the face. I think I bummed out the skinheads a little but the truth is like that. After the show the same drunk psycho who kept trying to talk to me all through the set kept trying to talk to me and eventually went away which was great because I couldn't figure out for the life of me what was on his mind. After three in the morning we're sitting on the bus and there's still a group of people standing out in the rain. They waved at me to come out and sign their fucking baseball caps. I wouldn't wait in the rain for ten seconds for some fucking guy in a band to sign my anything.

17 Richmond VA: Parts of this city look like a movie set for some old drama. Run down buildings, poor folks, people standing on corners doing nothing, waiting for who the hell knows what to happen. We played, they yelled and got onstage all night like we weren't even there. For the life of me I don't know what they get out of all this. I wish I could hear the music that they hear when we play. Tonight they are pretty lightweight on the soul level and it's hard to take them seriously at all when all they want to do is knock you over while you're trying to play. Finish playing and go back to the bus and await blast off to the next city. Don't want to talk to anyone, don't want to know. It's raining outside tonight. I was born and raised ninety miles north of here, the weather reminds me of a long time ago. I am looking forward to leaving. I'm always looking forward to leaving. I don't think of my room anymore. I used to think of being alone in my room with my records and typewriter but I don't remember what it feels like to be there so it might as well not even exist. That's good for me. The less I have the better. The less I know the less gets in my way when I need to hit it. I don't miss anyone or anything and that makes me a good touring machine and right now that's all I want to be.

18 Philadelphia PA: Got to this city. Woken up by the road manager. Interviews started a few minutes later. Later I left to go to soundcheck. King Sunny Ade was standing out in front of the hotel. I spoke to him briefly. Made my day. Went to the hall and did soundcheck. Was told that I had to go back to the hotel to do more interviews. I'm in here now waiting for the fuckers to call. I don't know why I am so full of rage. All I can think of doing is ripping that hall apart. Interviews have nothing to do with what the music and the death trip are about. Sitting in this fucking room watching a bunch of soft boys on MTV waiting for the world to start. Hours pass and finally we get to play. It was good when they weren't onstage. They were pretty good about it. After the show they were waiting outside. It reminds me how alienated I am from them. Signing autographs is so fucked up, how could you ever be friends with someone who wanted your autograph? Nice enough people but why they need to get something signed is beyond me. I can see meeting someone but that's it. Whatever. Now I'm back in the box. Vacancy is filling my life. The playing was good but that was all besides meeting King Sunny that happened today. Interviews don't count. My mother showed up tonight out of nowhere and it threw me a little but I still pulled off the show.

19 Baltimore MD: Played tonight with the Beastie Boys. L7 opened, they are as boring as ever, at least they're consistent. I don't think we played all that well. We didn't get a soundcheck and it wasn't a great set up with the monitors. I gave it all I had but I don't know. After the set I went outside and talked to people that were leaving because they didn't want to see the Beastie Boys play. I told them that they were missing a good band but they didn't want to see them. Ian showed up to the gig. As always it's good to see him. I wish we could have played better. We drive to New York tonight. I am sitting in the bus and there are people outside knocking on the windows. It never ends. You spend a good portion of the day and night dealing with all these people and they don't know about all the shit that you have been dealing with before they came up to you and they don't know what's going on in your head. Bullets, brains, headshots, horror. They don't know and you can't get mad at them for not knowing but you somehow wish they could read your mind. If I could open up my head and let it all fall on the ground it would make people throw up. There's nowhere to go on this bus where people can't see in and know you're in here except for the bunk you sleep on and the bathroom. I honestly don't see why anyone would want to meet me. I wouldn't want to know me.

20 New York NY: Did interviews all day right up until soundcheck. First thing was talking to Gilbert Gottfried the comedian for some television show that I have forgotten. After that was talking to a bunch of young people about drugs and stuff for PBS, that was great to be around positive people like that. Then an interview with the television show that shot the show tonight. After that there was an interview with Harper's. Then soundcheck and then time to get ready to play. The day went away. Playing was great until the bass player decided something was wrong and pulled an attitude and walked off stage one song before the set was over. It would be so cool to punch him out but then there would be no bass player for the rest of the tour. We are held captive by this child. I was hoping to be able to meet a girl but I never got out of the dressing room, I can't go out there without having to talk to all kinds of people. I hung out with Alan Vega and that was cool. Now the show is over and I just got back to the box that smells like bug spray. My body is full of pain and I am five pounds lighter than I was last week. I can feel my body feeding on itself. I felt bad on the cab ride back here. Tomorrow is more press and a gig.

21 Asbury Park NJ: Did a photo shoot for Harper's and then went to the gig. Got there late and made soundcheck. Asbury Park NJ is a hard place. The club is a depressing dive, don't know how the evening will go. The boardwalk is empty with only the occasional jogger to break up the lack of humans. I got stomped on, kicked and whacked around by people getting onstage. Managed to play anyway. I don't remember waking up this morning. I have started to think of women again. No one in particular. It doesn't matter anymore. I am thrown into the fabric of the road and I am not anyone that anyone will ever know. When I think of other people I know that I'm from another world. I'm too tired to think of anything to write. We played and we were good and I'm alone as always and sometimes it's hard to take. My body is in pain, I am still sitting crooked from the kick in the ribs I got from one of the people who claims to like us so much, yea right.

22 Trenton NJ: I got kicked in the mouth and spat blood on the stage for a few songs. Otherwise it was a good show. I watched some guy walk on people's heads until I told him to stop. He did. Did some thinking today, most of the shit that occupies my mind space is dragging me down. Nothing is on my mind at all now. We play the same place tomorrow night and then I'm off to the UK. I'm looking forward to walking the streets of London by myself and getting some time to think. It will be good to get out of America for awhile. Now in the box waiting for sleep to set in. Had some meaningless sex a few hours ago. Learned a good lesson there. It's not worth it. The need for female companionship that I was feeling last night is gone. I know now that it's all in my head. It's like I've been saying in that song Almost Real. People need to make life seem large at times just to survive it at all. We use lies and dramas to keep distracted from the fact that life itself is without moral or meaning. The very act of sex itself makes me see that. I don't know maybe it was just a bad night.

23 Trenton NJ: I am looking forward to getting onstage tonight. I am because I am curious to see if I will be able to do it. I feel so shitty right now I don't know how I'll be. I am exhausted. I don't know whether it's the fact that it's the last show or that I'm beat. I'll feel better when I get to the hall and smell that fucked up club smell. Later: I got to the place and that was all I needed. We were going to be filmed for a show to be televised in Spain and Portugal. The opening band was so bad that it got me in a great mood to play. I was sweating before I was on. Played hard and that's all there was to it. Spat blood most of the night from getting hit in the mouth last night. After the set I walked around the side of the club so I wouldn't have to go through the crowd. Sat in the backstage room and sweated into the carpet. Two sold out nights in Trenton. Body was wracked after show. A few days off now. Hoping to get some rest in the next few days.

26 London UK: Tonight was a talking show. Six hundred people sold out. All day long was interviews. I managed to get away from them for awhile and went to a local gym and got a good workout in. Before I knew it I was at the venue nearly falling asleep with little time before I went on. I did well. Went for about two hours, didn't notice. I emptied myself out and left the venue depressed and blurred. I don't know if I can do these shows anymore for a while, they get to me. I walked around the streets for a while after trying to get something of myself back. People passed in cars and told me it was a bloody good show. The air is nice out tonight and I would be out there walking still if I wasn't so depressed and tired. Tonight's show ripped a hole in me. Another night on the trail.

28 London UK: Interviews all day. Taxi cabs, people stopping me in stores for photographs. Shitty club PA and monitor system. Stinking back room with fucked up food, oh yeah I forgot we're in England. Played with jet lag pounding my legs. Did the best I could while people rolled past me. Don't know what they thought of us. After show were leg cramps and people's cigarette smoke, no room to move around and a bunch of people that I don't know in my face. Depression set in as I walked around the streets before soundcheck. Thinking about Joe too much these days. It gets to me. I miss him so much sometimes, it's unbearable. I never think about him while I'm playing so that's a temporary escape. I don't know what to write, I don't know what I feel right now. So many things have fallen out of my brain. The cities win always. I am blank and beyond loneliness, I am full of horror and it keeps me on my own planet.

29 Reading UK: Reading Festival 1992. We drove past hundreds of people who were doing their best to look fucked up and filthy. It looked like they had rubbed shit into their hair. We got to the compound and waited for our passes. The press bullshit never stops, Started as soon as I got my pass. Talked to the shithead from Kerrang and he has no idea how close he came to getting smacked like a bitch right in the teeth. He's asking me all this shit about now that I'm a big rockstar he reckons all of our new stuff will suck. If I was going to interview someone, the last thing I would do is try to get on the guy's nerves. I got suckered into a tent with a bunch of people who wanted autographs. I stood behind a table like a propped up asshole and signed pictures like a human xerox machine. All I could think of was getting on with the gig. Finally I got to get ready and hit stage. Played as hard as I could. Sure was a lot of people, about thirty-forty thousand. As far out as I could see there were people waving. After the set I had to do some photos and then I got the fuck out of there. I was amazed at how hard it was to do the autograph thing, it was unbearable. The people were cool and all but I can't stand making people stand in line to meet me and get their little thing signed, it makes me feel like such an asshole. I'm out of here.

September

11 Brisbane Australia: Brisbane is always a taste of the waste. On jet lag I was sleeping up until an hour before the show. I woke up in a dark room with the show yet to do. When we got there, it seemed unreal. Like this whole evening had been going on while I was asleep. I looked out at the other band and watched the stage divers push them around, it looked like the band didn't give a fuck about it either way. The people at the show were either beating the shit out of each other or beating up the bouncers or throwing up or drinking. Tonight was no exception. Not as many fights as last time. There was about fifteen hundred in there tonight, I think they all got on stage at least once. I played a little. I spent most of the time at the back of the stage keeping out of their way. What utter bullshit, having to stay out of their way. I don't care about them because they don't care about the music. So we played and I stayed in the kitchen until nearly three a.m. so I wouldn't have to meet and speak with drunks, they always make me mad with their slurred speech and bullshit talk. Finally we leave the kitchen area and I look on the floor of the hall. It's covered in beer cans. The green Victoria Bitter can was all over the place. Over two thousand sold tonight. One girl told me that she stocked 2400 cans herself earlier in the day. I'm glad to be by myself right now. I hope I don't dream tonight, the moon is full and it's shining down upon the water. I wish someone knew me.

12 Burleigh Heads Australia: Tonight was pretty much like last night but without the belligerence factor. Instead it was the annoying youth must get on stage all the time thing. We played well and I got off, but when I know the music isn't being taken seriously then I start getting annoyed with how lightweight people can be. Someone will think nothing of getting in your way all night and then expect you to be nice to them when they ask you a million questions. I stood outside hours before the show and watched the sun set against the Pacific Ocean and waited for the show to start. For several hours I was in the club, watched videos until too many people would notice me then I would have to move locations. That's how it is these days. I have to keep moving every few minutes otherwise I have to answer all these questions and I'm tired of answering, answering, answering. It's the truth. It's not "part of the job" either. So I had to just sit in the small room backstage and wait. Can't go anywhere around the venue. They get into back slapping here. People come up from behind you and slap you on the back and start in with the questions, startles the shit out of me. I wiped my shorts on some guys that chose to sit on the stage. I don't think they liked my sweat being scrubbed into their heads, they got off stage. If only they knew how heavy this trip is, but they'll never know because they're too busy with the bullshit. Life will pass them by like it passed their fathers and mothers by.

13 Sydney Australia: About three thousand people in a hall where you could see your breath. We were the last of four bands. I played hard as hell. I watched bouncers cheap shot young people that were giving them no resistance whatsoever. Drunk people backstage afterwards. Some guy back there with his compliment machine coming out of his mouth. I always wonder how they get back there. I think you should never ask for autographs backstage. If you somehow get back there, you should leave the bands alone, at least leave me alone. They have no idea where you're coming from, they never will. I left as soon as I could. Now I'm back in the box. Every part of my body is sore. It feels like someone has been kicking my legs all night. Sometimes this happens, my body gets sore from head to toe. Tomorrow is a day off. I went and found food after the show. The man behind the counter at the all night place had a blue dot tattooed on the tip of his nose. As I ate I wondered what the blue dot was all about. I thought that maybe in his younger days he had it on there so people would say, "Hey you've got a blue dot on your nose," and he could punch them out for laughs, you never know, Australians are pretty hard bastards. I sat on the edge of the bed for awhile trying to understand what my problem is. Sometimes I feel so lonely after shows that I get desperate but at the same time I am so relieved to be alone. I am afraid that I would freak someone out if they got too close. I wonder if you could shoot enough people to make the horror stop. If you could find a space that was large enough to where you could get all the bullshit out of your mind. All the sounds of traffic and screams and television static. What if you could live on the moon?

15 Canberra Australia: Today we drove from Sydney, we saw kanga-roos and desert. The air is so clear here. I thought about Joe and what he might think of this scene as it flew by the window. Another night of them getting onstage all the time and me getting out of their way instead of playing as hard as I could. We played well anyway. After a show like this one I will not talk to them, I will not sign anything. I take it personally that they will not let me play hard. They don't respect the music so I can't respect them, end of thought on that. Too bad though because last time we played here I remember it being a lot better in that respect. Maybe I take this too seriously, I don't think so. Life is so short, why fuck around. Charlie Parker, Coltrane, Miles, Monk, Hendrix, they didn't fuck around, I must aspire to that weight at all times. Tomorrow is a day off. I go to Melbourne to do press. I see things differently now. Press doesn't matter, the punters and what they think doesn't matter, the only thing that matters is the music. The rest is just ego and entertainment. I think you can do a lot more if you sidestep the ego trips and the entertainment bullshit factor. The music is enough, if it's not then you're in the wrong business.

17 Melbourne Australia: It was another night of them getting onstage and the set not getting very intense. I have bruises on my hand from hitting a guy in his face. I watched some guys beat another guy, about four on one. I don't understand the need for them to antagonize the band. I thought that they would have come for the music. I told them a few things. I told them that I wished it was one of them that got killed and not my friend and I told them that I'm not impressed by how lame they are. I'm not. Fuck these people and their lightweight bullshit. I'm tired of dealing with them. The music doesn't mean anything to them so they get onstage and waste my time, I can't be expected to take them seriously at all. Too bad that the music isn't enough for them and they have to bring their bullshit with them to my world. We should put a fence up and let them deal with themselves. I'm not part of them and they're not part of me. I don't want to know about their drunk pathetic lives. I don't know them and I don't want to touch them and I don't care about them. Perhaps it's time for me to stop being around people. I guess I'm frustrated at how weak people are. I think that people should have more soul. I can't see how they settle for so little. I don't like feeling like this. I don't like being mad at these people. I don't want to carry around this negativity. I don't know how to deal with people anymore. I can't understand them at all. I come from a different planet. No relation whatsoever. Alien blues is what I play.

18 Melbourne Australia: Same shit as last night but the place was different and they couldn't get onstage as easily so it was a good show. Someone still tried to fuck it up. A few songs into the set I started coughing and I thought that I had something in my throat. I looked into the front row and a lot of the people were coughing as well as the bouncers. Something about the air seemed strange. All at once it hit me that someone had sprayed mace in the air. I told the fuckers that they had their chance and they blew it, they should have killed me last year. Fuck you, you didn't stop me. I coughed and kept on playing. My eyes were burning and it was hard to keep my breath but I kept playing. Later on in the set it was sprayed again but a little stronger but I concentrated on the music and I kept playing. After the set was over I left through the back and was barely recognized. I didn't want to stick around. I can't talk to any of them. Any one of them could have been the one that had the mace. Having to deal with any of them would have been a weakening experience. The only thing that would have made sense would have been to smack the shit out of the first one who said shit. You always lose when you touch them, when you punch them, when you push them out of your way when you're trying to play, you always lose. Their weakness beats your strength every time. Best thing to do is leave and get back on the trail and move out. They aren't individuals to me. When a few get onstage all night and turn the whole thing into a lightweight pose out and spray mace then all of them are those people. I can't separate. It's them and me. Fuck you all, you should have killed me last year you human pieces of shit. I would like to get Sonic Youth, Nirvana, get all those bands on one gig and open for them and run their shit up the flag pole. I guess I'm like Mike Tyson, I guess nothing blows me off a fucking stage, I guess I'm pretty unstoppable when it comes to this shit. Fuck you. I'll be at that gig tomorrow bitch.

19 Melbourne Australia: No mace today. We played an early show. I was amazed at how well behaved the audience was. Sometimes I think they know the exact time to get onstage and fuck me up. It's always at the one point where the vocal stands alone and I have to be careful, like in Blues Jam where there's that part where it's just me and I want to get it good, right then was when the guy got onstage and stomped on my foot. Perfect. Flowers in the dressing room with a card that had a girl's name and address and the words "Try me" on it. I left them in there. Someone left flowers in the lobby and called me twice to ask me what I thought about that fact. I told her to leave me alone. I don't think that she got it at first but I straightened her right out. I talked to the man in the lobby and he told me that all evening he's been kicking people out of the lobby who were looking for me. When I walked in there was some guy in there waiting for me and I got rid of him by the elevator. I don't know what it is with these people. I must not like myself very much because I can't see why anyone would go to the trouble to bother with flowers and all the other bullshit. That's all it is to me. I don't want to know anyone. I just want to play the music and then crawl away. I don't think that anyone in a band has to be a nice guy. If I was a nice guy then I wouldn't be playing the way I do. Fuck it, it's not worth going into. I would like to go out tonight for a walk but I don't want to because I don't know who might be outside waiting for me. I don't want to hurt any of them, I don't want to do the time. Some people are better left alone. I sat in here tonight and tried to figure out why it makes me so mad when people give me things like flowers. It makes me lose my temper. Shows of gratitude anger me and I don't know why. Something fucked up about me, pick a number and stand in line. People like me don't have friends, believe it.

20 Hobart Australia: As we were starting the set, Sim looked over at me and said that he was reminded of Budapest. He was right. Strange vibe in this place, you can tell that they don't get much music here, not stuff like us at least. They were drunk but ok. We played pretty good. I had a good time playing, it would have been better without the barrier in the way but still it was ok. I barely remember getting here in the early afternoon. We leave in a few hours on an early flight to Adelaide, one hell of a depressing place to play. I hear that bands avoid the place big time these days. I remember the first time we played there. The first thing I thought as we were into the first few minutes was that we were going to have to endure two nights at the same venue. The bouncers had lead pipes and were fucked, but then again so were the people at the show. The air is cold and clear tonight. On the way in to the box I was reminded of a night on the road with Black Flag. It was 1983 and we had no place to go. We were driving to a town in Germany called Osnabruk where the owner of the place we played a few days before told us that we were welcome to stay there any time we wanted. We went there to see if she was going to make good on her offer. I remember sitting in the back of the cold van with a stash of yogurt and bread and cheese that I was keeping and trying not to eat too quickly because I couldn't be sure when we were going to eat again. We were playing a tape of the Velvet Underground and it was depressing in that van with the cold air and the headlights and all the miles to go and not knowing if we had any place to go and knowing that we didn't have much money and just sitting there knowing it, feeling like a piece of old shit. These people can't tell me anything at this point that can make me feel bad about myself. I was good tonight, I kept my hands to myself and when I did deal with them I was cool. One for me.

21 Adelaide Australia: For some reason they like us here. Last time we were here we played two nights and no one showed up and this time we sold this big place out completely. Go figure. It was uphill for me. I just stayed out of their way all night. People seemed to get off on what we were doing, or trying to do. A band called The Mark of Cain went on before us, they were great. I was distracted by having to look out for people all night. On the good nights I get to go into my own world and play from in there and play my guts out. Other nights aren't as good and all it amounts to is getting through the set as best you can and not get hit in the head. I am alone in the box and am glad. The questions wear me out. I had to wait for a while to get out of the hall tonight. It was question and autograph time until I went and hid in the backroom. After a while I hate the sound of my voice. I hate having to explain myself to people all the time. I'm wearing out piece by piece. I keep writing so perhaps I will have some kind of map to use to re-trace the steps if I ever get time to go back and pick up the pieces that are scattered on the side of the highway. Blank.

22 Perth Australia: All night long they were onstage and who gives a fuck about the music besides us? At some point I apparently pissed off the bouncers by taking a kid away from them and not letting them beat the shit out of him. I told the kid to jump off stage because the bouncers wanted to beat him up and he took the tip and did but then the bouncers went into the crowd and beat the shit out of him anyway. The opening band's singer was saying shit like "The music is black and that's the way it's going to stay", or "Our clothes are black and that's the way they're going to stay." Something like that and then they would plunge right into another Metallica sounding song. Of all the bands in the world why would you want to be like them? It was a bad scene all night. I didn't get off at all. All I did was try to get through the set and get the fuck out of there. After the show, the bouncer that was pointing at me during the set came back and got in the promoter's face. Fuck all of these people. It's not worth it, it's not worth trying to play music with all these lightweight people who can't handle it. Tonight it really hit me. I was sitting backstage thinking about how much bullshit we go through just to play. So much bullshit just to play music. I asked them to let us play but they are more into the bullshit pose than the music, some nights it's hard to take. Right now I don't want to know anyone, don't want to play music in front of anyone. After the show people were trying to talk to me but I just walked away or told them to leave me alone. Fuck them all, the bouncers, the bullshit artists, all of them. All I want to do is play. Tonight I think I should just get a job and get the fuck out of sight. I think I'm in the wrong place at the wrong time because I don't feel anything for these people.

25 Sydney Australia: The day started out in a television studio. I didn't want to do this shit but we were doing it anyway. It was Andrew who really wanted to do this. I knew it was going to be the same bullshit as it usually is. If every piece of equipment isn't exactly what he wants then he throws a shit fit. He was told that the equipment for the TV show was going to be the best gear they could get and he said that was ok. I knew that it wasn't going to be ok. I hate listening to the complaints. Of course there was the prima donna bullshit, no surprises there. "Tearing" three times and "Low Self Opinion" three times and then on to the hall for soundcheck, then back to the television studio to do it again as a dress rehearsal and then through it again "for real". After that back to the hall, a little before midnight. Stretch for a few minutes and then go out and kick it. Spit, ice cubes, beer, the endless chain of bodies onstage. A guy who would fill up beer cans with water and bring them to the front and cover our equipment with it. Can't play too hard because that would involve too much concentration and that means taking my eyes off of them for a few seconds and like the ocean, you can't turn your back on a crowd like this one. I spent the night looking out for the flying beer can or the ice or the punker. At one point I told the people up front that I wished they were all black. I knew that would piss them off and I was right. Funny as fuck to see them get mad like that. Even with all this lightweight element at the show we still rocked out. I don't stick around after the last song is over. I get the fuck off stage, I can't be sure what they will be planning. Maybe that one shithead is waiting to throw his glass right on the last note and there I'd be standing there with a fake ass grin on my face like a sitting duck waiting to get what I deserved for giving them an inch. So I play and split, make the hit and leave. I learned that this bunch isn't about music so I do the trip and get the fuck out. Might be a long time before I come back here again.

26 Manly Australia: Tiny stage tonight. Played ok and had a good time. Set clocked in at over two hours. One of those nights where everywhere you go someone is waiting to gawk at you for unlimited minutes. Young folks never get tired of seeing some old man warming up his body to go play. I always tell these young guys not to bother watching me, but rather they should go out and check out the women, they never take my advice. I like these people but I can't take the talk, I always come off sounding like a grouch. I avoid them because I know that I don't work well with people. I hate some of the things that come out of my mouth. I am good at being a tool and that's it. On-off, the intellect of a shark. I'm not good at hanging out. So as far as gigs go it was a good one. The crowd wasn't as belligerent as they were last night. Good for us. Put in a hard workout today so I feel tired from that. The next show is in Singapore. There's only one way to walk this line. It's all in your head. You can have all the good sleep you want, to do this all the way, you have to have the one idea. One strong thought is all you need.

29 Singapore: Nothing worked well tonight. The bass amp blew out a few songs in and the bass player made a big scene out of it, as if it wasn't bad enough already. He was told that this gig was going to be a wastey one and he still wanted to do it. So the gig gets wastey and he can't handle, typical. There was no real PA and it was a drag all the way through. Didn't see much of the city since I did interviews all the way up until soundcheck, which lasted 4 hours because we couldn't locate a bass amp. It's as if everyone in the country needs an autograph, they come from everywhere, they all have cameras as well. The BMG rep who was driving me around to all the radio stations was a nervous guy that had a tape of Suicide going for him and that was about all. It was a long day. People were waiting for me everywhere it seemed. My heart is heavy and I don't give a fuck about anything but the playing. It's the only thing keeping my head on straight right now. The interviews are getting to me. Tonight after the show we went and got some food and we saw a car crash. Mo said that it was going to be a hassle. I said, "It wasn't us." Me and Joe used to say that to each other all the time. "There are going to be a lot of dead people around after we get done and none of them will be us, so it's cool." Now it is. Now it's us, now it's me and I want to die all the time. It's all I thought about today while I talked to these journalist fakes and watched the nervous BMG guy walk around the room. Now it's me. I wish I could throw this night out. We leave for Japan in two hours and fifteen minutes and I don't even care. I'll play Tokyo, Pittsburgh or Hell, it's all the same to me.

October

02 Nagoya Japan: Finally a gig where no one got onstage and we could play. The rented gear was the stuff that we asked for and the gig went without a hitch. Between songs it was so quiet. I couldn't even hear a single conversation. We finished playing "Blues Jam" and they just stood there. I don't think it was apathy. It seemed more like respect or something. During the lowdown parts of the songs they were dead silent out there. It really let us get deep into the music. I had a great time playing. People were pretty cool to us as well. The hang up is the way people follow you around and want to meet you but when you say hello to them they shrink back like you were going to hit them or they are too afraid to approach you. It makes me feel uncomfortable. I like Japan. These people try to play you off like they like you and they're your friends but I know better. They are cool professionals and I like that but I can see how it would be easy to take it the wrong way and think that they're sincere about they way they act. Like they way they are all running over each other to get you shit. Fuck that. I know better. You're not my fucking friend, so just do your trip, whatever it is, promoting, interviews, whatever. I like it because I see the real you and you don't even know it. It makes me see the girl I went out a long time ago differently. I see where I got fucked up. I would like to play here more and shove it right down their throats every time. I think it's funny when people front themselves and they think that they're getting away with it. I don't trust anyone in this business except myself.

03 Osaka Japan: Tonight was another good playing experience. It feels great to rock hard and not have to think about getting whacked around. Some kids kept flying over the barrier and as they flipped over their boot tips would slam against the stage and if my feet were there they would have been broken by now. Japanese fans are the most intense I have ever encountered anywhere. I did an instore appearance at Tower today and it was a heavy experience. People out of breath when they would come to the front. All of their hands were cold and wet when I shook them. They were everywhere even at the train station when I was on an early train I took ahead of the guys to go to Osaka from Nagoya. After the show we went to the van and they were there and there was one guy crying and telling me he loved me. Tonight they were in the hotel lobby as well. I took the stairs, twelve flights just so I wouldn't have to wait for the elevator and get told that someone is sorry again. They always say they're sorry when they want your autograph and picture. They were in the lobby of the hotel when I got there this morning. It would be too crazy if you were in a big band and came here. Imagine someone like David Bowie or Prince, insane. After the set we went and ate food in a restaurant where you take your shoes off and sit at a low table and the ladies come out with the robes on and all, it was great. If I had a real room to live in that's what it would look like. I got a good workout in today. When I got to the gym they wouldn't let me in because I had tattoos and they had some problem with my shoes. They had a discussion about it and they gave me a sweatshirt and some shoes that they had around. Some gym. These guys would shit themselves if they went to a gym in America. In the gym here there were no weights that were heavy. I was doing shrugs with a couple of hundred pounds to warm up and I looked behind me and all the people had stopped and were staring at me. One guy came over with a calculator and showed me exactly how many pounds I was lifting. No one made a sound except me. They looked at me like I was some kind of monster. Honestly it felt good. The gym is the only place where I feel totally at home. People in a room sweating, lifting up shit and making animal sounds. I don't have to apologize for the way I am. I don't have to be nice to fragile people. It's the only place where I feel natural. I like working out better than sex, it's only second to music. Right before we went on this strange thing happened. I had bought a Jane's Addiction bootleg CD in the store underneath the club and I had the DJ put it on. I was standing in the hall and the CD came on. At first it was just the sound of a huge Jane's audience waiting to see the band. The bass line for "Up the Beach" came on and the crowd went nuts. Every time I ever saw them that's the tune they opened up with. For a split second I thought I was at Lollapalooza. It was an intense flashback. It only lasted a fraction of a second but it was intense. I'll have to tell those guys about it if I ever see any of them again.

04 Tokyo Japan: Another great night of not getting bugged while playing. The only pain in the ass were the Americans up front showing off the fact that they thought they knew us. Last night there was some

English guy talking shit and I said, "Shut up round eye," and the place broke out laughing. Dave Navarro just happened to be in Tokyo and he came and jammed out with us. We did "Crazy Lover," "Move Right In" and "On the Road." I hid from the autographers pretty well. Playing the same place tomorrow night, looking forward to it. It's the only thing on my mind. Let the fucking bull out of its cage and get the fuck out of the way.

05 Tokyo Japan: Tonight was a good time. The only hang up was the American element of the audience that feels the need to show off the fact that they're major assholes. I kicked them back pretty hard. I'm too good at verbal abuse. I learned from the best. Dave Navarro played with us again tonight. We did "Killin' Floor," it was cool. After the show there were girls waiting in the rain to get their paper signed. I did press all day and went to soundcheck. Now I'm back in the box. The rest of them leave tomorrow. I stay to do press for another two days. So what else is new. Burned out and blank. Didn't go out to eat with the rest of them because I just wanted to be alone. I am finding out things about myself more and more. I am sometimes dismayed at how hardened I have become but I guess it's part of the process. I don't care. If you stick around too long you get your ass shot off that's all I know. I'm glad we're getting out of here. I like playing here but the apologizing nature of the Japanese fans I don't like and I don't believe. I am reminded of the line from *Blue Velvet* where Frank Booth says, "Don't say please fuckhead!"

09 Honolulu HI: Back in America. Playing here feels like playing in Santa Cruz or San Diego. The PA was onstage and it made the entire stage shake. Couldn't hear any one instrument, just heard a huge dull roar. Still got off on the playing though. People in the crowd were cool but I could tell that they didn't know what to make of us. After the show I stood on the second floor and watched people dance. Some girl that had passed a note backstage came up and started talking at me. I kept telling her not to talk to me because I was dead. Finally I ignored her and she still stood there. It's at the point now where I cringe when they want to shake my hand. I find myself wiping my hands off on my leg. Their hands are always moist. I play and the rest is bullshit. I like to play and then I like to shut the fuck up. Standing around shaking hands and saying thank you has nothing to so with the music. I wish I could vaporize into a bloody mist after I play.

10 Honolulu HI: I go to the toilet and they come in and start the talking. We're in a toilet and I have to answer questions. I am a fucking idiot for being in a place where this can happen to me. They yell we play, what the fuck. I had a great time tonight. They throw ice and yell the stupidest shit I have ever heard but they stayed off stage and that was great. The guys always want to touch me. After the show they find their way backstage and put their arm around me. A woman keeps patting me on the back and she tells me that from what she heard me say tonight she thinks I would be an interesting person to talk to. I just stare at her until she leaves. What did I say tonight? I asked if there was a difference in the smell of rape and normal sex. That I didn't want to unite with anyone because humans smell like blood and brains. I am the Death Star and everything that comes out of my mouth is from darkness.

25 Tucson AZ: I don't know if they know. The sun sets and I sit outside waiting for the soundcheck to start. Small groups of youths come up to me and stand around like I am some museum piece or some wall hanging. One will speak and I will stare and use one word answers. One by one they will go away wordlessly. I don't know if they know. Pain is the only thing that will tell you the truth about yourself and the rest of them. The pain shot through my body like electricity tonight. After the show I sat in a puddle of my sweat on the floor of the arena. People looked over the barrier and yelled shit I couldn't understand. I felt like a boxer. I don't care what they yell. I'm just an animal. Just meat, experienced meat. They don't know that underneath my skin the pain is screaming the truth to me. So loud that it shuts out anything that they are yelling. Pain is my friend because it has never lied to me. It never leaves me for long. When pain is with me everything becomes clear and life has meaning. I know something about myself. I see deeper. Pain makes me stronger. Fire fills my body. After I get dressed I walk out and talk to people from some radio station. They are alien to me. Pain is the great isolator, the almighty truth teller. Fuck spirituality. It's all in the flesh and how much you can take. You want to transcend? Burn.

26 Albuquerque NM: The reverb in the hall was over five seconds in decay time. One of those places where you play the song and you hear it off the back wall for a few minutes afterwards. We played a few blocks away from where the Bush rally was. I went over there and listened to a man talk over the PA system about how we have to get back to Christ. He said things were looking bad when they hand out condoms in schools. A smattering of applause. Secret Service men all over the place. A bad scene. After I left Bush came onstage and kicked some spoken word. Tonight's show was good. Played hard despite feeling the shortness of breath that comes with the elevation out here. Some drunk guy shook my hand four times until I finally told him to cut the shit. I wince at the thought of shaking hands these days. It's like having to kiss strangers. I don't like having to touch strangers, it's fucked up. What if you were running for office, you would be doing that shit all day every day, working hard to get people to like you. I can't see how you could live with yourself doing that shit. Now I'm sitting in the bus in back of the enormous reverb chamber waiting to get on the road to Dayton, Ohio. The bouncers were fucked up tonight, strong-arming kids out, they have no idea what their job is —none. I am tired and sore, looking forward to getting some sleep. The last time I ever saw D. Boon was in this town. In fact I walked right by the spot today. It's so good to be out on the road again. I was home for two weeks and it was apparent to me that I can't handle that life. I was getting more bent out of shape as the days passed. Couldn't get good sleep, couldn't think straight. There's nothing like warming up getting ready to play. Nothing like being out there kicking it live night after night. You either do this all the way and take the pain and learn to be it all the way or you step off. I cannot see any other life other than this one.

29 Dayton OH: Another night at the Hara. Played here with Jane's Addiction a while back. Tonight was nowhere near as crowded as when we played with Jane's. I gave it all I had. The opening band is this rap group from South Central LA called Da Lench Mob. Ice Cube came out and sang with them tonight. Even he couldn't save them. They suck flat out. They are on the hate whitey trip. Apparently a few of them were talking about kicking our white asses. They carry guns and are no doubt some bad motherfuckers who can kill you like it's no big thing just like they say in their songs. With all the guns in the world they still suck. They have to go up against the hardest band there ever was and they lose every time. It was great to walk by them tonight when we finished. Fuck that rap shit. They can't cut it where it matters —live. All they do is that wave your hands in the air shit. Losers. I will keep playing and I will keep destroying all these weak fucks. After the show I try to sit in the bus but I can't because there's all these people outside banging on the window. I go out there and sign things and say thank you. Nice people but I can feel my skin crawling and I have to fight the urge to bolt. I can't believe how much that shit upsets me. I don't want to be that person that gets thanked all the time. I will forget who I am if I can't get away from the rockstar bullshit. I have to work hard to keep away from them. They don't know what I know.

30 Kalamazoo MI: The best part of tonight's show was the part where we're playing and I see that Ice Cube is watching and between songs I say in a cracked falsetto, "Put your hands in the air and wave them like you just don't care!" And then started laughing in my own voice. He got up and left. The playing was good. I had a good time. We got a short set but still it was cool. The opening band has some piece of shit song where they name off people that are "on my shotgun" or some shit. Apparently they have used my name in their list a few times. Not even the use of my name can help them. They still suck and they still get their shit shown up every night by us. I'd love to see them have to do a real set. That shit is so boring. A bunch of guys posing out, singing to a tape. How intense. Tonight the crowd threw shoes, shirts and hats. I spat on them and threw them off to the side making sure they never get them back again. Tonight there was one of those "meet and greet" radio things after the show. People call in to the station and win a ticket I guess. They come back to meet the band after the show. This kind of thing rubs me the wrong way. The people are always really cool but I feel like an ass hanging out making up fake conversation. No one told us about the one tonight. I was on the bus and someone came and got me. I went back into the hall and into the dressing room and there were a bunch of people standing around. I immediately felt uncomfortable and my mouth shut tight and I couldn't get my eyes off the floor. I stood around for about a minute and then a few of them came up to me and stuck their hand out and I shook it and I said thank you a few times and then I kind of drifted out the door. I told the road manager that I don't want to do that anymore. I think the playing is enough. I don't want to be someone's expectation. You can see that they're nervous and you want to make them feel ok and you don't want to bum them out, at least I don't. I don't know how to handle these situations. It's a drag to see that these people know how tired you are and they don't want to be a bother but at the same time they are thrilled to be where they are and I want it to be a good memory for them but I don't know if one of the requirements of being in a band is to be a public relations man. I do the best I can.

31 Indianapolis IN: Happy Halloween. The crowd looked the same as always. Kicked it as hard as I could. Now I am the hole. After the show I sat shivering in a corner and shook my head no when they came to interrogate me. They take and take. They can't get me all the way. You finish playing your guts out and you're sitting there steaming and they will come up immediately and start in with the questions. I get sick of my mouth. I get sick of answering endless questions, some nights it's all I do. Scratch, pry, dig, scrape. Sign this. Wring his bones until there's no juice left. No. You won't get me. The radio guy comes out of nowhere and tells me he has some people he wants me to meet. I tell him that after shows all I want to do is kill people. He goes away. They have no idea. You work with people for years and they have no idea what's going on with you. You just go on talking hoping that somewhere someone gets it halfway the way you meant it. Wince when they don't, run and cover when they do. Some Nation of Islam guys were here tonight. They were an intense crew to say the least. Immaculately dressed with bow ties and full length leather coats.

November

01 Chicago IL: We get to the venue and there's kids outside waiting for something. There's no tickets and they stand there in the pissing rain all day. Hours later soundcheck starts. Tonight they're up close and they throw Oh Henry candy bars and tell us that we suck. We play hard and

I can't tell what they're saying. The bass player pulls one of his infant attitude trips for the encore and no one kills him. That's it. It's a good thing that I do this for myself because if I was an entertainer I would be looking for their approval. How fucked up is that. They would hand me my head. Steve Albini was at the show tonight hanging out with the opening band I guess. I never met the guy before but once read an article he wrote that put me down. I was considering breaking his face up for him but when I moved in on him I saw that he was just a skinny punk. It wouldn't have been a good kill so I let it slide. He'll never know how close he came to getting his face fucked up in front of his friends. After the show is over I leave the venue to get some food before we leave for Toronto. People are outside waiting in bad weather. I sign whatever they have and do my best to be nice to these people knowing they have no idea how much I want to puke my lungs out of my body when I get asked to sign an autograph. I go to the restaurant up the street and people put pieces of paper in my face as I'm eating. I get on the bus and we leave.

02 Toronto Canada: We get to the venue after a drive that ends up taking about fifteen hours. People are waiting for the bus in shitting rain and wind. I go to the dressing room and shave. People are looking in the window. Hours later the doors are about to open and someone throws a rock through the window and covers me with glass. I notice that "the Da Lench Mob" as we now call them has incorporated a "We love y'all" rap into the show. No doubt high management has told them that they need to cross over and kiss some white ass to make the record and t-shirt sales go better. The audience eats it right up. Finally we get to play. I give it all I have. By the end of the set my bone marrow was screaming. Pain makes it go better. I get out of the shower and I'm still out of breath. My legs are burning. As long as I can maintain the present pain threshold, none of these fuckers will ever get to me.

03 Montreal Canada: There's something about us that the Beastie crowd doesn't like. Tonight they spit and flip me off. Good thing there's a barrier. It would be pretty satisfying to meet up with one of those spitters after the gig and show them something. Again we play hard and right through them all. Tonight was the end result of four interviews.

Sometimes I think if I have to talk about myself with one more stranger I'll explode into nothing. After the show I'm eating and I get called outside the bus to meet this guy who is partly retarded. I talk to him but his friend is freaking out and yelling so the retarded guy apologizes to me. I shake his hand which is covered with something that smells like rotting milk. I try to wash it off but it doesn't work. The smell makes it so I can't finish my meal so I throw it out. You get too close to people and they will cover you with themselves, with their lives. I don't want to touch. I want to play hard and play through but I don't want to touch anyone and I don't want to know what they want to tell me. I don't even know what I think anymore. I feel tired after saying thank you. I want to puke and sleep.

04 Durham NH: The DLM couldn't go on at their correct time because they were afraid of the check that the university was going to pay them. We have to wait for them to get their shit together. Finally we are allowed to play. I guess they don't know that universities never pay a band in cash. These guys are amateurs and won't even be around next year so who cares. There is a similarity night to night on this tour. People up front who are waiting for the Beasties are not tolerant of our brand of music. They have proven to be very abusive. Tonight they were in full effect telling us to get off stage and that I'm not as good as I used to be but looking at the age of the crowd I don't think they ever saw me the way I used to be — however and whenever the hell that was. They tell me that I'm a junkie and all kinds of other shit. I asked them how many of their fathers are in the Klan. I called them all white boys and that bummed them out big time. It's easy to get a rise out of people like that. It's a good thing that we don't play for the people and that we play for ourselves. Grab your dick whiteboy here comes the next verse. That was a good one. I played my ass off anyway. It was good to get out of there — you get the feeling that you would have to show one of these dung producers some real hostility. These food wasters are lucky that there are laws and barriers keeping me away from their necks. They have no idea how close they are to getting hurt by someone who wouldn't give a fuck if they died. I remember the Canadian guy who was giving me all kinds of shit one night in Rome. He walked out of the venue and got his drunk ass run over and killed by a guy in a car coming around the bend.

Sounds like the death of an asshole to me. So I played another show and I'm still alive.

05 Boston MA: Andrew pulled out all the stops on this one. He lies down to play, he solos through all the songs, he jumps through rings of fire, anything but play with the rest of us. He always talks about never selling out and he's the biggest sellout there ever was. He's so full of shit, no matter what he'll ever say I'll always know that he's weak. I am proud of myself for not attacking him. I know the importance of completing the shows that we have in front of us. I would like to swarm him so hard he would have to get his crippled wife to feed him. It's a disgrace to watch this punk make our stage a disgrace. There is a friend of the band's that's up here from NJ. He came to the show tonight and told me he was disgusted with the bass player's bullshit. I felt bad for him, worse for myself however, having to put up with him until the end of the tour where he will be unceremoniously dropped. I played hard as I could though and had a good time. At this point I am pretty hard to stop.

06 New York NY: Good time playing tonight. Got fucked up on the time because we played one song too long. Met some people. Met Ron Delsnor, the promoter, he was really cool. Lenny Kravitz had some pretty woman with him. Other than that, it was just a night. I didn't watch the Beasties because I kind of got trapped down in the basement with these people. I should have left the place as soon as I finished playing. It's a bad idea to stick around. You have to talk to people and get thanked or whatever. A few girls asked me out tonight. I did my best to be polite and say no without making a big deal out of it. Walked back to the hotel through all the people coming out of the show. Slaps on the back and clapping follow me down the street. I like the people here. They are cool and they don't hang on you. They have a sense of themselves it seems. Another night on tour.

07 New York NY: Here for the second night of the NYC shows. I would like to live here. It's great in New York. I walked by Carnegie Hall last night wondering if Charlie Parker had stood where I was standing. I tried to imagine standing in line to see Miles play there. Down the street a man was lying in the street, hit by a taxi cab. Police were there, several onlookers watched the man cry out in pain. They all came to New York. Miles, Parker, Coltrane, Roach, Monk, Mingus, Gillespie, Ayler, Coleman, Shorter, Prez, Blakey —all of them. The longer I make the list the more I show my ignorance by the number of greats I would be leaving out. I went past the Village Vanguard club once, I remembered the photo of Coltrane standing out in front of the place that's on one of his records I have. I tried to find the exact spot on the sidewalk where he stood in time. I walked outside today until it was too cold to go on. The sun is setting and the sirens are screaming by. It's dangerous to live here. Don't fool yourself, it's dangerous to live anywhere in America now. They all want to kill each other it seems, hell, me too. I want to see some of them dead for sure. Later: Did the show tonight and it rocked hard. I played as hard as I could. Vernon Reid came out and jammed with us at the end of the night and that was great. Iggy was at the show and we hung out and talked for a good while. He's so cool. It means a lot to me to be able to hang out with him. He's going to come to our show in New Orleans and play with us if he has time, he'll be down there recording. Iggy said that he wants to do a lot of shows when his new record comes out, he says he's feeling good. He was looking great. Other than that it was a good night. Some pretty women backstage. I guess they were there for the Beasties. All I know is that none of them looked at me twice.

08 New Brunswick NJ: Many were politically correct and a little unsure. I've never seen so many youths in baggy clothes. Hide the body's form and remove the idea of sex. Remove the threat of sex, something that might kill you. Campus anxiety. Young people losing the language of their bodies, sexuality muffled, stifled under layers of clothes. Nice people at the place tonight. Same security crew as the guys in NYC. Now that is a great crew. They know the difference between being a bouncer and being security. These guys do not get into hurting people. They are total pros and they like the people that come to the gigs. I talked with several of them. Too bad we can't take them with us, it would be great to not have to worry about that aspect of the shows. Played as hard as I could. Kept slipping on the carpet but what the fuck. Other than that there was nothing to remark upon. We came to their gym and we played and I left several minutes later. One of those gigs that are good but don't leave any marks. As I drove back to the city I thought about this girl that I actually loved. The pain of some of that shit never goes away. It sucks to be mortal and to have a heart that can break.

10 Raleigh NC: Played hard as possible. Ran out of time before we got to finish. Showered and got out of there. I don't know what else happened, been playing hard to the point to where it blasts out the rest of the thoughts that I have. After the show was over I sat on the bus and waited to leave. People looked inside for a long time. I felt like I was living on display. It was good to leave. I am falling apart in some ways.

11 Atlanta GA: Another night of good playing. Crowd was great. Not much to remark on. I didn't get outside much after we got to the gig. I got in a good workout in the gym they had there. After the show I watched people leave the hall. I feel so far from them. I don't know the language, I don't know the moves, I don't know anything about this version of the world.

13 Orlando FL: Outside gig tonight. First night with Cypress Hill. Good band and cool people as far as I can tell. I played as hard as I could and watched the Beastie Boys play as well, they were great as usual. They don't play bad ever —if they have I've never seen it. The backstage area is just a bunch of fences so as you stand around, people from all sides call out to you and then you realize you're just on display like some fucked up zoo trip. I guess it doesn't matter, in the end you're just ashes to scatter. Another show down. I like playing as much as ever but it's the other stuff that I don't handle well.

14 Miami FL: I sat out back of the exit door tonight and watched groupies wait for the Beasties. People disgust me sometimes. They tried to play that weak shit with me and I told them to get fucked. Played hard tonight and I think we really bummed out a large portion of the crowd. I like the idea of us and the Beasties playing together but I don't know if it makes much sense for the person in the audience. I can tell that we are too heavy for people coming to see the Beasties. I kind of feel sorry for them to have to sit through our set when they want to get into the party mood. After the show I was sitting on the side watching people do their thing and a few of them started coming up to me. They were Beasties people, people waiting around for the poor guys to come out and go to their bus. They were talking to me and all I wanted to do was hurt them. People were asking for my autograph and I was telling them no, that the autograph thing was stupid. I see things clearly. It's not about signing shit and being all charming to women that you want to fuck. It's the sword, following the sword and adhering to the line of the blade. That's all there is for me. When I talk to people I disgust myself. When they anger me I disgust myself further. Finally I got so sick of watching the women and their antics that I had to walk away. I sat for minutes thinking that all I wanted to do was give away all my possessions and throw away all my meager savings and get a job as a dishwasher. Perhaps be in a place where people wouldn't make me hate so much. As it is now all I want to do is play and get away from them before they make me do stupid things. I feel dangerous and devoid of sex appeal. I feel like the definition of the word ugly.

15 Tampa FL: In the parking lot of a hotel waiting to go down to the venue. Tampa is beat down. The streets are tired. No one knows it yet but America is worn out. I see it when I come to Florida. The coasts are going to go down first and the rest will slowly fall apart as the years go by. The midwest will end up being as bad as Los Angeles in a short while. I don't think I've been through Tampa since I was here with Black Flag. It's a Beasties show so I don't think there will be any bad experiences with the skinhead boys. Not many shows left on the tour. The year is winding down. I don't remember a lot of it. I wonder what next year will be like. I wonder if I can keep this up or if I will fall over. It doesn't matter because I know that in the end I will keep on going insanely until death. Later: Did the show and had a good time. Cypress Hill were great. I gave it all I had and felt good afterwards. I watched the Beasties for a while. I was on the side of the stage when some girl who was looking for a good place to see started stepping on my legs. I kicked her legs off of me and told her to get the fuck away from me. After that I couldn't have a good time watching the show so I had to bail. Now I'm on the bus listening to Clifford Brown play with Max Roach and Sonny Rollins. I'm alone and all is well.

16 Jacksonville FL: Gave it all I had tonight. Got in a good workout before so my spirits were high. The rest of the day I forget. I woke up in the parking lot of the hotel that also is the parking lot of the venue. Tonight is the first night the place was open. They were still building the front today. So we played and I don't know what they thought about it. Another night on the road. It's all starting to run together. I know you can go until the muscle falls off the bone and no one would notice. The road is open ended and will allow you to do every stupid thing to yourself that you want. I'm burning out slowly but I still want to keep playing, it's just now getting interesting. I'm beyond loneliness and my thinking is short term but clear like a real animal. There was a beautiful moment tonight when my body was screaming in pain and I kept riding it. I did not back off. Through loss and the Iron I have learned to make friends with the pain. It is my only friend at this point. I came up with an idea while we were in the middle of a jam about how good it would be to be able to have my own skull in my hand and still be alive. I would have someone to talk to. I am like all of them in that I am a desperate animal trying to escape fear.

18 New Orleans LA: Iggy Pop played with us tonight. It was cool as hell. When we were in New York he said that he was interested. He came to soundcheck and we kicked a blues jam that felt good. After that he asked me if I wanted to come sing some on a song he was working on. I went with him to Daniel Lanois studio and he and I sang on this song called Wild America. It was great to be standing next to him singing along. We did it without headphones, using the monitors over the desk. It was one of those situations where you are trying to concentrate on the work but you really can't believe what you're doing and who you're doing it with. We were just going for it and it was a great time. I hope that they keep my vocal in when it comes time for the final mix. I went back to the hall and got ready to play. I gave it all I had like I always do. The bass player was playing so loud that in some of the songs I thought my ears were going to explode. Can't wait to get that guy away from me. During the last song the generator blew out and we had to wait for them to get their shit together. It was wild to be waiting to play and see Iggy on the side of the stage with his shirt off jumping up and down waiting to get out there. When we finally got the power on we hit it and it was great. Iggy was all over the place. I'm glad Ricky Powell got it on tape. Crowd was pretty boring but that's ok. I don't have to live with them. It's a bit of a drag being in the band with this bass player but his days are numbered so it's no big deal.

19 Dallas TX: It rained all day and I watched the men load the gear into a fucked up old wrestling arena. I sat in the bleachers and thought about how many times people had sat there and yelled for one redneck to rip the head off another redneck. Water was coming in through the roof. There was a hole in the floor right in front of the stage. A girl I know came early to talk to me and I was lame and had little to say. I felt like a jerk sitting there not being able to say anything. I don't get along with people as well as I used to, it's like I have turned into another person. Right after Cypress Hill finished the barricade was broken almost immediately. Great to see it handed piece by piece across the front of the stage. After a long time and a lot of people onstage talking to the crowd telling them to get back we finally got to play. Our set was cut to forty-five minutes. We pulled off a few songs and did the best we could to get the crowd to be cool. It was like one of our regular shows, people all over the place. Other than that it was a good night. The Beasties were great as usual, it's great to see them every night. I didn't have to talk to too many people after the show and that made things pretty easy to deal with. I find it hard to say thank you over and over. It makes me want to rip my lungs out.

20 Houston TX: Tonight was Mike D's birthday. The Beasties were great tonight. They brought out a cake and smashed Ricky Powell in the face with it. Mike D sang "Georgie Girl." Cypress Hill were great tonight as well. I wish they could play longer but they only get twenty minutes. I wonder what it's like to play for that little amount of time. Eric, the percussionist with the Beasties, played "Obscene" with us and both he and Mark the Beastie keyboard player played "Next Time." It was a good set and I had a good time playing. After the show I sat and shook the hands of people that I didn't know and I noticed that without thinking about it I always wipe my hand on my leg. I get tired of people touching me. They were outside near the bus tonight screaming my name. You would think that they would have something else to do than to stand outside and wait for fellow humans to walk ten feet out to their bus. Now I'm in the box. We play in San Antonio tomorrow night without the Beasties or Cypress. There is only one thing to do and that's to keep hitting it hard and not let the normal bullshit hang you up. You have to keep away from the women to keep clear minded. I'm only interested in being relentless. The rest is just bullshit.

21 San Antonio TX: Tonight was a headlining show as the Beasties Boys are off tonight. The place stinks and it's cold like a lot of places in Texas. Hours pass and I go from the bus to the backstage hopping from one boring environment to the other. There are only about four hundred people tonight. Not such a big draw in old San Antonio. Finally we get to play and after straightening out a few stage divers we had a good time playing. Played a long set too. It was a good time and the crowd was very cool. After the show they were waiting around the bus in cold weather so I talked to a few of them and tried to talk them out of the autograph thing that makes me so sick. I stood there in this alley and told them the truth as best I could. I told them that I like them but the autograph thing makes me feel like an asshole more than usual. They just stood there and laughed nervously and held out the pieces of paper anyway. Some girls took us to a Mexican place and we ate a lot of food. It is now past six in the morning and I can't sleep. I will be in my own bed tonight. In a few hours I fly to LA and have all of Sunday to myself. I'm looking forward to being in my room alone with my stereo. I will try to get in a workout in as well. My body is sore and I am tired but unable to sleep. I missed the presence of the Beasties and Cypress tonight as the opening band was crap. Not much to tell. I feel good inside myself. I feel fucked up around others though. I can't handle women very well anymore. When they want to hug me it makes me freak out. I think they're control freaks. It's hard to talk to them because they are always talking shit to me. It's never real, always some bullshit trip. I don't do well with people and it makes me mad because I don't want them to think badly of me. But I am tired of answering the questions all the time. I know how fucked up I am. I am fucked up with other people's trips. I like the work and that's all. The rest is too exhausting and sickening.

23 San Diego CA: We played outside. People were cool. We played well and it was a good night. One of those ones where you play and nothing happens besides you going out and playing. That's it.

24 Los Angeles CA: We start playing and Chris' guitar lead starts to cut out and we have to stop through a song. We start again on another song and already the set is losing a little steam. Another song goes by and at least I'm going for it as hard as I can and someone throws a shoe at me and hits me in the face. It rings my bells good. We keep playing and a guy up front spits at me and it goes right into my mouth. I take the mic and swing it at him and hit him in the face and call him every name I can think of. Fuck these people. Take them out and shoot them. We finish the set and after the show the bass player starts talking shit about what I did. He always does it the same way. He walks away while he's talking and gets to the punch line when he's out the door. He never confronts. I can't respect him because he's a bitch. He lies down onstage, he solos through entire sets. He does all this sellout shit and then he tells me how fucked up I am. He's so weak. It's pathetic. Tomorrow is his last show with me. No longer will he disgrace my stage with his weakness. Let him do it to someone else. Hell of a gig though. I am unstoppable. Fuck you.

25 San Francisco CA: They threw large plastic containers of pepper, garlic, you name it. There were about four spices thrown up there all in all. Missed my head a few times. Close. I caught one. I spent the gig watching the crowd, inhaling pepper and waiting for the next projectile. I got hit in the head with a coin. Good shot. Tried to play with all I had but couldn't because of a few pieces of shit in the audience. Play all year and it comes down to your last show and they shit on you all the way. It would be nice to have a way to shit right back on them. It would have been so great to have found the guy, imagine the hospital bill. So like Iggy once said, "You're paying five dollars and I'm making ten thousand so screw ya." I hopped a ride with the crew bus and wound up at the airport in LA. We saw Ray Charles, it was cool. He was being led by this guy. They were walking real fast. I took a cab to my room. Sure was a good year for playing. It was great playing with the Beastie Boys and Cypress Hill. I wish we were playing tonight. I don't know what I'll do with myself.

HOLLOW MAN: 55 NIGHTS

#1: I keep telling myself that if I keep to myself a little longer everything will be alright. I don't know what this feeling of alrightness entails. I don't know why it occurs to me that I must be alone as much as possible to feel better.

It seems to me that the best thing is to keep things to myself. I have tried to explain myself to others and it always ends up being an upsetting waste of time.

My loneliness has never burned with more intensity than now. I wish there was someone that I could identify with. I don't look because I know how I am. I want something and as soon as I get it I don't want it anymore . If some woman told me she wanted me I would immediately go as far away from her as possible. But alone in this room, alone on the planet, the way I always find myself, I wish for a warmth that speaks to me. I don't know where it would come from.

Sometimes I think that I have been cut out of a mold to perform some duty or task. I'm not talking about some kind of weird destiny bullshit. It just seems like all the things that have been happening to me are part of some story. All the bad things that have happened recently are like the plot to a large drama.

I am not one to take things as they come. I don't have the time. I have learned that one can be put in situations where one must hang on and keep from going overboard into the raging torrent of life's events.

The loneliness that I feel fills me completely. I feel it in everything I do. I don't mind loneliness anymore. I have made friends with it and I can handle. Loneliness adds beauty to life. It puts a special burn on sunsets and makes night air smell better. It is the only thing I've ever really known besides pain.

#2: I called your number tonight even though I know it's disconnected. I just wanted to hear the sound of the tones the buttons made. I thought if I called maybe you would pick up the phone even though you're dead. Maybe I could hear you being shot over and over. Maybe you would answer and tell me that you don't understand what all the fuss is about. You would tell me what it's like to be dead.

The guy from the LA Weekly left a message on the machine telling me that they want to pay me for the obit that I wrote about you. Isn't that something. I can call in and they'll send me a check. I'll call them in the morning and tell them that I don't want any money from them.

As a reflex I called your number again. 392 2063 just to hear the sound the tones made. Now my eyes are stinging. I'm glad no one's here right now.

#3: The other day I was doing a video in Los Angeles. A few hours into what would be a 14 hour work day the pigs came by to show me pictures of potential suspects in Joe's murder. I spread the pictures on the floor and looked at 8x10's of fucked up guys who were too stoned to focus. After looking at their faces for a while and knowing that I'll never be able identify the guy I gave up. One of the pigs said that by time that all of this was over they would know as much about me as I did. Some of the shit that comes out their mouths is hilarious. I can't wait for them to find out everything about me. I would like to help fill them in on how much I think pigs should be taken out of circulation.

After we looked at the pictures one of the pigs took out another notebook and showed me pictures of the scene of the crime. He turned the page and came to a few pictures of Joe lying on the front walk with a sheet over his body. The white sheet covered almost all of him except the back of his head which was torn up. He looked so pathetic and small lying there. So lonely. His body fell in this fucked up position that made it look like he had been thrown to one side like some piece of insignificant garbage. He looked like an afterthought. I wanted to crawl into the picture and get him out of there.

Soon after the pigs thanked me for my cooperation and left. I sat in silence and thought about the picture. Seeing Joe like that made me want to die. Soon I was in front of a camera screaming along with some song. Every time I looked into the lens all I could see was that white sheet and Joe underneath it.

That was weeks ago and now I'm in Europe. I spend most of the nights trying to get to sleep in the bunk of a moving bus. I close my eyes and try to get to sleep. All I can think about is Joe and I start to cry into the pillow. I don't tell anyone about it. I keep seeing the sheet. Tonight I was in a book shop in the train station here in Munich. I saw the sheet on two books that were in front of me.

Tonight is a night off, the first one in two weeks. I wish we were playing so I wouldn't have time to think.

I am totally cut off from the rest of the world. I think of what it would be like to try to communicate with someone and I can't see it. I don't even want to anymore. I just want to keep moving. I feel good when I'm moving.

Tonight I was thinking, wondering if I will regret staying to myself all the time like I do. I wondered if I would look back and think that I blew it and should have ventured out into the world more. I look at women and some part of me wants to be with them, and then I see how at shows they don't come near me and never talk to me. I see that animals, dogs for instance, will instinctively stay away from certain people. It's as if they sense something about them. I think women do that with me.

Honestly I don't care. I am how I am and I should learn to live with it. Some part of me feels that I'm missing out on something. I realize that I'm a fucked up workaholic. I also realize that to do things you have to sacrifice other things. I can live with that.

What's hard to live with is my friend's death. I have been putting miles on the road ever since it happened but it doesn't do any good. I hate to admit how much it still hurts like it did right when it happened. At this point I can't tell how it will change how I live. I feel deadened and at the same time resolved to move forward towards my own death.

#4: I'm fucked up and changed since my friend died. Part of me died too. I see now that it's a bigger part than I can fill. I don't give a fuck about anything anymore. I know that's bullshit on my part, it's weak, all the things that I say I hate so much I am becoming. I am becoming a total hypocrite. It's hard to function with a broken heart, a shattered spirit. I feel so frustrated all the time. I just go with the program. I am the Hollow Man. I am the hollowgram. Fuck it. I have no hope, I have no one, nothing. I just walk with the wind. I am becoming smaller and smaller as times goes on. I don't remember how it feels to feel good. I look back at the writing that I was doing before Joe died and it's a lot different. I have less to say now. I think I should just stop. I can't write about anything except feeling hollow because that's all I am now. I am turning into a ghost. Soon I won't exist. I'm fading away.

#5: I feel guilty for the very fact that I'm alive. Today it really got to me. I no longer feel I have a purpose in life at all. I walked the streets today trying to get away from myself. It didn't work. I feel bad that I breathe. I keep thinking about my best friend in the plastic box. I no longer feel like a solemn warrior like I used to. I just feel depression, rage and bitterness. I feel let down that something like that could happen to someone like Joe. It gets harder to take as the days go by. For a while it was ok but in the last week it's been getting to me. I don't know if it's the exhaustion getting to me or what. All I know is that my life is dark and plain. I know that others have gone through much, much worse than this. I don't know if I feel or if I'm numb and in shock. I feel out of energy. I have been doing all the regular things I do but this time it's with a broken heart. I can't make things matter. It all seems so fucking stupid. Everything. Makes me think that all I do is take up space because I'm not in love with life's lie anymore. I used to feel like I should be doing things all the time and now I just do things to get away from myself and to get my mind off killing myself.

#6: At this point no one can tell me shit and have me listen. I'm tired of the words. I'm tired of the isolation sickness. I only get it when I'm around them too much. When I'm alone I feel alright because I can forget that I'm alive for a while. For now this is the only way that I have found relief. I do interviews, go on television and look into camera lenses. I heard once that Indians hated getting their pictures taken because they thought it took away a layer of their souls. I thought that for a few moments once. Seemed romantic. Now I know different. Nothing can take you out besides death. They can roll all the tape they want and it doesn't fucking matter. You can fuck all you want and it doesn't matter. None of it matters. You'll do what you'll do. You can fall for years and never hit the bottom. You can kill until you get caught. It's wide open. So much of what held me together I see now as total bullshit. A romantic dream. In search of some kind of approval. I don't care about it now and I'm more powerful than ever. I'm free and I'm over the edge looking back at them all. I'll never come back. They'll never, I'll never, nothing will ever bring me back.

#7: Back in LA for the first night in weeks. Rain has been hitting the streets for hours. I walk to a food place. The rain soaked sidewalks seem to take people's voices and fill them with a violent jagged current. I hear the words come hissing off the sidewalk and turn into threats hanging in the air like knives suspended. I sit in the food place not wanting to be near a window. I really do think of drive by shootings these days.

This is the place for paranoia. I think about the guy I nearly took out in New York the other night. He was hitting me up for change after I got out of a cab. He came around behind me and I thought he was going to jack me and I was going to try to kill him. I thought he was going to go for me. He had no idea what he was messing with. Not a clue. At this point I don't either. I think about the man I nearly hit at the record company office a few days ago. He was talking shit and I started staring at him, through him. He got a worried look on his face. He had no idea what he was fucking with. This city rips the heart out of humanity. It reduces people to desperate fear merchants. I want a gun so I'll never get messed with. I am scared of walking into a hold up in every store I go to. I don't want a gun because I don't want to end up one of those people that have guns and get their heads shot off. I want a gun because I feel the need for one every time there's a knock on the front door like the one that happened three minutes ago that I didn't open. My immediate impulse was to open the door and attack. Instead I sat stock still until the footsteps went away. I will try to sleep tonight. I wrote a girl tonight but didn't send the letter because I was embarrassed at the things I said. I was embarrassed and I pitied myself. I wish she would walk through the door right now and put her arms around me and never let go.

#8: Letter to a woman that scars the flesh and soul when she comes to mind. It's Friday night, a little after 9 p.m. March 20. I got here to LA this morning at 2 am. I went into this new apartment. The book company has moved into the living room. It's really good. My room was nothing but boxes and ghosts. A plastic container of blood and brain soaked dirt from Joe's head and a roach the size of a mouse was my company. I worked through the night unpacking all the stuff and building shelves. 14 hours later I finished. There were two milk crates of mail on the floor waiting for me. I found a letter from you. I was surprised.

I got back from tour last Sunday. The record company had me land in NYC and do 4 days of interviews. It was pretty fucked coming off a tour where I was on the road for 5 weeks with three days off. I wasn't in the mood to do stuff. It was hard to deal with all these people every day when I was trying to come down from tour. It's something that I've never been able to explain.

I am sorry for the last letter that I wrote you from Munich. If you got it or not it was pretty fucked up I guess. It's been difficult for me the last few weeks. I have a lot of things that are trying to rip me apart and I confide in no one so I spend a lot of time on my own. Whatever.

I am confused as to why you are writing me. You never really come out and say anything. You always seem to come off as vague. Perhaps I just don't understand. I would like nothing more than to understand you. I wondered if you were writing me letters to hurt me. If you're doing that please don't hurt me. When I think of you too much it hurts. It's embarrassing to say how much. It's pathetic at this point. I don't think you would want to hurt me.

Seems to me that you have been put through a lot of pain at other's expense a lot in your life. I imagine it was all men. You were probably a lot nicer at some point but someone whacked it out of you or scared it out of you, or humiliated it out of you. I don't know if you're mean or not but I think you're tough. I meet women when they come up and want to talk to me and they don't have it. They have nothing, so boring, so shallow. They make the world such a lonely place.

I don't know if it's a good idea for me to write you anymore. It's hard to think about you and not lose sleep. I have a bad enough time sleeping these days as it is. I have terrible nightmares now. I do all nighters now like I am doing right now because the dreams are so fucked. Going into the second night of not sleeping. I did a good workout tonight and I still don't feel tired. I have a headache that won't quit though.

These letters always go too long. Have you ever seen the Kurosawa film *Ikiru*? I imagine you have. If you haven't then you should. I have seen it three times now. I don't think I'll be writing you anymore, it hurts me too much. At this point I can't take it. Hope all's well with you.

#9: When I looked back I saw that the mountains I had spent so much time climbing had turned to piles of sand. The first gust of wind reduced them to desert. So much for glory and the past. Nothing to do but move on. The pack grows heavy at times and I wish there was some place to put it down and catch my breath. I look around. As far as I can see, there's no place to rest, not even for a second. I shoulder the pack and keep walking the trail of scars. My journey is to the wound, the great wound.

As I walk the desert spreads and grows before me. I see a man ahead of me shoot himself in the mouth and drop. He turns to sand and blows away before I can get to him. When I look for solid ground I start to sink. Only when I move can I survive. To be still is to know suffocation. I had to get away from your eyes. They were killing me. All I have to do is think of you and I start to choke.

I am the Hollow Man. I leave the hollow stare that stays with you long after I'm gone. I'm always gone. I am the echo on your phone. Your broken heart that leaks blood is my sound track. I am the annihilating silence that fills you with horror.

I can't look back. I can't take the pain. The trail's pull is so strong that to look back is to be emptied all the way. My heart was broken so many times that I went from shallow to hollow.

The urban landscape is my horror backdrop. The nights are filled with my loneliness. I long for a voice, a touch. I know that it will never come. I want to die all the time. I know that I will die pitiful and insane. Hollow.

#10: Just take me out and work me to death. I can't love anyone. I'm good for taking pain and dispensing rage. The nights pass and they remind me of books I have read about the ones that got fucked up in a war. I can't call anyone. I try to and then at the last minute I just put the phone down. I'm afraid of bumming them out. They might catch some of the horror that has taken me over. I feel like I have been dropped off on some other planet. I don't speak their language anymore. I feel better in the room staring at the walls, trying to make words work. I am the Hollow Man. I will be empty at the end of the trail. Nothing witty to say. I've got a bucket of dirt that's soaked in my dead friend's blood. I keep it in the closet. tonight the whole room smells like the dirt. It's hard not to go insane. I think I slip a little every day. I must be. As time goes by I feel less and less. I sink and become more hollow. Soon the sun will shine right through me. Pure.

#11: Tonight during one of the songs I talked about Joe. It was a whisper, the whole place was silent. It was like I wasn't even there. I just listened to myself tell the story. After the show I sat and let the sweat dry. I usually feel lonely after shows but not these days. I feel totally inside myself. I don't want to know anyone, I don't want to talk to anyone. I feel fine on my own. Some girl wanted to talk to me. I just stared at my feet as she went on and on. I have no idea what she said. She was talking to the wrong guy. I'm always the wrong guy. I got out of the venue and there were people standing in the rain waiting for me so I could sign their tickets. I looked at them and could barely speak. I just signed the stuff as quickly as I could, tried to get my name right, said thank you and left. I don't know what to do in those situations. I like them but I don't want to know them. I don't want to know anyone these days. I don't even want to know myself. Sleep is my escape. It gives me a break from the ceaseless self awareness that I choke on. I used to think of a woman and that if I could be with her that things would be better but now I know that that's just a dead engine in the desert. Just a burnt corpse that never gets discovered. It's nothing. I could never be there for anyone. I couldn't do anything with this girl that would change the way I am. I am the Hollow Man. I can barely be there for myself. I have to pick myself up off the floor all the time now. Sort through the pieces and figure out who I am underneath all the ash and sweat. I am disgusting. I want to end. I want to be one with the shadows. I want to end the scream that tears at my guts. I will travel on a moving bed tomorrow night. I will feel safe knowing that no one can touch me. It's the only break I can see.

#12: Just for a little while be with me. Just sit next to me, I need you. Not anyone. I wish it was that easy, there's a lot of them around. It's you I want to be with. I don't think it will ever happen. I was with another girl today. I've been with a few girls in the last week. It's not the same. They're nice, real nice but they're not you. I know I could walk up to you with an arm cut off and blood pumping out with each heartbeat and you wouldn't notice. I know how you are, you're not bad, you've had it hard. You need someone to help you, if you would let me get close to you I could heal all your wounds.

#13: While I stagger away to puke: I put a wall behind me and a wall in front of me. The wall behind me has bricks three deep and no light comes in. The wall in front of me has peep holes so I can see out. I don't want to talk about back there. I don't look behind myself unless I can be alone and scream. My horror isolates me and leaves me stranded in the middle of my brain. No matter what I do or say I'm always alone in this room puking and screaming. Sometimes I feel nothing at all, nothing. I can't talk. She could touch me and I wouldn't feel anything. I can fuck but I can't feel. I can puke but I can't feel. I've been falling for a while now.

#14: At some point you'll ask yourself why she left you. You will not play all the typical games in your mind where you make her something that lives below you, cold and inhuman. You will sit in your room and stare at the floor as you turn over every time you talked to her. You'll try to remember what it was that might have made her leave you forever. You can't find a single thing. In your mind you are wounded and in pain. You cannot find an answer. You will find a lump in your throat because you feel so stupid and vulnerable and alone. You'll remember everything that you said and meant as being pitifully stupid and embarrassing. You hope that she'll never tell anyone the things that you told her. You become suddenly angry at yourself for ever having told her all the things you did. You accuse yourself of being weak and lame, unable to face the world alone. You feel overwhelmed at your own inability to handle anything. Life sucks since she's been gone. You can tell how good you felt with her by how bad you feel right now. The radio will play a sad song as if the DJ knew you were in there and is trying to get you to cry. You feel the lump in your throat swell and you cry. Hard and short, the tears fall from your eyes onto the ends of your shoes. Your nose becomes clogged and you wipe your face with your arm. You will not tell any of your friends about this part of your life. They have probably been through the same thing as you although you never talk about the naked lonely moments that you do on your own. Totally on your own. Like no one's ever been there before, not like you have. Everyone has a desert that they go to and watch the moon paint the sand. When she leaves, you will feel the miracle of humanity. The horrible intellect that you possess will turn you into a self torturing machine. You will feel the hollow bones in your body. You will know me and the depths from which I come to you always.

#15: I look into the mirror and think of what my face would look like if someone had shot me in the left cheek with a gun. I think of what a fragile thing the skull is. I think of my face shattered and mutilated. I'm lucky to have a face and that thought makes me want to erase my face.

What an awesome trip to get murdered. Stepping over the line. Stepping into nothing. To be dead, to be murdered and die.

The faces and the streets are blank. The words are meaningless. The world is extinct and dead. I have found the meaning and it's meaningless. I don't have emotion to rekindle. I'm in a walking coma. Partly dead. From now on, it's just documentation. I am beyond heartbreak. I am extinct but still breathing. I stab myself with my senses yet I feel no pain. My body keeps breathing even though my thoughts are dead. It's funny how I am able to live this lie. How I can go out there and talk to them and then come back here to this room and break down all on my own. I am alive enough to feel the pain in my face when I look off to nowhere and start to cry. My eyes burn at first and then it's easy after that. I can't talk because I'm cold and made out of wood. Part of my face has been shot off and I can't talk like I want to. I can't let the words go. They stay inside and kill me a little more every day.

#16: To the Hollow Brother. I see you in the mirror as I contemplate another night on the killing plane. So many years here. Neon sprawl, littered with humans. Broken and twisted. I saw a woman come out of the bushes near a highway overpass today. She was pulling up her pants. She was as ugly as the concrete she was walking on. She was as beautiful. She sat down on a bucket and held up a sign that said: Please feed me and Joe. I guessed that Joe was the small dog at her feet. The car ahead of me must have said something because she screamed, "Fuck you, you son of a bitch!" at it as it made a left. Now it's night and no one's here except me and the hollow pattern of my breathing. I can't hold onto the flesh lies. I don't call them, I don't need them. They fell away from my eyes. I could no longer live in their world. I live in the hollow desert. The howling sonic expanse. Rage is my sustenance. I cannot use their language to speak. I lie whenever I speak because it's their words, they will never be their words. The words were here before me and all I can do is use them and get used by them. I'd rather be here in the horror worlds of my screaming desert night.

#17: I passed a woman tonight as I was riding my bike the wrong way down Hollywood Blvd. Our eyes met for a split second. As I sped down the street I looked behind me. She had turned to look at me. I thought of what would have happened if I got off the bike and walked up to her. Hello my name is Henry, I don't like the name but it's the one that they gave me. I hope I'm not scaring you. I swear I won't hurt you. You have such a kind face that I felt ok about coming up and talking to you. Would you like to come to my place? I swear I won't hurt you. We could talk or what ever you wanted. I could make you some food if you were hungry. I just came from the store. I'm so lonely in this city, so lonely on this planet. I don't want to die but I can't stand it sometimes. I wonder if someone could meet someone else and have their life turned around. Do you think that kind of thing ever happens or is it just something that we tell ourselves to keep hanging on? We tell ourselves certain things to keep the carrot dangling in front of our faces, I know. It's a fail-safe that keeps us in pain. I don't know if I'm living real life or a movie. I don't know where I fit. Are you like me? Do you feel need like it's trying to kill you when you're alone in your room? Do you think it's possible to meet someone on the street in a city past midnight and make some kind of connection that could last? I missed this car that was pulling out from the curb by that much. I think it's better for me to keep my eyes on the road.

#18: She got up about an hour after I did. Everything I did pissed her off. Why don't you listen to me when I'm talking to you, where are you? You're so fucked up! For a moment she made me care. Care enough to contemplate wordlessly killing and dumping her after dark in the parking garage. All I did was tell her to shut up and get out. She asked is that it? That's all you're going to say to me after we spent the night together? You're fucked you know that? I didn't say anything. I was miles beyond caring at all. I didn't even notice when she left the room. I heard the hard slam of the door as she exited. I am hard pressed to remember a thing of what she said the night before. I would just nod my head and stare off into my jungle. I don't remember the sex, I don't remember anything except the things that I want to forget, those things I remember with alarming clarity that makes me forget everything else.

#19: I want to write you and tell you everything, that's how desperate I am. I don't even know you. You're just a face that talked to me, a voice that had a comforting tone to it that made me want to stay with you so I could hear you say more things. It wouldn't have mattered what you said. It's like talking to a dog. They listen to the tone. I think that loneliness is disgusting and it victimizes anyone it comes near. I feel lonely and I project it on you. What an insult. If I told you I wanted to spend the night with you, you might think that I felt something for you but that's not the truth. The truth is that I'm looking for a way to get through the time left on the planet. I don't know you, I don't hear your words, I only hear the tone. I talk to myself while you talk to me. I don't even need you here, just leave your tone and your body in this dark box with me and I'll clutch it and listen to the tone and lie myself into a coma.

#20: Then on the other hand you have to remember the reason that you do anything for. Even the smallest thing, you must know the reason. There's always a reason. That's the only way to deal with this meat mutilation existence. Like it should matter who thinks what. I never lived for them. I never lived until I lived for myself. The rest of the time was just that, time. Doing time in the darkness. Not waiting for anything, anyone, nothing. I could pour my blood and guts out all over the place for them, for you.....would it matter? Yea sure it would, I would get sold out in no time. It's lonely here but it's alright if you know how to deal with the time.

#21: When you think you have no more guts to be gutted, you find out that you have a few more chunks that they can rip out of you. If you think you're all the way empty, you're wrong, you'll run into one of those people that will be able to press you flatter, to squeeze out a little more juice. The pigs were in my room the other day asking the same questions again. I kept telling them the same things over and over again. I don't deal drugs, Joe didn't deal drugs. I looked over on the carpet, there was Joe's body lying there with his brains all over the floor twitching every time the pigs asked more questions. Finally the pigs told me that they wanted me to take a polygraph test. I told the pigs that I couldn't wait. I'll take any test they have. I hope they ask me if I hate pigs so I can scream yes yes yes until I pass out. Every time I think that I'm building myself back up and putting things into myself that no one will be able to take away from me so I do not have to be Hollow Man. They come in and squeeze it out of me and drag me back into the world of pig horror.

#22: You asked me what I wanted so here it is. For a little while, sidestep the scars and the past and love me. Put your arms around me. I need you so much. It's hard to breathe. I feel so alone. All these people pass me and I don't know any of them. They talk to me but I don't understand anything they say. I hear but do not listen. I smile and shake their hands. They empty me, they pull my guts out. My mind is hollow, I cannot lie. I have been broken down. My shadow has been stolen. I can be your friend. I know they have hurt you. I know you expect things to go wrong. I know you expect pain first, so much that you create situations where it will be brought upon you so you can get it over with. You have been taught by example to take the beating. I could never hurt you.

#23: She was able to turn herself into plastic whenever she wanted to. I would put my arms around her and all of a sudden she would get hard and slightly cold. A few seconds later she would turn back into flesh and everything would be alright. She liked being plastic better then being flesh. I would wake up in the night and she would be sleeping plastic. If she sensed me looking at her she would turn to flesh in the speed of an eye blink. We would never talk about it. I was afraid she would leave me. I thought that if I loved her she would remain in flesh. If I ever brought up subjects that were too intense, she would look away and her skin would take on a slight sheen as her pores disappeared. Sometimes she would go between plastic and flesh with every breath as if she couldn't decide which she preferred. Nothing I did was enough. Too many beatings and abuse had scarred her forever. From my dark box I wonder where she is now. I wonder if there was anything I could have done differently to have made her stay with me. I know that love has no great power in the world. The wrath of abuse and pain are far more decisive influences on the flesh. We will go to great lengths to deny and hide. She is living scar tissue.

#24: I'm losing tonight. I'm in this room in Seattle and I'm looking at Joe Cole's book and it hurts. I have a lump in my throat and I want to die because I miss him so much. I look at the picture and I read the words and it hurts. Sometimes I wonder how I'll make it without killing myself because it's all I think of doing a lot of the time when I'm alone at night. I am finding it hard to give a fuck about anything at all. I miss him. I don't know what to do with myself. I can't find a way not to lose over and over. Sometimes I feel like I'm suffocating inside, like I want to scream but I can't because there's so much scar tissue in the way of my throat. I'm lonely and fucked up. I'm losing this round. Sometimes I feel like I can deal with it and then there comes a night like this and it's hard to take, so hard. I think that the things that happen to people on this planet are enough to make you want to die fast. I will not talk to anyone about anything, I will write like hell and tell the truth. There is nothing else. They ask me how I can do what I do and I can't explain to them that I have no choice. I'm a wounded animal caught in the headlights.

#25: I leave another heartbreak hotel and make my way down the road. I went to the town thinking that something good was going to happen, something out of the ordinary. Didn't work out like that. The streets and the room all told me that I'm in a slow desperate moving psychosis. All I can do is move. I looked into her eyes and knew she didn't get where I was coming from. I am from the still moments that go unnoticed. The emptiness and the silent sadness. I couldn't say a word to her. I have no language that works with these people. I told her that I come from a different planet and I knew I was right. Hushed voices wait for me at bus stops. They see me and I hear my name behind me. The planet and all its cities wait for me. I know I won't be here long and that's fine. The silence and the alienation are refined. The blades are sharp and I never run out of blood.

#26: The airport makes me think that I can breathe again. Always good to see an airport especially on the way out. Going out. Escaped from another city before it killed me, wore me down and ground me out. I leave today to go to more dead cities on the planet. I like the idea of leaving cities. The freedom is in the movement. Between cities they can't touch you, they have to leave you alone when you're above the clouds. It's good to get off the earth for a while.

#27: I can hear the dirty traffic through the window. The sun burns my feet as I sit on the end of the bed and think about the idea of sleep. I can hear voices and movement out there. I want to walk around but the lack of sleep is getting to me. All I'll do today is sleep to get ready to do press. I will see nothing of Madrid except from the back of a car. I already know this. Kool and the Gang posters up everywhere. The room waits for me to fall and then closes in with paranoia dreams of a killer chasing me. Hours later I'm semi-coherent and they come and take me away to answer all kinds of questions. I wonder if the sun shined out there today. I wonder if I could have had a good time. All these rooms look the same after a while and you get used to being alone all the time.

#28: I thought I recognized a street as we sped along. I realized that the street I was thinking of is in Zurich. They all look the same after a while, you can go fast enough, long enough to where it's all the same. The guy next to me looked out the window at a large building and said that it was too large, a fascist building. I was going to say something about the building not being bigger than Guns and Roses, their logo loudly adorning the back of his jacket. I looked at the buildings flying by, lit up for the tourists. Last time I was here playing a boy was hit by a car and killed outside of the show. Outside my window they scream at each other and beep their horns. I do interviews most of the day and then fly to another city. I am homeless, hopeless, without care or love.

#29: Hollow recollection that drills me alone in this box. I'm standing in front of twenty-five plus press people answering questions. I wonder what the fuck I'm doing. I look out the window and see all the people that have heard that I'm in Rome at this record store doing a press conference. They watch from outside and try to catch my eye by holding up records that I'm on. I finish the press thing and there's record company people running around asking me if I'm alright. Yea sure, it was just some questions, what the fuck? They open the door and the others come in and then I'm signing things. Some piece of shit tells me that I only played the shitholes all these years so I could play with the

Chili Peppers in front of several thousand people. He said I used the shitty punker dives as a stepping stone. I tell him to forget the rest of the speech and let's go outside so I can smack him like a bitch. He bails. Smart piece of shit. More record company types rush over to see if I'm alright. It's just a piece of human garbage, what's the problem? I go to the airport. I am picked up by two young pigs with machine guns and am told to unpack. They are mad that I'm not scared. I want to punch the pigshit out of them. Finally they let me get out of their city. I leave the city, another one waits for me always.

#30: Hollow memo. I was riding in the back of a car going through the Alps. I had pulled out of Munich an hour before. The moon was staring in the window. I faked falling asleep so the record company lady wouldn't ask any more questions. All of a sudden a thought hit me. Something that I've always known but never thought about in a different way. I thought about Joe's mother Sally. She has been working so hard to keep it together. I never really knew her before Joe was killed. For no reason at all, all of a sudden I realized that she lost her only son. Her son was murdered and she'll deal with that for the rest of her life. She'll go through it every day. She must feel like some kind of horrible failure for bringing up someone who died before she did. I started to cry. It was so fucked. I felt so totally alone in the world. I hate this place so much.

#31: 2:46 a.m. Paranoia, depression and exhaustion have a hold on me. I was staring into the black of the room sweating and thinking that I would like to get some time off so I could go out and blow my brains out. I am hungry and there are places open to eat but I'm too paranoid to go out there and get food. I'm not doing too well I guess. I should have not come here for my day off. I sit in my room and I freak myself out. I wish to be happy but all I can do is make myself more angry and full of rage. I have no one to blame but myself. I am not looking for anyone to blame but I desperately need some kind of relief. I don't know how to get it and I don't know what to do with myself now. You can get so tired that you cannot sleep and all you do is get more fucked up. Believe me it's true. You can withdraw inside yourself further and further to the point to where you won't even be able to listen to a voice on a record. I get quieter every day. I don't know what to do. I don't want to kill myself but sometimes it's the only thing that I can think of. I have interviews starting in the morning and then I go to Arizona to play. I fear for myself. I don't know how I'll get through the next few months.

#32: In a hotel room far away from the real world I sit and think to myself while she is in the bathroom. There is only them. There is never anyone that is as close as a life away. I think about the stranger in the toilet. I think about what she's thinking, what she thinks of me. If she feels freaked out by the things that I have told her in the last hour. I wonder if she's scared of me and wants to find a way to get out of the room. I wonder if she's in there freaking out thinking that I'm going to hurt her. There's just them. No matter what you say, you'll always be on the outside. Always a stranger. All of a sudden life becomes a disease that rips you apart and leaves you on a strange planet. You go along with it because you know nothing else. If you think about it too much it makes you depressed because you see all the things that you have to do to keep your mind busy. You try to talk to someone and almost always you regret it afterwards. I think that I will hate myself in the morning. She comes out of the bathroom. Everything I say and do from this point on is desperate and pathetic.

#33: I am a stupid fuck up with no life. One more night here in my room and then I leave to go out there again for a long time. I'm glad that I'm leaving. I like my room, with all the music and the door that I can close. Mostly the music though. I like listening to Charlie Parker and Coltrane at three in the morning and getting left alone. But I don't belong here. I have been here a few days and already I'm getting fucked up in the head. My problem is that I have no idea how to get along with people. All I can do is play and move. I try to get along with them and it fails. I'm no good at being in one place. I get lonely on the road like anyone else but there's something about the movement that keeps me in one piece. Here I fall apart and I talk a bunch of stupid shit and I get weak and the loneliness gets to be too much. I was in rare form tonight. I tried to talk to a girl and all I did was insult her terribly. If I had the courage I would talk to her and tell her that I am sorry, that I acted in a dishonorable manner. Maybe tomorrow night I will. Of course I won't because by tomorrow night I will have found some way to justify what I did and I'll just say fuck it, so what. The only good thing that I do is cause myself pain by playing my guts out and pushing weights up and down. These people will never know how fucked up I am because I don't have the strength to kill myself or the intelligence to render it with words. I'm caught in the middle. Too stupid to do anything and too smart to know that I'm nothing but a no one.

#34: I dreamt last night that I came into a room and saw a girl that I used to go out with lying on a couch with my father. She was laughing in my face and treating me like a child. She was acting like my stepmother. I can't remember what my father looked like but I remember him staring at me and laughing. I won't see him again unless it's in a dream. I don't know what to do with myself except to make myself as hollow as possible whenever I can. The less I am the better.

#35: I'm getting good and empty. I have never been so empty in all my half life. I lie in my black box and I don't think about anything except killer's eyes. I have become comfortable with his eyes. I look into them and I wonder where he is and what he's doing. What he had for breakfast and if he thinks about what he did, if he has dreams like I do. I used to think of women I knew and now I don't. I came upon the great idea that unhinged me from life as I knew it before. The days are passing me and I can't tell one from another. They give me things and as soon as they leave I throw them out. I can't hold onto them and be free. You even touch them and you become part of them for a while. It's hard to get them off you. You have to be careful because they will kill you with words and actions. The only way to be free to live the half life is to be hollow. Otherwise it's just a gut stomp that kills you always.

#36: Night off in a New York box. Spent hours walking the streets. Students talking about "gender sanity". An old woman pushing her cart, me walking from street to street not knowing where the hell I'm going. No one recognizing me, thinking of things:
I don't want my brain to explode and all the murder to come out
I don't see any other way other than to put their brains all over the street
I don't want to hurt anyone

I know I'm the kind that hurts people
Stupid animals know not what they do to others
The two guys staring at me in the diner make me want to reach over and grab one of them by the throat, the feeling immediately leaves me. I don't want to hurt anyone, I don't want to touch anyone and I don't want anyone to touch me. I see a sign with a picture of a father and son weather forecasting team on a local news station. The father has his arms around the son. I think of my father touching me and it seems unreal that it ever happened. I makes me think of my mother and the rage that she makes me feel. Hours pass and I'm back in the bug spray smelling box. I am determined to write truths from my guts that will make me sick and violent when I read them back to myself. Stab that shit talking bitch in the stomach so many times that she'll never have children. Never being touched by one of them again. I inhale the bug spray and feel the claustrophobia of the room set in. Have not slept in a day and a half and I feel fine. I'm free, that's the thing I've got in my favor tonight and all nights from now on.

#37: I told her: Most of the people that I know I pay a salary to. I would never ask you a favor unless I was paying you. Like if I was hungry I would ask you to get me some food and I would pay you for the food and your time. I pay the guys in the band because I know how fast they would be gone if I didn't. My parents taught me from an early age to depend on no one but myself. I never felt they supported me in any way besides the food and housing. I pay people to do things and I usually only know others from business that I do with them. I told her that the phone doesn't ring at my place on the weekend. She started to cry. Right there during an interview on camera. I don't understand the problem. Seems to me I have rooted out the truth pretty well. Some life.

#38: I am doing the best I can to strip away the excess and get to the point. Existence is the muscle pulling away from the bone. Pure animal pain. The rest is just television to me. Death is the only thing that I answer to. Death calls out to me at all times. I am always aware of its presence. I have made friends with my nightmares, they are just dreams now, part of me. I fully understand what Kurtz said about making friends with horror and moral terror. They were my enemies and they plagued me and now they are my friends and they are my allies. They do not judge me like people do. I am of horror and terror.

#39: On the nights when we're staying in a hotel and not on the bus moving across some black highway I will have short moments of panic right before I fall asleep because I don't know where I am. Right before the eyes close I'll choke from not knowing where I am in the darkness. It happened the other night in London. I looked into the darkness of the room and started to spin. For a few frantic seconds I didn't know if I was alive or what. Geographic location was secondary to just being alive. Wouldn't it be great at a moment like that to be able to have someone with you to tell you that it's alright, some kind of human buoy, a reference point. Someone who wouldn't laugh at your cold-skinned horror life. Someone to tell you where you were. Someone to take away the panic need to blow my brains out right then and there feeling.

#40: I just came back from a woman's house. It was a good time with her. She is beautiful and kind, intelligent and has a great sense of humor. I am glad to be back in the room. I have found that I prefer to be alone. I have taken this thought further and found that I like to be with the dead. I like to be alone with music and memories of things and people that are no more. I am playing Thin Lizzy in the headphones. I have to use headphones because the human shit bag upstairs freaks out when I play anything past a certain hour. Phil's dead, Monk, Miles, Trane, Parker, Lightnin', Joe Cole, all the greats, all dead and here with me. I feel closer to them than I do with anyone living. I wonder if there's anyone else like this out there. It was good to be with the woman but I feel separate from her, the closest I can get is next to her. I feel like a dead person next to her. She really has no idea what my reality is. I don't know what hers is either. We are equal in our strangeness to each other. The dead will take you just the way you are and there doesn't have to be any lies or game playing. I think more about dead people than I ever do about the ones that are living. It's good to be in this box alone with Phil. In the morning I do a television show to talk about Joe's death so they can show it and try to stir some kind of local consciousness to inspire someone to come forward and give information. It will be ok, I'll know what to do. At this point I know a lot more about the dead than I know about the living. I am beyond life. It was horrible at first. It felt like a curse of some kind but steadily it became a welcome fact. I feel good somehow through all these empty nights.

#41: For the last two nights the old Black Flag truck has been parked outside the apartment building I live in. This truck belongs to the sound company that supplied Black Flag with its sound system for three years, from 1984 through to 1896. This is the truck that Joe and I drove in almost every day for seven months in 1986. Last night it sat outside the building like some huge black horrible reminder. I imagine that the sound company is working at some local club off the Blvd. It seemed like a bad trick. Maybe it drove itself over there and was waiting for me to come out. I wanted to walk over to the window and look into the cab at the place where we sat and spent so much time running down the miles. The Black Flag logo was still on the back. I sat on the steps and looked at it for a long time. I don't know what I waiting for. Maybe I was hoping to see Joe in there waving me over so we could get on the road and get out of here. It sits outside the building watching me. I know how stupid this all sounds. Sometimes I feel so ruined. I can't sit still for too long or it gets to me. I have been throwing out memories as best I can. Sometimes I'm not hollow enough. I'm working on it.

#42: Hosted KROQ's Love Line show tonight. It's the number one show in the city of Los Angeles. You call in and talk about your hang-up no matter what it is. High lights include: A fourteen year-old girl caught giving her boyfriend head and has been kicked out of the house and can she have some tickets to the band's show tomorrow night? A fifteen year-old girl that gave eight guys head and wonders about the legion of sores around her mouth. A white guy who is scared of getting the shit kicked out of him by his black girlfriend's brother. The manic depressive boy who is scared of what he might do to his girlfriend. Endless faxes come in from people all over who are listening to the show. Afterwards people call in to talk to me while I'm waiting to get out of the station. At the ground floor we are informed that there are people outside that have been waiting all evening. I duck them and we see them as we go speeding out of the parking lot. I get back home and go out to the store to get food. I go by the diner where the blonde was a few months ago. She's not there tonight. I go west on Sunset and look at the whore come out of the car wiping her mouth. I go into the supermarket and someone in each aisle knows me. One guy says he's just moved here from Buffalo and he trips out on seeing famous people. I give him a confidential look and tell him that WE ALL shop here. He says, "That's cool" and leaves. I get back on the bike and weave through the whores and the drug dealers and go back to the apartment.

#43: I sit in this room in a silent clear eyed state of horror. In my mind my mother walks towards me with buckets of aborted children. She screams at me that she hates me for surviving her. I see cameras and my friend's blood being eaten by flies. Police fucking with me. I sit in the room and wait for the night to go by. I sometimes wish for someone who could help me but I have tried that and I know that you ride out horror on your own every time and you never talk about it because no one gets it unless they've been there and if they've been there you don't want to know them and they don't want to know you. You can smell it on each other and you both know the same dull ringing ache and the insanity that you've been through and continue to go through. I constantly amaze myself that I'm still alive. I know that the most dangerous thing to my health is me. I know that I are capable of great harm to others. The ones that I like and the ones that I don't. I only hurt the ones close to me as well as the ones at arm's length. I see people stepping over bodies to get on the bus. I'm in bed with a woman and I roll over onto Joe's dead body. I turn into a silent human scream. If you understand then I feel sorry for you because you're fucked up. If you don't, then I suggest you stay away from me because every move I make is a warning signal, a prelude to violence.

#44: Sometimes life is a recurring nightmare. Sometimes every thought that comes through my head is horrible. Like right now. I'm in Sydney, Australia. I have the curtains shut and I have been in bed for a few hours just lying under the covers trying not to think because the only things that come to mind are Joe Cole getting murdered and this woman that I wanted to be with that didn't want to be with me. Death and rejection. I don't care how it sounds or how it looks. Earlier today I went out there and did the work that I needed to do and now I'm back in the box and feel no need to ever leave again until the morning. I feel safe with myself, even if I feel like killing myself all the time. Behind the hollow eyes there is a hollow, thoughtless, desperate scream. I've been dead for months and none of these people can tell. A few of Earth's women have fucked a dead man. It wouldn't have been the first time.

#45: After the night they spent together he thought about the woman constantly, not knowing what she thought of him or if she even thought of him at all. She called him and told him that the night meant so much to her, that she had been waiting years to be close to him and even though they had met on several occasions she had never seen fit to tell him of her feelings. She had kept them to herself for years and finally told him. Now she calls and tells him of all the times she had watched him when he didn't even know she was there. She tells him that she wants to know where he's at with her because she doesn't want to lead herself on. She is open and totally honest. She tells him that if he just wants to be friends with her, to please speak now and she'll tone her feelings down and not hope for anything. He likes her, he really likes her. He knows himself. So many empty miles have hollowed him out and he knows that he'll never be able to be there for anyone else. He can't even show up on time to be there for himself. He has no needs and no longer has an understanding of how to deal with anyone else's. He stammers and tries to find a non committal answer that will give her hope and keep her around but will allow him to get out quick if he feels he needs to, like he knows he'll need to a few weeks later. He knows well the suffocation that he always feels when he gets too close to one of them. When he gets too far away from himself. Too many years driven like a nail into himself. He never gets too far out of his head. He breaks the silence and listens the words come out of his mouth: No, I don't think I could ever be more than a friend to you and not a very good one at that, I'm not very.........I'm just not good with......I'm sorry. He tells her that he'll see her next time he comes through. He hangs up with relief and slight pride from having told the truth and sparing someone his beneath the skin behind the eyes desperation that spares no one. Ever.

#46: In a box in Melbourne Australia. It's too late for a lot of things. Too late for me to care about the things that don't matter because I have seen them with my hollow eyes for what they are. I smell my own fear and coiled animal panic when I think of my father and my mother's boyfriends. I can't give a fuck about what happens to them. All I can do is be ready if any of them come forward to try to destroy me. I cannot love and cannot be loved. Love is for humans. I know what I am. I am a sociopathic predatory animal. Either you're looking to make the kill or you're looking to get killed. I thought I loved some people before but I now see that I did not. It was just one of those things that happens when there's nothing else to do. Just something to take up the time until death comes. With my hollow eyes I see you, with my hollow eyes I see myself, falling away. Human pain is 99% bullshit. I have freed myself from human pain. All I know is animal pain. If they hit you, you have to take it because it's illegal to kill them when they fuck with you. You have to take it and swallow more animal fear and grow more scars. Life is hollow. Leaves in a box. The shrink's office was in her house. I used to sit in the shrink's waiting room and watch her children come though the hallway on their way home from school. They would look at me and laugh. I wanted to kill them and the fucked up shrink bitch that was picking my brain. I would go home from that and listen to the bitch mother tell me how much money she was paying to have the shrink bitch tell me what my problem was. I would see my father on the weekends and he would tease me about what a sissy I was to be getting talked to by a shrink. We are now partners in mutual disgrace. The only thing we have in common is self disgust.

#47: Hollow walk on late night streets. Charlie Parker in New York. Bloody explosions of liquid fire scorch the sides of my skull. Dead men in cars drive by looking for the meat sale. A group of men come out of a bar smelling like aftershave, scuffling feet and quick violence. They expand and contract near their car. The two men look at me in the diner. They talk to each other and look back and laugh. Blocks later, groups of men pass by and the smell of beer comes off their clothes. I fool myself and think that I'm invisible until a few people call my name out and then I see that it's the wrong planet for me. Charlie Parker nodding off on the bandstand, sweating backstage. His music full of beauty, fury and death. Why can't they see it in everything? Why doesn't it drive them to small rooms all over the world? Why am I so alone on the planet?

Blocks go by. I see death everywhere in everything. I see them walk by on the street and I think of savagely attacking them with blunt instruments. Tough guy in a coma, put there by a guy who cared less than anyone he ever met in his half life. I think of women that don't exist. I kill strangers in my mind and walk late at night in bad neighborhoods because I am a bad neighbor. The pigs filled up three notebooks on me from all the things that the people in my old neighborhood said I did, said I was. Now I'm hollow for all to see. Thoughts explode and disintegrate in my head as I listen to my footsteps hit the street. I feel like stalking them. I don't look for friends anywhere. I don't look for kindness because I know more about humans than they do. I've had my head blown off by words for years. The only thing that could make me notice is guns. That's what it's come to. The words are meaningless when they fall out of their mouths. They love you, they hate you, it's all the same in the real world. Don't cling, don't attach to them. You'll rip yourself to pieces. Let their words fall to the ground, let them break at their feet so they can see where they are. Let them break their own backs, if they don't, the only back that will get broken is yours. I'm waiting for the world to fall over and quit. I'm waiting for the sun to run itself into the ground. There's that scene in *Deer Hunter* where the Green Beret is sitting at the bar and the guys are trying to get him to talk and all he says is "Fuck it" and keeps looking away. That's all there is to do, keep looking away, right through the bottom, right into the eyes of the Abyss. Call nowhere home. Unhappy misanthrope kills them to ease the pain. Finally he kills himself.

#48: Singapore. Tonight as we were walking out of a restaurant we saw a small car wreck. Someone said what a drag. I said that it wasn't us. I felt like something had kicked me in the side. I remembered how me and Joe used to say that to each other all the time. We would read something in the paper about something bad happening to someone and we would say that it wasn't us so we really didn't care. We thought everything was funny. That's all over now. I've never felt so alone in my life. I am Pain's errand boy.

#49: I'm surrounded by car exhaust and neon. Night time in Tokyo and people are all over the place, walking and laughing and breathing. None of them know that Joe is in a small box in the ground and the silence and stillness in the box would be enough to give them nightmares for the rest of their lives. I am pretty pathetic at this point, I know this.

#50: In a box near the airport in New Orleans. Walked along the highway looking for a gas station to get something to eat. People were inside but all the doors were locked. People are afraid of getting shot in the head. Afraid of men coming into the Quikmart, looking past them, and all of a sudden telling them to lie down on the floor or they'll get their fucking heads shot off. Afraid of a man that wants to kill for the fucked up sake of killing. The smart ones know that others will do that. Paranoia is everywhere, it's been hammered into a reality. In fact it's no longer paranoia that we feel. It's the honest knowledge that things can happen to anyone any time. Paranoia used to be something that would crawl up the back of your spine and bite, now it's just the weary reality that violence never sleeps. I walked along the highway. I was alone and hollow: I don't want anyone to know me. I don't want to know any one of them. I want to speak in hushed tones and avoid the light of day. I feel hunted sometimes. They know me, I don't know them. They have the advantage always. I used to think that if I knew one person that I would be alright. If I had one person to talk to that all things would be well with the world. I know now that you don't need anyone to get by. All you have to do is know how to duck and avoid places where they can see you. If I'm alone I start to forget. I forget myself. I forget my mother and father and I forget all the things that the humans have said and done to me over the years. I forget all the things I have done to them. I usually regret dealing with people. I lose my control and do things that I hate myself for later. It's obvious to me that I don't know how to be around them. When they come to talk to me I keep my distance and treat them like a curator at a museum talks about the paintings on the walls. More so around women. I feel that if I don't keep my distance that they will think I want to rape them and they'll call the pigs on me and I'll go to prison. When they talk to me I either cross my arms or put them in my pockets and I try to be as unthreatening as I possibly can. Sometimes they ask if they can kiss me or hug me and I politely say no because I don't want any of those fucking women touching me and then telling the pigs that I tried to do something with them. Sometimes they give me notes and ask me to go out with them so they can talk to me. They want to take me somewhere so they can have their own personal interrogation session. I always say no because I don't want to talk to them and I hate answering questions. I like walking alone on the highway at night.

#51: Rebirthed after death. My father hacked out my lungs and stripped me of courage. He gave me only fear and a few words to live by, words like: Yes sir. My mother and her boyfriends ripped my arms and legs off making it hard to move. I learned to crawl very well. I gave the guts my parents gave me at birth to strangers from the stage at an early age. I had to grow my own guts to replace them. One time I took out the intestines that they gave me and nailed the end to the edge of a stage and let the audience pull them out and take sections home as souvenirs. I dumped all the brains out of my skull and grew new brains. I lifted weights and pounded words into the air and onto paper and learned about pain, the first thing that was truly my own. I forged myself out of a vacuum. I crawl along the highway on hacked off stumps year after year. Some wonder how and why. I never do.

#52: So I go out and smash myself all the time. I put myself in places where I'm up there and they're down there. I put myself under their scrutiny every chance I get. I get spat on, dented up and hollowed out. I hit myself in the face while I play to make myself play harder. I sing and wreck my throat. I see through people when they talk to me. I have the nerve to wonder why I'm so lonely and isolated from people. It's funny, sometimes I'll feel like some kind of victim, like poor little me. It's no wonder anymore, I do this shit to myself and that's what happens. Right now I'm sitting here in my little box thinking about the piece of shit that spat on me tonight and how I cracked him in the face with the mic like it wasn't anything big. It wasn't. I don't wonder why I couldn't talk to this girl I know after the show. How I just looked at her and said some bullshit hoping that it would relieve her of any stress I might have put her under by being so weird. It was easy to see that I had confused her by being fucked up. I excused myself and left. I am banged up and smashed up. I don't make sense and I shouldn't get too close to people because there's just no way it works anymore. I talked to one guy I have known for a few years and he wanted to hug me and I felt myself want to run. I could tell that I had alienated him. I can't help it. I didn't want to talk to him but I did anyway because I could see that I was freaking him out a little. He asked me how someone could get in touch with me on an intimate basis, he said he wanted to phone me because we lived in the same town and he shouldn't have to write me. He was right but all I could do was stare at him. I wasn't going to give him my phone number, hell he might use it some time. I was too fucked up to talk to this guy and even be a human being so I walked away. I go out and smash myself around all the time. I pride myself on being able to take a lot of pain on a regular basis. How the fuck can I expect myself to be able to be cool to someone else when all I do is self involve myself? I get lonely and have the nerve to wonder why. What a joke. I should get off the bullshit and get on with it. If I wanted to do something different with myself I would. If I'm going to go this route I should go, go and take it and deal with it and not complain that I'm not getting the comfort of the world that I left behind. How typically weak of me. I must get stronger. I must listen to my scar tissue and follow the silent instructions and cut the bullshit.

#53: All the hollow nights filling me. I have been back here for a few days and tonight it hits me how useless I am off the road. I wake up in the morning and work at things but I can't remember any of it. I look through the mail and all the voices from the letters crowd me and I have to put it down. I have all the time I want to do whatever I want. I keep myself busy as best I can. I try not to think. The night comes and around 8 p.m. I start to feel nervous even though I have worked out hard a few hours before. There's no gig, no chance to push against myself. I fall in on myself. I look around my room and don't recognize any of the belongings. The only thing in here that doesn't belong is me. Someone calls me and it's all I can do to get them off the line and turn the phone off. I'm too fucked up. I sit still for a few minutes and then look for something else to do. Somehow experience has failed me. I am a bullet lodged in a wall. Time spent moving constantly makes sitting still all but impossible. I have painted myself into the corner of a portrait of myself. Discipline and repetition waited and got me into this room before they turned on me. Experience has made me into a confrontation addict.

#54: I didn't want to get off stage tonight. I'm in the box inside Hollywood. I felt like my guts were flying out of my body. I've been cooped up in the box for a few weeks and tonight I was part of a benefit and I got to do some talking for fifteen minutes. It wasn't enough. Now I'm back here and I want to break shit. I don't know when I'll be getting tired now. It was hard to be back in my element for a little while and then to get ripped out of it and thrown back into the box where nothing moves, nothing happens. I still smell like tobacco smoke. I want to be on tour. I need to have more self control. I am afraid that I am addicted to touring. When I'm home I can't deal with things. People are either too hard or too soft. Too soft in that they can't deal with it or too hard in that you can walk outside and be in the wrong place and have some eighteen year-old example of the species shoot you in the face. It makes me hostile and confused. I have thrown out the idea of what is fair. I'm in this box right now and I want to be out there. I need relief. The year is almost over. They didn't kill me. To paraphrase Ice T: You should have killed me last year. I feel inadequate and I don't know why. It seems like I can't get hit hard enough. I feel out of place in this day and age. I have pulled back. I got sick of getting pinned to the floor by midgets and being in a position where I was forced to care about things that didn't matter. It's a weakening experience. I've got to get back on the road, I can't stay here too much longer fooling myself every day. It's a trip realizing that there's no other way for you to go.

#55: 1992 staggers down the hallway clutching its side where it has been stabbed. The lights are growing dim. The drug dealers and the whores in my neighborhood know each other. It's the only community I've seen on the streets near my house. Ugly, fat women in hot pants standing on the corner laughing and talking with quick faced young men always looking side to side. They talk and laugh and inhale car exhaust and watch the lights change and then a car pulls up and one of the whores gets in and waves goodbye as the car pulls away. Shucks, so heartwarming. The other day I watched two pigs with their guns out in the parking lot of the video store, they were looking into one of the stores. One pig had a shotgun and the other had his handgun out. All the drug dealers just stood in the parking lot and watched. I don't want to live around here anymore. 1993 is almost here and I find myself in

Hollywood and out of Venice for a year. I never liked Hollywood but here I am anyway. I moved into the present box because it was there. I had nowhere else to go, all of my stuff was in storage and this place became available. The nights here pass slowly. Sirens and chopper blades. Don't know how long I've been here this time, a few weeks, a month, I don't know.

1992 feels old and haggard. 1992 feels betrayed and tricked, no one told the year that it had only a year to live. I stay up nights until the sun is almost coming up. I like to get up early and work during the day but night after night I have found myself unable to sleep even after a hard workout and a day of office work. I stay up and look at the wall. I barely know this room. I have been out on the road almost all of this year. I feel like a fish out of water. A bullet lodged in wood, inert and unmoving. I imagine exchanging words with a woman that understood me. I wish I had something to say that I wanted her to understand. I feel bad that I am so empty that I can stay in this room only to leave and lift weights until exhaustion makes my limbs shake. Then it's to the kitchen for the same food every night. After that it's back to the room and wait for sleep. I search my mind for something that doesn't make me recoil in shame, rage and horror. I come up empty. Touch mc. Lie on this mattress with me and do something that makes me feel something else other than that I've made a big mistake letting you come here. I'm stupid and I don't know what move to make. Teach me how to think again. Please. Please. Please....leave.

1992 hears people in all the apartments celebrating 1993's approach. 1992 lurches to the side and collapses, gasping with the roar of cheering and clapping ringing in its ears. I throw out magazines without bothering to read them. The animals out there. The animals driving by in their cars. The animals mistaking me for prey. I don't know which one has the gun in his pants. I don't go out there much anymore. I go out there every few days for food and then right back to the room. Out there they come up and ask questions. They touch you in the supermarket. Touched by a stranger on the streets of death. I'm sorry. Please understand me. I don't mean to harm, I don't mean to do damage. I am an animal in pain, stricken with fear and I will fuck you up. If you love me I'll let you down. I'll turn on you and make you hate me. I'll do it because I'll think it's what I have to do to survive you. I don't trust love.

I feel hands around my throat. Mother's boyfriends. Father, step-brother. You can have it, save it, shove it, taste it until it makes you choke. I sit endlessly. I wait to leave again and again. I live the same horror trip over and over. I have to move so I can unplug myself from thought and disappear into action and pain. The rage builds again, obscuring any thoughts of balance and self control. I want to feel muscle pull from the bone. I want to make my body scream. I want to learn the lessons in pain that expand me. Last longer, move faster, with more clarity. I will go until my body quits. Panicked and charged with blind fury, the bull sees the gate come up and he stomps and bellows in an arena full of strangers. It was always simple combat, one against all. One never relenting, knowing no other way to go but until collapse. 1992 dies.

LIVE DATES 1992

Band Dates

February
11 Rotterdam Holland
12 Hamburg Germany
13 Hamburg Germany
14 Gronningen Holland
15 Deinze Belgium
16 Paris France
17 Amsterdam Holland
18 Nijemagen Holland
19 Munster Germany
20 Kassel Germany
21 Hannover Germany
22 Saarbrucken Germany
23 Zurich Switzerland
25 Munich Germany
26 Munich Germany
27 Frankfurt Germany
28 Innsbruck Austria
29 Vienna Austria

March
01 Milan Italy
02 Lyon France
04 Birmingham England
05 Liverpool England
07 Dublin Ireland
08 Belfast Ireland
10 Glasgow Scotland
12 London England
13 London England
14 London England

April

01 Fullerton CA (also Dennis Miller show taping)

02 San Diego CA

03 San Diego CA

04 Los Angeles CA

05 San Francisco CA

06 San Francisco CA

07 Los Angeles CA

08 Los Angeles CA

11 Phoenix AZ

12 Dallas TX

14 Cincinnati OH

15 Chicago IL

16 Chicago IL

17 Detroit MI

18 Toronto Canada

19 Toronto Canada

21 Washington DC

22 Washington DC

23 Boston MA

24 New York NY

25 New York NY

27 Atlanta GA

28 Atlanta GA

June

02 Berlin Germany

03 Dusseldorf Germany

04 Stuttgart Germany

05 Bielefeld Germany

06 Eindhoven Holland

07 Rotterdam Holland (plus day show at Dynamo Festival, Eindhoven)

08 Brussels Belgium

09 Paris France

10 Amsterdam Holland

11 Florence Italy

13 Fribourg Switzerland
15 Sheffield England
16 Newcastle England
17 Glasgow Scotland
18 Birmingham England
19 Manchester England
20 London England
26 Houston TX
27 Dallas TX
28 Austin TX
29 Oklahoma City OK
30 Columbia MO

July
01 ST Louis MO
02 Lawrence KS
03 Omaha NE
05 Denver CO
06 Salt Lake City UT
08 Seattle WA
09 Portland OR
11 Sacramento CA
12 San Francisco CA
13 Santa Clara CA
14 Santa Cruz CA
16 Phoenix AZ
17 Santa Barbara CA
18 Tiajuana Mexico
21 Los Angeles CA
23 Anaheim CA (cable television shoot)
27 ST Petersburg FL
28 Miami FL
29 Gainesville FL
30 Pensacola FL
31 New Orleans LA

August
01 Nashville TN
03 Minneapolis MN
04 Racine WI
05 Grand Rapids MI
06 Pontiac MI
07 Cleveland OH
08 Columbus OH
09 Pittsburgh PA
10 Buffalo NY
12 Toronto Canada
13 Ottawa Canada
14 Montreal Canada
15 Providence RI
17 Richmond VA
18 Philadelphia PA
19 Baltimore MD
20 New York NY
21 Asbury Park NJ
22 Trenton NJ
23 Trenton NJ
28 London England
29 Reading England

September
11 Brisbane Australia
12 Burleigh Heads Australia
13 Sydney Australia
15 Canberra Australia
17 Melbourne Australia
18 Melbourne Australia
19 Melbourne Australia
20 Hobart Australia
21 Adelaide Australia
22 Perth Australia
25 Sydney Australia

26 Manly Australia
29 Singapore

October
02 Nagoya Japan
03 Osaka Japan
04 Tokyo Japan
05 Tokyo Japan
09 Honolulu HI
10 Honolulu HI
25 Tucson AZ
26 Albuquerque NM
29 Dayton OH
30 Kalamazoo MI
31 Indianapolis IN

November
01 Chicago IL
02 Toronto Canada
03 Montreal Canada
04 Durham NH
05 Boston MA
06 New York NY
07 New York NY
08 New Brunswick NJ
10 Raleigh NC
11 Atlanta GA
13 Orlando FL
14 Miami FL
15 Tampa FL
16 Jacksonville FL
18 New Orleans LA
19 Dallas TX
20 Houston TX
21 San Antonio TX
23 San Diego CA
24 Los Angeles CA
25 San Francisco CA

Spoken Dates

January

17 Sydney Australia

18 Sydney Australia

19 Melbourne Australia

20 Melbourne Australia

21 Adelaide Australia

24 Brisbane Australia

26 Sydney Australia

Jan. 23 & 25 sang with Australian band The Hardons in Sydney

March

06 Dublin Ireland

09 Glasgow Scotland

12 London UK

May

04 Eau Claire WI

05 Chicago IL

06 Cleveland OH

08 Denver CO

09 Salt Lake City UT

28 Los Angeles CA

August

26 London UK

December

23 Los Angeles CA